ENGLISH CATHOLICS AND THE EDUCATION OF THE POOR, 1847–1902

Perspectives in Economic and Social History

Series Editors: *Andreas Gestrich*
Steven King
Robert E. Wright

Titles in this Series

1 Migrants and Urban Change: Newcomers to Antwerp, 1760–1860
Anne Winter

2 Female Entrepreneurs in Nineteenth-Century Russia
Galina Ulianova

3 Barriers to Competition: The Evolution of the Debate
Ana Rosado Cubero

4 Rural Unwed Mothers: An American Experience, 1870–1950
Mazie Hough

Forthcoming Titles

The World of Carolus Clusius: Natural History in the Making, 1550–1610
Florike Egmond

The Determinants of Entrepreneurship: Leadership, Culture, Institutions
José L. García-Ruiz and Pierangelo Toninelli (eds)

London Clerical Workers, 1880–1914: Development of the Labour Market
Michael Heller

Financing India's Imperial Railways, 1875–1914
Stuart Sweeney

Mining and the State in Brazilian Development
Gail D. Triner

Global Trade and Commercial Networks: Eighteenth-Century Diamond Merchants
Tijl Vanneste

ENGLISH CATHOLICS AND THE EDUCATION OF THE POOR, 1847–1902

BY

Eric G. Tenbus

Routledge
Taylor & Francis Group
LONDON AND NEW YORK

First published 2010 by Pickering & Chatto (Publishers) Limited

Published 2016 by Routledge
2 Park Square, Milton Park, Abingdon, Oxfordshire OX14 4RN
711 Third Avenue, New York, NY 10017, USA

First issued in paperback 2015

Routledge is an imprint of the Taylor & Francis Group, an informa business

BRITISH LIBRARY CATALOGUING IN PUBLICATION DATA

Tenbus, Eric G.
English Catholics and the education of the poor, 1847–1902. – (Perspectives in economic and social history)
1. Catholic Church – Education – England – History – 19th century.
I. Title II. Series
371'.0712'42'09034-dc22

ISBN-13: 978-1-138-66129-5 (pbk)
ISBN-13: 978-1-84893-038-4 (hbk)

Typeset by Pickering & Chatto (Publishers) Limited

CONTENTS

To Kristy and Conor

PREFACE AND ACKNOWLEDGEMENTS

While the historiography of nineteenth-century English Catholicism has been a rather crowded field filled with general overviews, biographies and narrower monographs, as well as what a scholar once warned me were landmines both professional and personal, the field has lacked a systematic book-length study of the educational efforts of the Catholic community to provide elementary education to the Catholic poor in the important half century following the entry of the Catholics into the state grant system in 1847. While much of the earliest work done on this topic fell under the category of educational history, I like to think that this study is as much or more about religious history and the positioning (or repositioning) of Roman Catholic identity within that elaborate milieu we call Victorian religion. If the subject of English Catholics and elementary education has filled several pages of an overview or a chapter of an edited volume or biography, it has not been viewed, as it is here, as a facilitator of change in the identity of that English Catholic community. That said, I owe a tremendous debt to the scholars who have marked the historiographical trail before me and provided glimpses into the Victorian world of English Roman Catholicism with its historical richness and financial poverty, its Irishness and Englishness, its intellectuals and industrious working class, its eccentric personalities and sober leaders and finally its determination to make life better for its flock amidst the turmoil and progress of nineteenth-century Britain.

For a project that has occupied so much of my post-private-sector career, I will be hard-pressed to remember all who have helped me see this to completion. I would like to thank those professors at Florida State University who participated in this project at the dissertation stage, namely Jonathan Grant, Peter Garretson, John Kelsay and Victoria-Maria MacDonald. More intricately involved was my major professor Eileen G. Lyon, whom I thank for introducing me to modern British history and for her love of religious history, as well as her guidance and advice in both the classroom and the research and writing stages of this project at both the master's and doctorate levels.

Along the way I have received tremendous support from colleagues within the Department of History and Anthropology at the University of Central Missouri, who helped keep me focused on my research despite our heavy teaching load. Thanks to John Sheets, Gersham Nelson, Bill Foley, Carol Heming, Paul Rorvig, Sean Kim, Dan Crews and the late Raymond Leonard for your own individual ways of encouraging the path towards publication. Thanks also to the University of Central Missouri for its internal grants that allowed my travel to England in spring 2005 and 2009.

Without the kindness and dedication of many in England who assisted in my collection of primary source materials, this project would never have moved beyond the prospectus stage. I thank most heartily the following archivists: the late Sister Ann Burke (Sisters of Notre Dame, Liverpool); Sister Mary Campion (Faithful Companions of Jesus, Salford); Brother Malachy (Irish Christian Brothers, Altrincham); Brother Damian (De La Salle Brothers, Oxford); Ian Dickie (Westminster Diocese); John Sharp, PhD (Birmingham Diocese); Meg Whittle, PhD (Liverpool Diocese); Robert Finnigan (Leeds Diocese); and Graham Foster, PhD, and Anthony Dolan (Nottingham Diocese). While my access to the Westminster Archdiocesan Archive was somewhat limited and not as open as the others listed, I was able to make up for some of that through use of the relevant correspondence contained in the British Library and the English Catholic records at Pitts Theology Library, Emory University. I also thank Professors V. A. McClelland and Jim Sack for reading and commenting on drafts of the manuscript. My special gratitude goes to my good friend Father David Lannon, Archivist of the Salford Diocese and PhD in history, who has been a model of kindness, encouragement and expertise in the ten years we have known one another, as well as a generous host during my visits to Burnley. Whatever may be found useful in this examination is from the combined efforts of these scholars, advisors and friends; what is in error is my responsibility.

To my family I owe the most. All my love and thanks to my Mom and late Dad, who gamely read through the dissertation but did not live to see this book. Most importantly, everything I have accomplished professionally could not have been done without the constant love, support, patience and good humour of my wife Kristy and son Conor. It is to you both that I dedicate this book. Thanks for keeping me grounded in the present when I was lost in the past.

1 A CHURCH DIVIDED AND THE EDUCATIONAL SOLUTION

'The Catholic Church is springing up again', boasted the Archbishop of Westminster, Cardinal Nicholas Patrick Wiseman, before a captive audience of European Catholic leaders in Malines, Belgium, on 21 August 1863. 'It had left its tap root', he continued, 'under the religious soil of England, from which new suckers are now shooting upwards; the sap which was believed to be drained out is rising in them once more. The old plant scents again the waters, and revives, endowed with a marvellous fertility.' As Wiseman regaled his audience with the triumphs of the Catholic faith in England since the restoration of the hierarchy had placed him at the titular head of English Catholicism thirteen years before, he realized he had to step gently around the one matter that he uncharacteristically described in rather blunt, truthful terms which betrayed a certain lack of success. That issue was education. 'Our weak side is the education of our children', he declared, 'whom our poverty prevents us from bringing up as we would desire'.[1]

These statements comprise two of the central messages of this study. The first is the enthusiasm and confidence reflected in Wiseman's portrait of his Church in mid-nineteenth-century Britain. The second is the sober realization that, despite recent advances for Catholics in England and Wales, education, namely education of the Catholic poor, was an issue in need of tireless effort and one that had to be a priority for Catholics. This same feeling was aptly expressed in a notice in the July 1850 issue of the *Rambler*, a notoriously provocative liberal Catholic journal from mid-century.[2] With the paper's characteristically hyperbolic and alarmist tone, the editors wrote, 'Without the Catholic education of the Catholic poor, all our other efforts are something very like a mockery and a self-delusion'.[3] Within this dichotomy of Catholic exuberance and cautious reflection on education lies the heart of this project. This book argues that the English Catholic community evolved in its pursuit of the education question.[4] This pursuit was a long, tiresome and challenging ordeal which left an indelible mark on the Catholic community. As a result, the Catholic community that witnessed the historic Balfour Act in 1902, which removed many of the most troublesome remaining educational grievances for Catholics, bore little resemblance to that which had welcomed the Catholic Emancipation Act in 1829 or even that which restored the Church hierarchy in 1850. Other factors such as a growing Catholic middle class and economic prosperity, the extension of political reform, and changes in Catholic forms of devotion contributed to that evolution in identity. However, education predominated.[5]

Understanding and monitoring the identity of a community, even one as small as the English Catholic community, can be a daunting and arduous task given the intricacies of human behaviour and the dangers of generalization. Yet an understanding of the complexity of the Roman Catholic community in the 1840s is essential to an understanding of how education may have helped change the face of Catholicism in England and Wales. Much like other English denominations in the early nineteenth century, English Catholicism contained disparate identities split along ethnic and socio-economic divisions. Beginning with the first Catholic Acts in the last half of the eighteenth century, a series of events occurred which allowed for gradual changes in the Catholic community. The Emancipation Act followed by the Oxford Movement in the 1830s and its wave of conversions in the following decade and the Irish Famine in the 1840s all exerted pressures on the English Catholic community; these events kept the community in a continual state of flux. The three important groups which comprised the English Catholic community in the first half of the century were the old English Catholic gentry, the Oxford Movement converts and Irish Catholic immigrants.

English Catholic society following the Glorious Revolution was burdened by the onerous penal laws which severely restricted the religious and political rights of Catholics in both Ireland and England. Although enforcement of the penal codes, which connected civil disabilities with religious constraints, was sporadic and often non-existent, the government treated Catholics as second-class citizens, even if they happened to be wealthy members of the gentry or nobility. In 1778, in the midst of the War of American Independence, Lord North's government passed the first Roman Catholic Relief Act which allowed Catholics to serve in the armed forces and also gave them rights of land ownership. Further Acts removed restrictions on the franchise, entrance into the legal profession and the practices of Catholic clergy in England. By the end of the eighteenth century, most of the civil disabilities and religious restrictions on Catholics had been removed, except for the final indignity – the prohibition of Catholics sitting in Parliament. However, the identity of a community that spent the better part of a century under severe penal laws would undoubtedly be reflected in its actions.[6]

John Bossy's authoritative work *The English Catholic Community 1570–1850* has long provided English Catholic historians with a valuable revisionist interpretation of the nature of the Catholic community just prior to the hierarchy's restoration in 1850. His argument detects a healthy, growing Catholic community throughout the penal era. This is an argument that may be used to temper somewhat the ebullience of Cardinal Wiseman's remarks on the recent growth of the Church in England. Bossy's work did the same to that strain of historiography that used John Henry Newman's famous Second Spring sermon as its starting point, which Bossy argues was not grounded in historical evidence.[7] Since Bossy traces the English Catholic community from its Elizabethan roots, he paints the most complete portrait of the early nineteenth-century Catholic gentry, who had dominated recusant Catholic history. Gentry families were losing their control over the faith in England, due mainly to behavioural changes brought on by the Industrial Revolution. One of those behavioural changes was rural to urban flight which led to their separation from fellow rural Catholics of a lesser economic status. This occurrence was accompanied by a renewed clerical mission chiefly to those same rural Catholics who had relied upon the gentry for leadership. Both of these phenomena lessened gentry influence so that by 1820, Bossy contends, the gentry were no longer a significant contributor to the Catholic community.[8]

Nonetheless, Mary Heimann has shown more recently that Catholic devotional practices of the gentry-dominated recusant period did not disappear when the gentry lost their pre-eminence. In her examination of devotional literature in the nineteenth century, Heimann concludes that it was popular recusant devotions such as benediction and the rosary that dominated the faith of Catholics in the nineteenth century, even after the restoration of the hierarchy. Her strongest piece of evidence that English Catholicism did not become 'more Roman than Rome' was the continued use of Bishop Challoner's *Garden of the Soul* prayer book, first published in 1740 and thereafter until 1899.[9] If we are to accept her thesis, we might clarify some details here. The political and social influence of the old Catholic gentry may have diminished, but the religious traditions from the period in which they dominated with their quieter spirituality did not, even under the glaring light of late nineteenth-century hierarchical ultramontanism in England.[10] Yet the question remains, what would happen to that identity, which was held together for so long by political disabilities, once those disabilities were removed?

Part of the answer is found in Bossy's description of the gentry's waning influence. As the gentry's leadership role declined, Catholic identity evolved as a whole, a process that Bossy explains 'managed to combine fidelity to its tradition and openness to its environment with a rare ... measure of success'.[11] Another part of the answer is found in the gentry's contribution to the education question, along with other members of Catholic society, after their power as a social class had been eclipsed. This part is most relevant to the present book since education played the most important role in the evolution of the Catholic identity because it dominated Catholic interests from the restoration of the hierarchy until the end of the nineteenth century and beyond. A survey of the Catholic press in that period bears witness to its thematic dominance. Whereas Bossy concludes that between 1780 and 1850 English Catholicism experienced several 'processes', all working towards the 'creation of a complicated whole',[12] this book will build upon and extend his conclusion. It will be argued that education was *the* major change mechanism or agent in the evolution of that 'complicated whole' – that new late nineteenth-century Catholic identity. The education question continued to transform the Catholic community fifty years beyond where Bossy ends his study, becoming the dominant issue of the last half of the century for the English Catholic Church. This was especially so for the hierarchy which picked up the mantle of leadership from the Catholic gentry and made education their top priority.

Since the decline of the gentry's influence opened the door to other Catholic leaders and other Catholic influences, it is important to examine the other two dominant components of the Catholic population. The Oxford Movement converts who began to enter the ranks of English Catholicism in the 1840s can be viewed as one of the more obvious examples of the 'Catholic advance' in the nineteenth century. Emerging from the internal conflicts that plagued the Church of England in the early nineteenth century, Oxford converts were a diverse group. Many were men and women of education, public schooling and university, who held diverse religious and political opinions. They included eventual ultramontanes like Henry Edward Manning, William George Ward and Frederick Faber, as well as men like Newman and Ambrose Phillips de Lisle, both of whom exuded a less Roman, more independent style of Catholicism.[13] Interestingly, women played a more substantial role in convert Catholicism compared with old English Catholicism, especially considering the many who funded, founded and joined the numerous religious orders that flourished in the century and added so much to the Catholic educational effort.[14] One historian has interpreted the Oxford conversions as coming in two distinct waves. Earlier waves of converts associated with Newman consisted of those more closely tied into the Oxford intellectual nexus and were clergymen or had very close ties to that world. The later wave brought a wider variety of converts, from clergymen to business professionals to aristocratic women, all of whom converted for a myriad of reasons.[15] It has also been argued that this later wave tended to draw more converts from nonconformity than from Anglicanism.[16]

While the converts were a small group, their contributions were significant, including social and intellectual standing and financial means. The initial wave of conversions convinced emerging ultramontanes like Wiseman that the conversion of England was a possibility, albeit a remote one. However, the energy they infused into the faith contributed to that overall confidence Catholicism began to exhibit after the restoration of the hierarchy in 1850, a confidence represented by their public call for that conversion. Lastly, converts also brought a high level of educational expectations from their Oxbridge experiences that, when applied to the current condition of Catholic education, caused them to question the seriousness and ability of English Catholicism to wage an effective battle for education. This was just one of the issues that led to the profound antagonism that developed between converts and old Catholics, a conflict, for example, carried out publicly in the pages of the *Rambler.* This vehicle of convert ideology consistently violated what old Catholics and burgeoning ultramontanes deemed acceptable. There is no question that consistent points of dissension about education existed between old Catholics and new from the middle until the last two decades of the century, plaguing the educational efforts of the Church. But afterwards, Catholics ended the century with a significant degree of unity, a significant result of the arduous struggle over education.

The Irish Catholics who emigrated to England are the final group.[17] They began moving to Britain late in the eighteenth century in small but steady numbers. Three waves of Irish immigration occurred: around 1790, in the 1820s and in the 1840s. The 'point of equilibrium' between Irish and English Catholics throughout England occurred around 1818, with the percentage of native English Catholics dropping to 20 per cent by 1851.[18] Irish immigrants to Britain tended to settle in three main areas – London, western Scotland and Lancashire – and, by 1851, were a predominantly urban phenomenon, with over 80 per cent living in towns with populations above 10,000.[19] Much has been written about the immigrant Irish Catholics in England during the nineteenth century, which has helped to create a portrait of Irish Catholic identity. Generally, the Irish Catholic immigrants arrived poor, uneducated and unskilled in the labour market. Large numbers of Irish lived in squalid conditions in the industrial towns ridden with disease, overcrowding, alcoholism and a host of other social ills. Lynn Hollen Lees's excellent urban history of the Irish community in London argues that the Irish practised self-segregation and existed in a sub-culture that resisted assimilation into English and English Catholic society. This occurred despite the wishes of the hierarchy, which wanted assimilation and the severing of their cultural attachment to the Irish countryside. Lees concludes that some practices, such as the use of the Irish language, were discarded but others, such as the wake, were continued, even against the wishes of the hierarchy, thus creating a unique community premised on pre-famine tradition as well as the changes that an alien, industrial and urban society forced upon them.[20] M. A. G. O'Tuathaigh also writes convincingly of Irish resistance to assimilation into English society, a resistance based on factors such as lack of education, proximity to home, disappointment of not making it to America, suspicion of the British and the belief that British meddling in Irish affairs caused them to leave in the first place. The Irish segregated themselves from the remainder of society, even Catholic society, purposely, and in this separation were likewise viewed with suspicion and disdain by not only their English Protestant neighbours, but their English Catholic co-religionists as well.[21]

Another more interesting attribute of Irish Catholic immigrants that has also received ample study is the nature of their Catholicism. The idea is a myth that all Irish Catholics regularly practised a robust, orthodox faith by virtue of their having come from a country that had remained Catholic after the tumult of the sixteenth and seventeenth centuries. As Bossy argues, to assume that all Irish Catholic immigrants were assiduous churchgoers before they arrived and only fell into non-practice after experiencing the degradations of the English industrial town is to buy into the myth. His estimates put the rate of consistent religious practice at about 50 per cent for all Irish Catholic immigrants, no matter where they settled.[22] Lees places this number at around 30 per cent in metropolitan London at mid-century.[23] The kind of Catholicism practised by immigrants relates to this argument. Both Bossy and Gerard Connolly dismiss the notion that Irish Catholicism in the form of Irish immigration inspired and saved a dispirited English Catholicism in the nineteenth century. Connolly argues that the opposite was true; Irish Catholic immigration actually weakened a thriving English Catholicism on account of Irish non-practice of many of the sacraments and non-attendance at chapel.[24] Bossy adds that Irish Catholicism bordered on the nature of being a 'folk religion, barely touched by the counter-Reformation ... and unfamiliar with the obligations of regular religious observance and sacramental practice', a thesis first developed by Emmet Larkin, who argued that Irish Catholicism did not begin its 'devotional revolution' until after the famine and under the direction of Archbishop Paul Cullen.[25] Larkin's thesis, however, has been judiciously countered by Thomas McGrath, who saw in Ireland not a post-famine 'devotional revolution', but the last stages of Tridentine reforms that had been delayed in Ireland due to the penal laws.[26] Into this heady historiographical mix is added the notion that although regular attendance at Mass and adherence to the sacraments were lacking, one cannot discount the Irish immigrants' strong psychological attachment to the Catholic Church, even if that attachment was loose enough to cause a decline in religiosity.[27] Clearly, the Irish dimension presented an enigmatic challenge to Church leaders in England, especially since their sheer numbers, most in dire poverty, required the greatest attention and use of Church resources.

If the Roman Catholic communities had little in common with one another besides their faith, the challenge for the Church would be to unite these disparate groups so that English Catholicism could benefit from their collective strength rather than be hindered by their respective differences. The one issue that drew interest from each of these Catholic communities was education. No other issue but education could have possibly served to bring together Catholics, rich and poor, cradle and convert, liberal and ultramontane, English and Irish. The evidence will reveal that support for education crossed ethnic and socio-economic barriers, although contemporary commentators like William Bernard Ullathorne, Bishop of Birmingham from 1850 to 1888, highlighted the notion that poor Irish parents were not as interested in the education of their children as they should have been: 'it is impossible to deny that ... the Irish poor have not, as a body, the same zeal for the education of their children that they have for their religion'.[28] Perhaps Ullathorne's condemnation was not simply a case of blind generalization springing from his experiences in the Midlands, since Catholic primary school logbooks from Lancashire also reveal a certain lack of urgency on the part of parents in getting their children to school with school pence in hand. Even if there was some truth in Ullathorne's accusation, it is fair to say that the importance of education still crossed those barriers. Tens of thousands of poor Irish parents did send their children to school, and the average attendance figures in Catholic elementary schools across the country prove it. Perhaps the singularity of the education struggle was enough to raise the issue above the jealousies and misunderstandings that plagued the different communities within English Catholicism. Evidence of this internal antagonism is seen by the consistent denunciations of Catholic intellectual sophistication by the liberal convert editor of the *Rambler*, John Moore Capes, who offended both the recusant-minded Ullathorne and the ultramontane Wiseman.[29] The one issue, however, that could mollify those divisions and bring some sense of agreement and unity, even if only temporarily, was education, especially of the poor.

Education was one of a few focal points where Church and government were drawn into more frequent contact with one another. As Catholics recognized the need to build, among other social wants, more schools, they saw in that effort the necessity to enter into negotiations with a central government in the process of becoming more collectivist and present in the ordinary lives of its citizens.[30] Contact with the government had not been a priority of old Catholic recusant society so it was just as well that control over English Catholic affairs had passed from the gentry to the more activist vicars apostolic whose positions were replaced by diocesan bishoprics with the restored hierarchy in 1850. The bishops recognized education as the way to prepare Catholics for this world and the next, while also realizing that the effort could possibly have a unifying effect by bringing English Catholics, including the recent Irish arrivals, together for a common goal. O'Tuathaigh argues that the Church in England actively tried to bring unity to its Catholic flock as witnessed by its multitude of educational and social organizations, the object of which was the 'creation, as far as possible, of a self-contained Catholic community of sobriety and solid good behaviour'.[31] This analysis, if broadened beyond the Irish factor to the entire Catholic community, requires repositioning. The hierarchy wanted more than sobriety and good behaviour, even for its most downtrodden. It wanted to prepare its flock spiritually for the challenges of temporal existence and for the glory of eternal life.

Another historiographical argument that has relevance here comes again from Heimann. In her work on Victorian Catholic devotion, she suspects that it was through practices of Catholic devotion, such as the rosary, Stations of the Cross and prayers taken from *The Garden of the Soul*, that Catholics transcended their differences and accepted their faith as a unifying factor. She writes, 'Catholics of all classes, intellectual abilities, and ethnic origins were encouraged to join together in a distinctively Catholic experience which became increasingly accessible in order that it should become more widespread'.[32] My argument, however, comes at this unification from a different angle. Yes, devotional practices may have led to a new spiritual identity, one marked by greater homogeneity that helped break ethnic and socio-economic barriers between English Catholics. Yet, perhaps part of that new Catholic identity to which she points came from the increasingly assertive and self-confident, some might even say aggressive, position on education that dominated the writings and agendas of the hierarchy and the Catholic press in the last half of the century. It could be that neither argument reaches fulfilment without the complementary effects of the other, but the real-life brick and mortar effects of school-building and the high-stakes political manoeuvring involved in the pursuit of the education question cannot be discounted in the transformation of the Catholic identity. In fact, these manifestations led the way.

The examination of nineteenth-century Roman Catholicism in England and Wales continues to be an active field, as witnessed by a number of recent studies beyond those already mentioned, although a comprehensive study of Catholicism and elementary education has been conspicuously absent. In addition to the general overviews by Bossy, Edward Norman and J. Derek Holmes, which touch upon education intermittently, there are other volumes in which education has comprised chapters of larger general examinations of English Catholicism.[33] V. Alan McClelland began nearly half a century of research on English Catholicism and education with his revisionist account of Cardinal Manning, whose reputation had been so damaged by his late Victorian biographer E. S. Purcell.[34] Further important examinations of Manning but not necessarily education have come from D. E. Selby, Robert Gray, Dermot Quinn, James Pereiro and Jeffrey von Arx.[35] Other useful but narrower examinations of the topic that have added to our understanding of the community but have not traced the transformation of English Roman Catholicism into the bolder, more militant, politically active community as this book does have been written by Josef Altholz, Mary Griset Holland, Dermot Quinn and Mary J. Hickman.[36] More recently, Maurice Whitehead has augmented the earlier work of McClelland by stressing the hierarchy's emphasis on education as being one of self-defence, meaning that if Catholics did not educate their own poor, someone else would.[37] John T. Smith has recently provided a valuable comparative examination of late nineteenth-century clergy and the schools by investigating the overlooked educational motivations of Anglican, Catholic and Wesleyan Methodist clergy and the relationships they had with schoolteachers in Victorian Britain.[38]

Kester Aspden's recent analysis of Roman Catholicism in the twentieth century argues that by 1903, the year with which he begins his study, the Church, while still retaining some of its historical defensiveness, had become more confident and assertive in the fight against secularism, and that the twentieth-century bishops often obsessed over the education issue.[39] This book will bridge the gap between Bossy's and Aspden's studies by explaining how the Church and Catholic community evolved while pursuing the schools question into one that was confident, assertive and perhaps even aggressive and obsessional. This educational obsession of the twentieth century was born in the challenging post-restoration period when the Church was simply trying to get its footing amidst a besieged Church of England, an energized nonconformity and the ascendancy of secularism.

The tendency when examining this kind of movement is to focus on the individuals who were the community's leaders. Sometimes that focus can provide a warped image that does not accurately reflect historical reality. In this case, such an exclusive focus would highlight the work of the Catholic episcopacy, while neglecting the important educational struggle waged at the parochial level by lesser members of the clergy and local laity. However, since the bishops took the issue of education and pursued it as their most important goal, a large focus on the bishops is essential. That focus will highlight the efforts of the second and third Archbishops of Westminster – Manning, who served from 1865 to 1892, and Herbert Alfred Vaughan, who served from 1892 to 1903 – to whom improved education seemed essential to the survival of the English Catholic community. It will also reflect the great care and labour of Bishops William Ullathorne, William Turner, Robert Cornthwaite, Alexander Goss, Bernard O'Reilly, Edward Bagshawe and others towards education of the poor in their dioceses. As a result, most of the primary sources for this work consist of books, pamphlets, sermons, pastoral letters, speeches, correspondence and other writings from the pens of the Catholic leadership, some of which were published in the voluminous Catholic press or reported in the mainstream newspapers like *The Times* and the *Manchester Guardian*. Within these tracts, one can discern a distinctive philosophy of education that stood in clear opposition to the centralizing and secular currents pushing for a state-sponsored resolution to the social and educational problems that plagued Britain in the mid-nineteenth century.

To provide a more complete picture of Roman Catholic educational efforts, however, this work will also examine efforts at the regional level, primarily in the dioceses of Salford, Liverpool, Leeds, Birmingham and Nottingham. Other than central London, no part of nineteenth-century Britain had a greater population of Catholics than Lancashire, due to its history as a recusant enclave for old Catholic families and its proximity to Ireland from which immigrants funnelled into the port of Liverpool.[40] With the large Irish population in these dioceses, the Church retained its missionary focus as it had to administer to the great needs of the poor living in areas of Lancashire where

> the cottages are old, dirty and of the smallest sort ... masses of refuse, offal and sickening filth lie among standing pools in all directions; [and] the atmosphere is poisoned by the effluvia from these, and laden and darkened by the smoke of ... factory chimneys.[41]

Improving educational provision for Catholics in areas such as these proved a daunting challenge, but the evidence reveals that the local Catholic clergy and laity in these areas, in part at the direction of the bishops, were actively involved in the struggle for the schools. Local parish communication, including but not limited to a great amount of primary materials related to the educational efforts of religious orders, helps to provide balance to our glimpse of nineteenth-century Roman Catholicism in England and Wales. Most helpful in providing insight into the everyday complexities and impediments of the classroom are the numerous poor school logbooks from the two northern dioceses which open our twenty-first-century eyes to the educational laboratories where policy and rhetoric encountered and often clashed with reality. Finally, this study acknowledges the recommendations and evaluations of Her Majesty's inspectors of schools, many of whose reports were copied into the school logbooks or quoted extensively in the annual reports of the official Catholic school organization.

The reader also needs a solid understanding of Roman Catholic educational philosophy in order to grasp this work's arguments concerning Catholic education and identity. This will add much depth of understanding to the actions taken beginning in the 1840s and continuing to the 1902 passage of the Balfour Act. The next chapter will examine the state of Catholic education at mid-century and the underlying tenets that supported the Catholic position on education to provide a basis from which to validate the central argument: that the struggle for education helped to transform the Catholic identity towards one marked by obstinacy, defensiveness, tenacity and, occasionally, aggression.

Towards the close of Cardinal Wiseman's lengthy speech in Malines, the Cardinal turned reflective about the future. Acknowledging that Catholics, especially in England and Wales, often did not share opinions on political or social issues, he offered to his listeners the maxim that, when problems concerning justice surfaced, those divisions must melt away: '[we must] all unite as in one common cause, and concur in one uniform course of action'. Hitting a note that could have been identified specifically with the education struggle, he continued with hopefulness: 'when the Church has need of our services, especially on behalf of her poor, the same unanimity will prevail, without any admixture of political contention'. He ended on an inspirational note: 'Be united in loyalty, fidelity, and community of interests ... be one in faith, in charity, in zeal, and in adhesion to the centre of unity; and you will carry all your just claims, and attain all your sacred ends'.[42] In reality, Wiseman was trying to inspire Belgian Catholics to overcome their own difficulties. He may as well have been speaking to his own flock.

2 THE STATUS OF CATHOLIC EDUCATION AT MID-CENTURY AND THE CATHOLIC EDUCATIONAL PHILOSOPHY

The Status of Catholic Education at Mid-Century

From the years prior to Catholic Emancipation to mid-century, the state of Catholic education, much like the Catholic community itself, existed in a decentralized, irregular and poverty-stricken condition. This was a time of rising Irish immigration into London and the western port cities but before the great wave of immigration induced by the Irish famine. Without an established Church hierarchy with an organizational centre, Catholic England and Wales remained in the decentralized mission status that had emerged from the penal era following the tumultuous sixteenth and seventeenth centuries. Educational provision was haphazard at best. Yet one historian has shown that despite the disorganized and muddled state of schools prior to 1847, the Catholic community was slowly creating an embryonic system of Sunday and day schools from a variety of funding sources to provide education for some of the Catholic children crowding the Irish slums.[1] More recently, Brian Carter has shed more light on the condition of Catholic charitable efforts and, specifically, education in the first half of the nineteenth century by highlighting the importance of the Catholic middle and working classes and the relative absence of the Catholic aristocracy in that benevolent work.[2]

The year 1838 witnessed an upswing of bigotry towards Catholics from both the Protestant-influenced press and Protestant organizations such as the proselytizing Reformation Society. In response, Catholics founded the Catholic Institute to provide organized administrative and financial support for the informal religious education of Catholics prior to the acceptance of Catholic schools into the state grant system. As Charles Langdale, born of a prominent Yorkshire family, a Member of Parliament, first chairman of the Institute and arguably one of the century's most important lay Catholics involved in educational matters, noted in a letter to the Catholic vicars apostolic suggesting the idea for the first time, 'The press, the pulpit, and the lecture-room, teem with libels on our Church; and even within the walls of Parliament voices are continually raised to swell the tide of calumny against us'. Acknowledging the increase of religious prejudice and the dire need for such an organization, the vicars apostolic cautioned in their reply to Langdale that such efforts should be done with dignity and sobriety.[3] The Institute listed as its goals: repelling the 'calumnious charges' against the Catholic religion; defending Catholic doctrines by publishing and distributing affordable informational tracts; placing in the hands of the poorer classes of Catholics books of piety and devotion; and securing for Catholics the full enjoyment of rights of conscience that the law guarantees. Also listed within this fortress of defensive rhetoric was the cause of Catholic education for the poor, primarily at the elementary level.[4]

When the government announced its plan in 1839 to create the Committee of the Privy Council on Education and thus streamline the grant-giving process, Catholic anger surfaced. The new administrative system was designed to continue the exclusion of Catholic schools from grant programmes unless those schools consented to the use of a Protestant Bible.[5] Foreshadowing what would become a staple of the Catholic educational effort later in the century, a great meeting was held on 15 July at Freemason's Hall, London. Lay leaders of the Catholic community, both Irish and English, as well as several members of the clergy attended. At this boisterous six-hour meeting, amidst several inflammatory speeches and great bouts of cheering, participants accepted and passed nine resolutions on education. These nine resolutions amounted to a declaration of support for government-funded education, a demand that religion be part of that education and controlled by each denomination, and the right of each denomination to receive state funds based on political equality.[6] No speech was as well received as that of the Great Liberator, Daniel O'Connell, the most famous Catholic in the kingdom, who assailed the government:

> They insist upon excluding us from what is the money of all. We are ready to accede at once to the proposition, that so much as is the money of the Protestant let the Protestant have the benefit of it; but so much as is the money of the Catholic it is swindling and robbery to deprive the Catholic the benefit of it.[7]

One of the vicars apostolic who could not make the meeting was the Benedictine Peter Baines of the Western District. His letter, read aloud to considerable cheering, argued that the 'established Church of England has no right to arrogate to itself the education of those who choose to dissent from it; and that every sect has ... an equal right to participate ... in the public grants'.[8]

Catholic outrage, indignant speeches and numerous resolutions, however, had little effect on Parliament in 1839. For the next eight years, the Catholic Institute struggled to provide building and maintenance grants to Catholic schools, a tall order for a community struck hard by the 'hungry forties'. Often, the Institute's reports complained about the lack of contributions; an 1843 article in the *Catholic Magazine* angrily asked its readers how it was that the Institute had received 'not one penny ... during the current year ... from the numerous congregations of Liverpool, Manchester, Birmingham, Glasgow, or Edinburgh'.[9] Further, the Institute's other obligations to support the faith by printing and distributing tracts, prayer books and catechisms compounded its difficulties in funding education. Catholic Institute records describe the meagre educational grants awarded to Catholic schools in the three years prior to the Catholic entrance into the state grant system in late 1847. Only three maintenance grants were awarded in 1845, totalling £50. With improved financial standing, the Institute awarded twenty-eight grants in 1846, coming to £660, but dropped to twenty grants in 1847, totalling £624. Building grants tended to be offered in larger amounts to fewer communities. None were awarded in 1845, fourteen were awarded in 1846 for a total of £1,500, and four building grants in the total amount of £320 followed in 1847.[10] As important as these financial contributions were to any forward progress of Catholic education, especially during a period of rapidly rising Irish Catholic population, much more was needed to meet the educational needs of the Catholic community successfully.

According to the Institute's records for 1843, 236 Catholic elementary schools educated 38,207 children in 571 congregations, an increase from a total of 122 schools in 1833.[11] In 1845 statistics from Catholic mission records reveal approximately 258 elementary schools; according to the *Catholic Directory*, that number fell back to 236 in 1847, leaving approximately 335 congregations without a Catholic elementary school.[12] Given the increasing Irish population, it is likely that by 1848 there were over 40,000 Catholic children being educated in Catholic elementary schools. The figure that alarmed Catholic leaders, however, was the estimated 65,000 Catholic children not receiving any education at all, a number corroborated by a government report on the state of education in 1840 that complained of the 'multitudes of Roman Catholic children ... [who] are consequently left in almost complete neglect, a prey to all the evils which follow profound ignorance and the want of early discipline'.[13] With that number in mind, it is clear the Church faced inadequate capacity even in those parishes where there were Catholic schools. St Helen's, in Lancashire, represents a typical example of this problem. In 1848, the Catholic population of this industrial town was 6,000, of which 1,500 were elementary school-aged children. The lone Catholic school had room for only 100 students, a deficiency of 1,400.[14] Obviously, St Helen's – only 16 km from Liverpool's docks – was feeling the pressure of famine refugees pushing deeper into Lancashire, but similar deficiencies existed across the country. Bermondsey, in the London District, needed space for 2,000, but could provide for the attendance of only 260 Catholic children.

Birmingham, in the Central District, required 2,000 places more than the 570 available, while there was only room at the Central District's Nottingham schools for 210 out of approximately 1,000 Catholic children living in the town. Of the six parishes in Liverpool, approximately 3,200 students attended Catholic schools, but space was needed for another 2,000. Manchester presented perhaps the most dire situation: its schools accommodated only 855 of the more than 6,500 Catholic children living among its six parishes.[15]

The statistics from 1845 Catholic mission records provide further information on the condition of Catholic education, bringing additional deficiencies sharply into focus. Although these deficiencies came in all shapes and sizes, the most common problem was inadequately sized facilities which undermined teaching effectiveness. The Catholic school in the Central District town of Kidderminster in the Midlands consisted of a mere 4x4 m room inside the home of the schoolmaster. The Broadway Catholic school, Central District, held classes in the kitchen of the priest's home, while those at the schools in Nuneaton, Central District, and Poole, Western District, were held in chapel vestry rooms. St John's school in Manchester consisted of two rooms, one of which was too small, the other described as 'totally unfit, being in a miserable attic'. The Yorkshire District's Leyburn Catholic school was held in a small room above a stable, while the school in Cardiff was conducted in a loft above a cooper's workshop. Nor were the London District's Catholic schools immune to these problems: Guildford's Catholic schoolroom was too small and exposed to the weather, while those in Gravesend, Hendred and Chelmsford were actually small rooms located in private homes, a common dilemma throughout the country. In fact, the two most common complaints from these 1845 records were that schools were desperately needed or that existing schools were not large enough.[16]

As stated, funding the construction and maintenance of schools placed a heavy burden on the Catholic community. The pages of early to mid-century Catholic periodicals are filled with accounts of annual charity dinners raising money for schools, and the *Catholic Directory* annually listed the names, addresses and directors of each charity organization, along with a description of their educational needs. One of the most successful early century examples of these charity organizations was St Patrick's Charity School, located on London's Tottenham Court Road.[17] The original school opened in 1803 and privately provided Catholic education for thousands of destitute children through mid-century when the girls school entered into the government grant system.[18] By the 1830s, the charity also operated an orphanage, which extended its financial responsibilities. Its annual fundraising dinner, usually held in late spring, was an occasion for its patrons to meet the children and, hopefully, to increase their donations from the previous year. These often noisy affairs consisted of speeches about the condition of education, Protestant harassment and the increasing numbers of children who required attention, as well as robust toasting and cheering of the Catholic supporters and clergy present. A successful night could raise as much as £371, as occurred in 1837; only two years later, however, the annual dinner raised a paltry £150. In 1850 the St Patrick's Charity Schools entry in the *Catholic Directory* complained openly about the continuing inadequacy of its fundraising and hoped that the following year would provide the funding it needed for all of its programmes.[19] Other examples of such charitable Catholic institutions that relied upon the goodwill of middle- and upper-class London Catholics existed in Poplar, Spitalfields, Southwark, St Giles, Greenwich, Deptford, Hammersmith and Somers' Town. Outside of London, the larger cities of Liverpool, Manchester, Birmingham, Nottingham and Carlisle had comparable organizations, as evidenced by a similar and common complaint about deficient funds at St Patrick's School, Liverpool, in 1833.[20] Interestingly, several Catholic schools from all districts listed their sole source of income as coming from a single local patron, usually a Catholic member of the gentry, who built the school on his property. Catholic schools also employed a myriad of fundraising tactics in this pre-state-grant era such as special charity sermons, tea parties, balls, bazaars, day excursions, general subscriptions and children's pence.

Sometimes funding in these early days came from the most unlikely of places – Protestants. In 1835, at an annual fundraiser for Catholic schools in Poplar, London District, the Rev. Mr Barber spoke kindly of many in the Protestant community who had supported his schools that year through subscriptions. Two years later, at the same fundraising event, the chairman, Andrew Lynch, MP, thanked the local Protestant community for 'attending meetings to promote the religion and education of Roman Catholics' and a toast was drunk to the health of those Protestant gentlemen who had generously supported Catholic schools. A correspondent to the *London and Dublin Weekly Orthodox Journal* wrote of the amazing proceedings in Leicester in August 1836 when the Protestant mayor, Thomas Paget, and his Protestant councillors assisted in fundraising at a solemn high mass and sermon on education at the Catholic Church. Similar examples of extra-Catholic support for education are recorded sporadically throughout the Catholic press in the years preceding 1847.[21]

Another important facet of Catholic education was the handful of schools operated by religious orders, which provided a tremendous boon to Catholic education. Several religious orders returned to England when Revolutionary France chased them from the Continent in the late eighteenth century; the first half of the nineteenth century saw the return and growth of many more, some of which had once thrived in pre-Reformation England. While these orders would realize their greatest impact on secondary education, their role in providing elementary education to the Catholic poor throughout the century was indispensable. The Irish Christian Brothers, founded in Ireland by Edmund Rice in

1802 to educate poor boys, opened its first English school in Preston in 1825, followed by another twenty schools over the next two decades. The internal funding of these schools particularly benefited the English Catholic community. Often criticized by government reports as being too Irish and for being associated with Irish nationalism, these schools were, in fact, excellent centres of learning by the standards of the day. Unfortunately for the Catholic community, problems arose when, in 1850, Catholic bishoprics were re-established in England and the new bishops attempted to exert control over the activities of the religious orders, including running the schools. Additionally, the Irish Christian Brothers refused to accept grant aid (and the subsequent inspections) from the state due to their experience with and suspicion of state-funded and non-denominational schooling in Ireland. They also refused to open fee-based secondary schools for middle-class Catholics, and, as educational costs increased and teaching methods advanced beyond the monitorial system, the financial and educational viability of their schools weakened. The brothers had withdrawn from England by 1880, their schools taken over by less intransigent religious orders like the De La Salle Brothers or the Xaverian Brothers or operated by local priests and lay masters.[22]

Female religious orders began contributing to educational efforts when both the Faithful Companions of Jesus and the Sisters of Mercy came to England to open schools in 1839. By 1850 over twenty different female orders operated Catholic schools in the major towns and cities of England; that number increased after the restoration of the hierarchy upon the invitation of Cardinal Wiseman. Prior to 1847, as with the male religious orders, these institutions supported themselves; however, unlike the Irish Christian Brothers, orders such as the Faithful Companions of Jesus and, later, the Sisters of Notre Dame de Namur, wisely arranged for fee-paying secondary schools to help support their elementary schools. Most female orders also decided to accept grant aid from the government after 1847. Consequently, the female orders held a permanent place in the education of poor Catholics throughout the remainder of the century and beyond.[23] Yet, the need for schools and teachers remained much greater than these religious orders could provide.

One of the earlier political battles over education caused alarm in religious circles in 1843 when Sir James Graham, Home Secretary in Robert Peel's second ministry, proposed a comprehensive factory bill with educational provisions to provide greater national coverage for the fledgling and irregular system of government grants then supporting Anglican and nonconformist primary schools. Graham proposed that factory and workhouse children between the ages of eight and thirteen should receive three hours of education each day under Church of England supervision, while restricting factory time for children to six and half hours. The schools would receive funding from the poor rate and government grants. Even with Anglican control over the education, Graham inserted a conscience clause to placate nonconformists, thus allowing them to withdraw their children from Sunday worship and Anglican catechism. However, the resulting nonconformist and Catholic agitation against the bill prevented its passage and postponed the creation of a true national education system for nearly three more decades.[24]

The importance of this episode to Catholic education lies within the Catholic response to the bill, which revealed a community far from unified on the subject of education and willing to fight one another as much as they battled Graham's legislation. Yet buried in this reaction there is a glimpse of the defensiveness, the boldness and the aggression that would characterize Catholic educational efforts later in the century. Peter Augustine Baines, vicar apostolic of the western district from 1829 until his death later in 1843, caused turmoil within Catholic leadership with his vigorous denunciation of the factory bill and attack on those Catholics, notably the Catholic Institute's Langdale, who were searching for possible compromises with the Tory government. Writing to his fellow vicar apostolic, John Briggs of the Yorkshire district, Baines expressed his hope that Catholic leaders would unite to tell 'Sir Robert Peel (in the civilest possible language) that whilst this anti-Catholic legislation goes on the ministry may calculate upon the ardent opposition of every Catholic lay and clerical in the kingdom'.[25] While Nicholas Wiseman, then co-adjutor vicar apostolic of the Central District, had told Briggs that Graham had personally guaranteed the safety of Catholic schools under the bill, Catholic concern did not abate. Briggs received a letter from Thomas Walsh, vicar apostolic of the Central District, the same day as Baines's letter that articulated for the first time the Catholic desire to have their own schools supported financially by the state, much like Anglican and nonconformist schools were, to ensure a proper Catholic education for Catholic children.[26]

The internal acrimony came the following month when various Catholics actively responded to the impending legislation and found they were not in agreement. Both Baines and Briggs authored and circulated parliamentary petitions against the bill and criticized each other for doing so in a series of rather dramatic letters.[27] Baines's petition reiterated what Walsh had written to Briggs: that Catholics in good conscience could not enter a state elementary education system under the control of Protestants. In response to Briggs's notion that Catholics might help sway ministerial opinion, he replied: 'as to minimalizing ministers, you might as well minimalize your own gate posts. They care nothing for us. They wish to undermine our religion.'[28] A few days later, Baines admitted to Briggs that he did not expect the provisions of his petition to be granted, but simply wanted the ministry to realize that the best way to quiet the Catholics was to offer them grants for their schools. Flashing an assertiveness that was not yet a widespread

Catholic mindset on education, but later would be, Baines justified his demanding petition: 'There are cases in which quiet and determined furiousness are required together with a ... contempt for what men may say, and this is one'.[29] Baines later apologized to Briggs for his criticism of fellow Catholic Langdale, whom he had attacked for supposedly implying that Catholics could use the Protestant Bible, and he called for Catholic unity regarding the bill and education in general.[30] Baines would not live to see such harmony because he died just two months later, his health perhaps exacerbated by the strain of the 1843 bill debate.

Clearly, the state of Catholic education prior to 1847 was fragile. Tea parties, annual dinners and the charity and support of kind-hearted Protestants were not the most reliable ways to build a system of Catholic education with schools located in proximity to need. Competing and divisive answers to educational questions certainly did not help the situation either. While a skeletal system was slowly being built, something more was obviously required.[31] The Catholic community needed government assistance and finally began receiving it after 1847. The community also desperately required better organization and stronger leadership, both of which came with the restoration of the hierarchy in 1850. That leadership helped articulate and publicize the Catholic message on education and bring to the surface a consistent philosophy of education which was paramount to the development of a Catholic education system.

The Catholic Philosophy of Education

In the summer of 1852, the *Rambler* published in two successive issues a remarkable letter to the editor, in which an anonymous Catholic priest compared the goals and merits of state education to those of Catholic education. The letter is singular for its excellent summary of the differences between Catholic and state interpretations of education, the latter of which was steadily becoming influenced by secularism in Victorian society. Sensing that such divergent ideologies would eventually lead to a showdown, the priest outlined the greater benefits of a Catholic education:

> Catholic education has for its one and sole aim the training of the soul for its citizenship in the eternal kingdom of God; State education, the drenching of the mind with a diversified knowledge of facts and sciences ... The Catholic idea of education presupposes a state of moral and intellectual disorder, the fruit of original sin ... [and] it must combine guardianship ... moral [and] intellectual with its tuition. State education, ignoring the doctrine of original sin, appears to presuppose an original perfectibility; thus State education is tuition without guardianship.[32]

The fundamental difference noted here was the absence, in state education, of the guiding influence of religion and its permeation into all facets of the intellect. The fact that state education required Bible reading did nothing to appease this priest's criticism because that, in and of itself, did not equate to an education dependent upon and infused with the authority of God. He concluded that it remained to be 'shewn that the Bible, as used in [state] school education, is necessarily more than a means of teaching reading'.[33]

That letter provides particular insight into the Catholic view of education in the nineteenth century.[34] Because the small but growing English Catholic community was divided, the need for a unifying issue was paramount. Even though differing opinions on education existed within the community, there was much agreement on the essential core issues. The priest's letter would have been widely accepted from Archbishop's House in Westminster to the offices of the liberal Catholic *Rambler* to the Irish parish in the crowded slums of Manchester. The letter described the essential philosophy towards education which eventually unified the Catholic community: 1) education must be based on and built upon religion; and 2) education is more than the acquisition of knowledge and should have a salvific quality. Roman Catholic agreement on this philosophy developed in response to more than half a century of increasing governmental involvement and secular interference in the educational arena. The more the government attempted to wrest educational control from the denominations, the more determined the Catholics became to fight for a Catholic education. As indicated, Catholics did not agree on every aspect of education, but disputes usually arose in regard to peripheral issues as the finer details were resolved. For example, on the subject of secondary or higher education, some liberal Catholics, many of them converts, believed in greater scientific and intellectual freedom and a higher level of secular knowledge than the non-liberal Catholics would allow.[35] Or, regarding primary education, certain members of the hierarchy feared and rejected government aid, while others saw it as the only way to expand education with their limited resources.[36] But over the course of the last fifty years of the nineteenth century, Catholic views, opinions and perspectives began to converge as the elementary education struggle intensified and Catholics recognized that a strong offence consisted of a strong, unified defence.

An essential foundation of that defence was their educational philosophy, which was given formative guidance at the first Synod of Westminster the same summer as the *Rambler* article. This meeting of all the bishops set the agenda for the next fifty years by declaring education of the poor the foremost necessity and goal of the Church: 'Do not rest until you see this want supplied: prefer the establishment of good schools to every other work'.[37] With that in mind, an examination of the Catholic philosophy of education follows.

Education is a Parental Duty

The starting point for the Catholic philosophy of education was the concept that education begins at home. In fact, some Catholics actually stated this outright.

William Turner, Bishop of Salford from 1852 to 1872 and an ardent advocate of an improved and expansive educational effort for the Catholic poor, wrote on the subject of parental duties: 'Let it never be forgotten that, according to the natural and Christian law, the true place of the Education of children, is not the School, but the home of their parents'.[38] Turner further used the Bible for a deeper understanding of this parental responsibility, referring to Isaiah 38:19: 'The fathers shall make Thy truth known to the children'.[39] This reasoning for the parental right and obligation to educate stems from natural law theory as described in the medieval works of Thomas Aquinas. In the *Summa Theologica*, Aquinas wrote on this subject:

> so long as a child does not have the use of reason, he does not differ from an irrational animal ... So, according to the natural law, a son, before coming to the use of reason, is under his father's care. Hence it would be contrary to natural justice, if a child, before coming to the use of reason, were to be taken away from its parents' custody.[40]

Elsewhere, Aquinas speaks of the parents' obligation to educate: 'It is manifest that for the education of man there is required, not only the care of the mother by whom he is nourished, but much more the care of the father by whom he has to be trained'.[41] Taken together, these two arguments formed the basis for which English Catholics understood the duty of parents to educate based on natural law and without undue interference from the government. Accordingly, parental rights and obligations, under the purview of natural law, were also restricted by the requirement to raise and educate children with the knowledge of God. Failure to do so, whether intentional or not, was a religious violation by the parents and that obligation to educate could then be supplemented by the Church, which had the right to oversee the education of Catholics in both spiritual and secular matters.[42]

William Ullathorne, Bishop of Birmingham, told his diocese that parents who did not educate their children in the faith were worse than infidels because they had broken their pledge to God:

> It is therefore the inherent and sacred right and duty, which God has implanted in your souls together with your faith, that you educate your children in the Catholic faith. ... This duty is divinely imposed upon the souls of all Catholic parents, and makes you deeply responsible before God for its performance.[43]

Robert Cornthwaite, the prolific Bishop of Beverley from 1861 to 1878 and Leeds from 1878 to 1890, expressed a similar opinion when he cautioned his diocese that the state was attempting to relieve parents of their right and duty to educate.[44] When the bishops used such language, they were adhering closely to the Thomistic vision of education. Yet they were certainly not naive enough to believe that parents could provide an education to their children, and they believed the Church assumed the responsibilities of education by proxy under the consent of the parents. Although this modified the letter of the argument for parental rights, it did not alter its spirit. Catholic leaders were well aware of this and did not leave the concept unstated either.

Henry Edward Manning, Archbishop of Westminster, exposed the ridiculousness of taking the argument of parental rights too literally.[45] 'To say that fathers and mothers are to educate their children', he argued, 'and that their home is to be the school of Christian instruction, catechetical teaching, formation of conscience, preparation for sacraments ... is either the shallow talk of men who know nothing of Christian education ... or a mockery of the poor'.[46] Perhaps Bishop Vaughan explained this obligation in the strongest religious terms. He argued that when the parents baptized the child, they were 'recognizing the joint right of Christ to the education of the child'. As such, parents contracted a supernatural obligation to Catholic education that could not be abrogated by the government without revealing tyrannical intent.[47]

Education Must Mould Character

The second premise of the Catholic philosophy of education may be gleaned from another article in the *Rambler*, which stated unequivocally in 1856, 'Education, then – real, true education – is not, in its essence, imparting knowledge, but it is the formation of character'. Since character is comprised of one's habits, the purpose of education

> is to form and establish in the very soul of the child certain fixed principles and rules of conduct; rails, not indeed of iron, but of a material as unbending, laid down in the road of life ... to guide and support him ... until he arrives at the appointed terminus.

Salvation, of course, represented that destination.[48] Granted, the *Rambler* held liberal Catholic positions, was an organ of some of the converts and was unpopular in some important Catholic circles, but the same view of education can be found in the more mainstream and hierarchically approved Catholic quarterly, the *Dublin Review*.[49] In an article from October 1883, the writer stated that one of the most important features of a Catholic school was that the education should consist primarily in 'influencing the manners, conduct and character of the scholars'.[50] Another *Dublin Review* article argued that in a Catholic education, 'the mind and character ... [must] be formed upon the motives of religion', and that every aspect of a young Catholic's life must be 'moulded by, coloured and seasoned with Catholic principles'.[51] Bishop Cornthwaite aptly argued in an 1869 pastoral letter that education trains both the heart and the mind, preparing the student's character for citizenship on earth and in heaven.[52] The prominent convert Thomas William Allies, one of the most influential laymen to have worked for the progress of Catholic education in this period, provided answers to an educational questionnaire in 1859 that reflected similar views of this Catholic perspective on education.[53] To a question on whether any Catholics had certain objections to the current system, Allies responded that since Catholics viewed education as more than instruction, and 'as a moulding of the whole moral and intellectual being', they would always be attuned to the operation of the system and highly sensitive to any proposed changes.[54] Fundamental beliefs associated with the formation of character transcended the existing territorial walls between diverse Catholics and provided the first essential common ground needed for this community to bridge its differences.

A corollary argument emerged on the basis that education stood far and above mere instruction because it intended to inculcate morality into one's character. Bishop Turner warned that unless morality was embedded into the process, then education would simply consist of the acquisition of secular knowledge and our children's hearts would be 'dragged into the gulph [*sic*] of every vice'.[55] Archbishop Manning, who was arguably the single most important contributor to the Catholic educational effort in the last half of the nineteenth century, defined education as a civilizing force by which 'the reason, the conscience, the heart, the will, and therefore the character and the life, of the young are shaped and moulded'.[56] Manning, however, had developed a strong foundation for his educational position even before converting to Catholicism in 1851, when he served as the Anglican Archdeacon of Chichester. In 1843, he examined the growing controversies over education in the context of the Factory Act in an address to fellow Anglican clergy that year. Defending against the rising challenge of nonconformity towards Anglican educational dominance, Manning forged a solid argument to counter 'any scheme which thwarts or entangles the free exercise of the catechetical [*sic*] office of the Church', a threat he called 'pure evil'. Keeping education under the Church was the only way to save the next generation of Englishmen from being lost, he argued.[57] Such thoughts obviously influenced his later Catholic educational philosophy and provided Catholicism with excellent insight on the Anglican educational position.

This morality-inculcating role of education also surfaced when the Rev. Walter J. B. Richards, an oblate of St Charles and a diocesan inspector of schools, told a parliamentary commission that religion was the only basis for building character and that immorality would be the natural result of a secular education. He related an interesting example to the commission about a Protestant schoolmistress who brought her own child to be admitted into a Catholic school. When asked by the manager why she did not put her child into her own board school, the teacher replied 'that she could not give any sufficient teaching of morals to her [there]'. She believed, according to Richards, the security of her child's morals to be safer in the Catholic school. This example proved so unbelievable to the commission that they asked whether this was based on hearsay or not. Richards promptly answered that he heard it directly from the mistress of the Catholic school.[58]

Education Must Have a Religious Element

Catholics, lay and clerical, consistently stated that education must contain a religious element. Therefore, Catholics viewed as a danger any plan that threatened to supplant education founded upon strong religious principles with generic, non-doctrinal religion or secular education. The bishops were keenly interested in keeping doctrinal religion a part of education, and, as the history of the English Catholic hierarchy revealed in the nineteenth century, elementary education of the poor was the domain of the bishops. Birmingham's Bishop Ullathorne recognized the danger of education without religion in 1850 when William James Fox brought an education bill to the floor of Parliament. Fox's bill sought the empowerment of local governments to use local rates to 'fill any gaps' left by the denominational school system. In addition, the new schools were to be completely secular in nature, devoid of any religious training. With this bill Fox hoped to rid education of the sectarian impasse that plagued the system. The Church of England, however, saw this bill as both a threat to its hegemony over education, as well as a general threat to society, which it believed was founded upon moral and religious education.[59] The bill proved so radical to the religious sensibilities of Anglicans, Catholics and some nonconformists that it did not pass. In reaction to the bill's introduction, Bishop Ullathorne laid bare what he saw as the true nature of Fox's plan:

> By it you indoctrinate and familiarise the mind with a principle that only wants the force of passions for a momentum with which to outheave from the soul of youth both the principle of authority and the positive doctrines of religion together.[60]

Despite the failure of the bill, it awakened many to its possibilities and supporters of state-supported, nondenominational schools continued to push for a national plan.

Alexander Goss, Bishop of Liverpool from 1856 to 1872, feared that the Victorian emphasis on self-reliance in education would crowd out religion and permit, and possibly encourage, the youth to desire a higher station in life beyond their means, a station decidedly secular.[61] Bishop Turner stated the Catholic position to the faithful in the greater Manchester area using terms that could not be misunderstood. In a letter to the clergy in 1869 he wrote, 'Education to be genuine must always rest upon the foundation of religion ... An education that should not comprise religious instruction, would be a serious evil'. He then placed his admonition in a historical context: 'Trace the progress of those evils which, have devastated society, destroying both the Altar and the Throne, and see how these calamities have had their origin in the neglect or abuse of education'.[62] In the same year, Archbishop Manning wrote an important pastoral letter on denominational education that focused on one simple yet forceful message: 'Education without religion is impossible'.[63]

Not surprisingly, the lower levels of the Church hierarchy held similar views on education as the bishops. Inevitably, the further one ventured into the lower reaches of the Catholic Church, the greater the diversity of opinions stemming from the greater variety of backgrounds. Despite this caveat, however, elementary education moved priests to echo the views of their bishops. In addition to serving their normal duties in the church and around the parish, many parish priests also served as managers of poor schools throughout the country. As school managers these priests dealt first-hand with the myriad of problems encountered in operating a school for the poor, including hiring and replacing teachers, ensuring that religious and secular educational standards were met, raising money for construction and maintenance, paying off the debt and getting parents not only to send their children to the school, but to send them properly clothed and with their school pence.[64] Naturally, as the government's role in education increased and regulations and requirements added to the burden of operating a poor school, elementary school managers shared in the contempt of the bishops for any movement towards secular education or decreasing denominational control over education. Regarding the separation of religion from education, priests reiterated much of what the bishops were saying. The Rev. Canon Toole, a Manchester priest, told a group of educationists in 1866 that the growing support for separating religion from education, especially of the poor, was unsound.[65] He explained that only a religious education could control their behaviour and, by implication, keep social order:

> Hence the necessity of making religion a part of the only education which they can obtain, that they know and feel from the beginning that it is a necessary part of the training which is to fit them for the discharge of the whole duty of a man.

A secular education divorced from religion that might include 'the more polished intercourse of life, may give an exterior of propriety, and may refine, but cannot subdue the passions' of the poor.[66] Canon Frederick Oakeley of London published the pamphlet *Education to be Real Must be Denominational* in 1872. In it, Oakeley, a convert, expressed his view that education without religion 'is in fact no true education at all: it is meaningless, aimless, characterless. It is the form without the spirit.' He reinforced the prevalent belief that education without religion was how dangerous creeds such as 'Socialism, Communism, Fenianism, and all the various forms of political heresy and social confusion' were adopted and disseminated.[67]

Many lay Catholics played prominent roles in the education struggle during the latter half of the century, some as Members of Parliament, others, such as Allies, through a career in education. While lacking social diversity – most came from the upper middle class, gentry and aristocracy – this group of laymen consistently dedicated themselves to the cause of elementary education for the poor. Many of them represented old Catholic families which had survived since the Reformation. Charles Langdale's position on education was clear from the beginning of his involvement in educational matters: 'I believe you cannot have education, properly so termed, without religion ... Without religion I cannot but consider this valueless, and but too often worse than valueless'.[68]

The laity, lower clergy and the bishops all agreed that without religion there would simply be no education at all. It should be understood that this opinion was not unique to Catholics. Anglicans and some Wesleyan Methodists generally shared similar opinions on the subject with Catholics, resulting in these three groups forming the vanguard of the voluntary school movement, led by the Anglicans, in opposing the bulk of the nonconformists who had acquiesced to the idea that the nondenominational religious education given in the board schools post 1870 was acceptable because it was not controlled by the Anglican Church.[69] The solidarity of Catholic opinion so consistently and forthrightly expressed regarding the separation of religion from education reveals a community beginning to shed the chains of factionalism and, at least on the question of elementary education, to offer a unified front.

Education Must be Devotional and Catechismal

Not only must a Catholic education build moral character and be inseparable from religion, but it must also include certain devotional and catechismal elements. Catholic leaders feared that attendance in board schools or even in non-Catholic denominational schools would distance Catholic children from the faith even more than poor living conditions, tenuous family situations and itinerant employment. Attendance at Catholic schools ensured that children would have the frequent and consistent practice of daily classroom devotions that marked a Catholic education. The strategy, then, was to provide an education for each Catholic child that would meet with the following description from Cardinal Wiseman:

> Let their intellects be instructed by the Eternal Wisdom, speaking through His Church. We will have them not drily believing in the most blessed Trinity, but invoking it at the beginning of each daily lesson: we will have them not merely look upon

> the Cross of their Saviour, but impress it hourly upon their foreheads, as the pledge and badge of eternal life ... All this only a Catholic education can secure them.[70]

The hierarchy treated the duty of parents to send their children to a Catholic school seriously. Bishop Cornthwaite could not have been more clear when he announced to the Beverley diocese that sending their children to secular schools or 'to those where a false religion is taught ... would be a breach of duty, for which God will call them to a strict account'.[71] The stern tone was justified because only in the confines of a Catholic school could the children learn the catechism and the daily devotions.[72]

Devotions were non-liturgical, outward or physical expressions of faith learned in the catechism and could be viewed as forms of popular piety. As children learned their catechism, they were also trained as to the proper devotional actions that made Church dogma manifest. Devotions could involve physical items, such as crosses or rosaries, or could simply refer to prayers, but all had some basis in Church dogma as revealed in the catechism. For example, the schoolroom practices of making the sign of the cross on the hour or impressing the cross against the forehead were early Church devotions re-popularized in Richard Challoner's *The Catholic Christian Instructed in the Sacraments, Sacrifices, Ceremonies and Observances of the Church by Way of Question and Answer*. In this eighteenth-century catechism, originally published in 1737, making the sign of the cross was explained, with reference to Church fathers Augustine and Tertullian, as a devotion done many times throughout the day 'to show that we are not ashamed of the cross of Christ'.[73] In the *Abridgement of Christian Doctrine*, published in 1759 and revised in 1826, Challoner inserted the devotion of making the sign of the cross at the strike of the clock with the intention that children would follow his example.[74] Challoner's most famous work *The Garden of the Soul*, originally published in 1740 and republished several times until 1899, also supported this devotion. When English Catholics insisted upon devotional activities mixed in with the daily process of education, the evidence points to their citing *The Garden of the Soul*'s directive to keep God predominant in all of one's thoughts and actions throughout the day.[75]

Bishop Turner believed the crucifix and other religious symbols to be as necessary to the educational development of a child as the reading of lessons.[76] Manning conceded later in the century that the importance of finding suitable teachers was one of the most pressing concerns in the successful operation of Catholic schools because 'a teacher's office ... is that of a catechist, and an intimate fellow-helper in our pastoral office'.[77]

Thus, concern for spiritual education via the catechism was another point of agreement among Catholics. There was nothing that so identified a purely Catholic education as the teaching of the catechism and the performance of daily devotions in the classroom to outwardly express the meanings of the catechism. These actions were uniquely Catholic and marked the classrooms as places where religion held supreme even when secular subjects were being taught. They were a reminder that the ultimate purpose of this life, and thus any education one received, was to prepare for the next.

Education as a Defence

The decline of religiosity and the rise of secularism were two formidable opponents with which all Christian faiths battled in the nineteenth century.[78] Catholics had recognized the nascent danger of secularism by mid-century and, much like their fellow Christians, actively attempted to deflect it. Clearly religious education was the best bulwark against such a threat.[79] As early as 1844 the *Tablet* remarked on the declining religious spirit of the age and the growing appetite for secular ideas and attractions: 'When if ever there was an occasion, was there such a one as the present age? An age steeped in luxury and famine ... an age of unbelief ... in Christianity'.[80] At mid-century, Manning, then newly converted to Catholicism, approached this subject in a series of published lectures called *The Grounds of Faith*. In them, he asked what had contributed to Britain's greatness and concluded that the nation's success came from things 'material and not moral'. Manning further opined that 'the rule of Faith once lost, [then] souls wander and perish, [and] men ... come to state, as scientifically certain, that there is no definite doctrine in revelation'.[81] Catholics perceived a march of the secular, the spirit of which, according to Cardinal Wiseman in a pastoral letter in 1856, had grown much stronger and more invidious because it had 'assumed all the shape of a "denomination," imitates the forms of "religious bodies," ... has public meetings with chairman and lecturer ... [and] has printing-presses and its offices'. The solution, he believed, was the resuscitation and improved health of denominational education, given his belief that rising secularism was stealing Catholic children from the Church.[82]

Protestant proselytism also threatened the Catholic Church. Protestant organizations such as the Reformation Society had, by mid-century, begun targeting poor Catholics in the slums of Britain's largest cities.[83] Edward G. F. Howard, MP for Arundel and brother to the fourteenth Duke of Norfolk, raised this concern in a letter to Charles Langdale, when he was Chairman of the Catholic Poor School Committee. Published in the committee's official periodical, the *Catholic School*, his letter attempted to increase the awareness of Catholics to the dangers of losing their children to the Protestants. This threat, Howard warned, was a 'stimulus ... given to us ... to step in with heart and hand to rescue [the at-risk children] – to save them at once ... from proselytism'.[84] Wiseman described the same threat in a pastoral letter to his diocese a year later. Beware, he exhorted, of the

> fresh and energetic efforts made of late in London, to draw our poor children away from our own schools. If we sleep, the enemy will come and scatter tares among the hopeful seed which we have long been sowing, and spoil the future harvest of the Church.[85]

The peril was considered great enough that Bishop Turner reminded his parish priests throughout the Manchester area to caution parents about sending their children to Protestant schools where proselytism and imminent peril to their faith existed.[86]

While threats of secularism and Protestant proselytism were daunting, what Catholics truly feared was the end result of these two forces: the falling away from the faith.[87] This danger permeated much of the Catholic literature on education and other social matters from mid-century to the beginning of the twentieth century. The *Tablet* ran an article titled 'The Crimes of Apostasy' which delivered this dire warning:

> It is impossible to imagine a more awful and pitiable condition for a human soul than that in which, having once known the truth, it has fallen from it, and the intellectual conscience has become so perfectly purblind that it ... mistakes light for darkness, truth for error, heaven for hell ... [and] when the fall of the spiritual nature has been so complete that not a pulse beats.[88]

It has been argued that leakage became the dominant problem for the Church in the nineteenth century as baptized Catholics, primarily Irish, stopped practising their faith in a regular fashion.[89] Statistical evidence on apostasy was difficult to generate, but historians put the number of practising Irish Catholics at only between 30 and 50 per cent of the entire Irish Catholic population.[90] Such substantial, potential apostasies were not lost on the hierarchy, especially the parish priests who had daily contact with the Catholic poor.

The first annual report of the Catholic Poor School Committee proclaimed that the prevention of apostasy was an important part of their overall mission.[91] The same inaugural report included a pastoral letter from Wiseman to the Westminster diocese in London appealing for the invigoration of Catholic education because 'in spite of the great efforts which have been lately made, multitudes of children of Catholic parents are lost to us from their not receiving from us a religious education'.[92] Over a decade later, in the same year that he replaced Wiseman as Archbishop of Westminster, Manning penned a message to his new diocese. In it he offered a plenary indulgence to those who would work for the benefit of the thousands of poor children. Apostasy was his culprit, and he asked incredulously, 'How is it that Christians who believe in the supernatural grace of Baptism can neglect the Christian education of their children, and can even endure to see helpless, unconscious souls robbed of their faith?' Their work would not be done, he said, 'until the name of every Catholic child is inscribed in the books of our Schools, and not one shall grow up ... without a Christian and Catholic education'.[93]

Of importance is the consistency of the Catholic message concerning the threats of secularism, proselytism and apostasy. From bishop to parish priest to layman to newspaper editor, ultramontane and liberal, old Catholic and convert, the consensus was the same – they would only be successful in stemming the tide of those threats by pursuing an active, aggressive educational policy. This consistency helped engineer and bolster the new and emerging Catholic identity with intense commitment, a sense of purpose, rhetorical aggression and increased confidence. In the name of education, particularly elementary education, Catholics rose against common enemies of the faith and, in doing so, created a unified community from disparate parts.

Conclusion

Much of what defined a Catholic education was defensive in nature and was explained in reaction to governmental initiatives or legislation or in response to the gradually increasing activities of secularist education organizations. Catholic leaders did not set out to define (and redefine) education simply because they were not satisfied that their public understood it correctly. Much like the Church of England, which was equally insistent on this subject, Catholics believed their educational philosophy and practices were being threatened and that mobilization was a necessary defence. Pastoral letters, editorials, essays, pamphlets and parliamentary debates and testimonies were all part of the energetic and unwavering Catholic defence of the subject which mattered most to them. A profound tradition of religious obedience with the Catholic community may, in part, explain this unity – from hierarchy to parish priest to laity – on the education issues. The bishops, under the ever-watchful and guiding eye of *Propaganda Fide* from Rome, controlled the education debate and Catholic parishioners, understanding the importance of obedience, especially when they were a struggling minority in a sometimes hostile environment, followed suit. Yet beyond obedience, this unity can be explained by the fact that education was understood by the middle of the nineteenth century to be a positive contribution to the lives of the poor. And since Catholics believed that education was more of a preparation for the afterlife than for any temporal ends, there was no reason why all of the divisions within the Catholic community could not agree on the primacy of education and to do so more confidently and aggressively as the century came to a close.

A Catholic education had to be religious in nature, comprised of a combination of both secular and religious knowledge and had to prepare each Catholic properly for a life of devotion in order to reach an afterlife of salvation. Furthermore, even secular instruction had to be permeated with Catholic religious principles and supplementary to the entire religious atmosphere which included characteristic Catholic practices that could only be found within a Catholic school. This overall philosophy guided the Catholic struggle for schools, providing the bedrock upon which was built a community overcoming its quiet recusant past and developing verve and energy to meet the educational needs of its members.

3 EDUCATIONAL OBSTACLES TO OVERCOME

The visit of Her Majesty's inspector was the day for which the entire school year was spent in preparation. Even so, Catholic school logbooks, in which teachers recorded daily notes on events, visitations and other schoolroom incidents, reveal that the amount of secular instruction spiked in the months leading up to the inspection, often at the expense of religious education. As the examination neared, teacher entries in the school logbooks reflect the heightened repetition of secular lessons for all levels of students. The logbooks also reflect tangible classroom anxiety as teachers not only struggled to teach rudimentary skills in preparation for the examination but also battled daily attendance problems. Imagine the impact on the headmaster and manager from the following report – a report that affected a school's financial health – when it was published several weeks later:

> The state of instruction in the ... school calls for notice. I found the advanced children unable to copy letters from the black book and frequently their efforts were unintelligible. The progress of the children will be retarded seriously by not laying these necessary foundations. Sewing I found does not exist at all ... and there is no reason why it should not be taught here as elsewhere. Some of the seats in the gallery require backs ... [and] the walls require illustrated cards of object lessons. The Committee of Council will be unable to allow an unreduced grant to the Infants school next year unless Her Majesty's Inspector reports more favorably upon the instruction.[1]

Upon receiving such a report, the school faced reduced funding unless drastic changes were implemented to correct the highlighted deficiencies. Possibly because of his ultimate responsibility to the bishop if the school lost grant money and endangered its future and to the education of local Catholic children, the manager, usually the parish priest, might even replace the teacher after such a report.

Not all Catholic inspection reports were as dire as this. In fact, most earned adequate, some even exceptional, grades, but even the acceptable schools were reported to have deficiencies, usually stemming from a lack of financial resources. It is noteworthy, however, that this report, dire as it was, came not from an unfriendly Protestant inspector but from a Catholic inspector. More importantly, this vignette can serve as a portal into the state of Catholic education and the obstacles Catholics faced on a daily basis: the lack of adequate facilities and supplies, the inability of students to pass simple examinations and the conspicuous absence of required subjects. Reading between the lines of this report, one senses even bigger problems: a serious lack of funding, low quality of teaching and administrative frustration. These problems, and more, regularly confronted the Catholic educationist, thereby making the struggle to build, maintain and control the schools a daunting task. Such challenges necessitated Catholic entry into the political battle for education to secure a more equitable share of educational funding, a battle Catholics entered cautiously but in which they remained long into the next century.

Despite the diverse nature of educational problems, the foremost obstacle Catholics faced was a lack of financial resources, a problem not unique to the Catholics. This difficulty hampered Catholic education efforts from the building and supplying of schools to attracting, training and retaining teachers. Although still an impediment at the end of the century, the constant financial encumbrance forced Catholic educationists to find clever and unique ways to raise money. More importantly, it also forced them eventually to recognize the necessity of governmental aid if they were to keep their schools remotely competitive. Ultimately, it was their community-wide indigence that compelled Catholics to demand rate-aid for their schools, as well as to become active players within the system, rather than reluctant participants. Although it occurred among Catholic leadership, this shift reflected a more general and greater transformation of the entire community from quiet outsiders into more conspicuous activists. But by accepting an active role within the system, as exemplified by their call and struggle for rate-aid, they simultaneously consented to a further loss of educational control and independence as that rate-aid would mean some form of public management. Such was the necessary price to keep the schools operating and expanding in number. Yet, it was also a move that reflected confidence – confidence that they could relinquish some control while still firmly guiding Catholic education and maintaining an uncontaminated philosophy.

Lack of Unity

Early in the struggle, Catholics lacked educational unity. This situation improved as the century came to a close, but, at mid-century, Catholics still struggled to find agreement on how to educate their children. Of all the obstacles, this lack of unity required recognition and remedy; for the Catholic community unity meant strength and strength meant success. Disunity clearly reflected the contentious nature of Catholicism in England and Wales as described earlier. The *Rambler* spoke of the absence of Catholic unity as early as 1849 by referring to the community as 'notoriously the most disputatious ... in the kingdom, quarreling with one another on every possible opportunity'.[2] Of course, this very journal was a major contributor to and participant in that discord. Its liberal outlook conflicted with the ultramontane beliefs that the revived episcopacy would soon be taking, and its scathing criticism of the backward status of Catholic education and intellectual activity was laced with conspicuous contempt for the old Catholic community populated mainly by the gentry and aristocracy. Another example of its acrimonious hand-wringing came in 1856 when the journal criticized those Catholics personified by the 'couleur-de-rose man', who could not see the terrible danger awaiting English Catholicism and who always saw the glass as half full. The author argued that the future of the faith depended upon how the education issue would be solved.[3] At issue was the journal's belief that more converts should be afforded a greater role in educating Catholics, a situation the hierarchy wished to avoid. Cardinal Wiseman, taking great offence at this characterization and assuming it was targeted at him, penned a response in the *Dublin Review* the following month. He disparaged the *Rambler*'s divisive tone, stating that 'we greatly fear the differences, and angry discussions that are rising amongst us on the subject of Education'. He finished with this appeal and dire warning: 'Only let us keep united and trust not to man, and we have nothing to fear. Our real dangers can only spring within ourselves.'[4] The sometimes irascible and always outspoken Edward Bagshawe, Bishop of Nottingham from 1874 to 1902, asked for greater Catholic unity in a politically laced pastoral letter in 1883. Referring to a Papal encyclical to the Spanish Church that criticized the removal of religious influence from politics, Bagshawe pleaded with his own diocese to follow the Pope's advice to keep religious influence involved: 'it is absolutely necessary that we should use all our powers against those who war against the Church ... and, secondly, that we should do all we can to unite and combine in political action with our fellow-Catholics'. This suggestion included meeting together before local and national elections and, if possible, creating local Catholic political associations to prepare for political emergencies.[5]

Despite these pleas to the Catholic laity, disunity persisted when the subject was education. The lack of harmony had its roots in the historical, intellectual and ethnic divisions that plagued Catholic society at mid-century. It was certainly not a divide that could be resolved quickly and easily; in fact, it must be admitted that certain levels of accord came only with the deaths of the most intransigent Catholics. It must also be noted that success, in part, resulted from efforts to overcome other obstacles faced by the Catholic community, such as the necessity to raise money. Yet, healing these divisions became an unvarying priority for Catholic leaders such as Manning, Vaughan, Bagshawe, Cornthwaite and others later in the century.

Lack of Financial Resources

Unlike the lack of unity, the lack of sufficient funding was a problem for which the Catholic community would not find adequate answers by the turn of the century. The steady poverty of the community hampered educational efforts and, as a result, led to a deficiency of schools, teachers, supplies and other educational necessities. George Richardson, a prominent Mancunian lay Catholic, wrote that the community's poverty, coupled with the rigid rules of government aid, meant that 'education is amply provided where it is *little* needed, and entirely neglected where it is *most* required'.[6] Scott N. Stokes, a Catholic inspector of schools, argued as much in the *Rambler*. Catholics, he argued, simply could not furnish enough money to build sufficient schools on their own; therefore, he strongly recommended that all bishops and priests take advantage of government aid.[7] Cardinal Wiseman also recognized the desperate situation Catholics faced in raising money and building schools when he told his audience in Malines, Belgium, that his own diocese had over 17,000 Catholic children not in attendance at Catholic schools.[8] Further, a Catholic report in 1870 cited the appalling condition of Catholic education in Leeds where funds were 'manifestly insufficient'. Since grant aid from the state only matched that raised through subscriptions and school pence, the schools in Leeds faced insurmountable obstacles because of the extreme poverty of the more than 20,000 Irish Catholics inhabiting the city.[9] In October 1870, the *Month*, a Jesuit periodical, remarked that less than a third of all Catholic children were being educated and that nearly £400,000 was required to build the necessary schools to educate them.[10] After yet another insufficient collection for his Diocesan Mission Fund, Bishop Goss of Liverpool complained bitterly in his sermon about the inability of Catholics in his diocese to raise sufficient funds in contrast to local Protestants. He asked the congregation if there were no Catholics who could give more. Goss then examined the collection data from various churches based on their average attendance figures and determined that Catholics were subscribing between ½ penny to ¾ penny per head, a figure far below what he expected. He added sarcastically about the more fashionable Catholic parish of St Francis Xavier's, 'Why, they would give twenty times that amount to witness an execution at Kirkdale!'[11]

At the local level, a variety of money problems surfaced regularly. Very often the burden was most heavily felt by the local parish priest, who could be overwhelmed by the financial intimidation of a new project and required assurance from the bishop that with hard work and government aid, schools could be built successfully.[12] Sometimes that assurance was not enough and local priests wrote to their bishops despairingly. Timothy O'Connell informed Bishop Cornthwaite that the Keighley mission was in deep financial trouble in 1869: 'I can't pay it [the mission debt] more, especially at present as I have quite enough to do to pay current expenses!'[13] Similarly, in 1886 Rev. John Sherlock expressed to Bishop William Ullathorne in Birmingham the fear that his school might have to close due to debt. Sherlock listed four main causes, all of which were not unique to his location and might be found in any Catholic mission. First, his Catholic population had decreased but he was obligated to keep the same number of staff at the school. Second, they had had to forego the school pence for at least half of the children due to unemployment. Third, they had not been able to secure the assistance of pupil teachers and were forced to employ teaching assistants at a higher salary. Finally, his schools had lost £85 from the annual grant the previous two years due to poor record-keeping. 'If something is not done to lessen this debt', he argued, hoping for assistance from his bishop, 'I see plainly we must close St John's School after the examination next October'.[14] Further, in 1887, the master of Holy Cross School, Liverpool, Lawrence Conway, admitted that poverty was the main hindrance towards securing more teachers and more seats for children, and that priests in his area were reduced to begging door to door to raise subscriptions for the schools.[15] With necessity the mother of invention, more enterprising ways to raise funds emerged as needed, from, as indicated earlier, the holding of community bazaars to the bold suggestion from William Hogarth, Bishop of Hexham from 1850 (and Newcastle from 1861) to 1866, that the Church tax everyone over fourteen years of age ½ penny per week to go into the diocesan general fund.[16]

In 1883, the *Dublin Review* raised the concern that this continued lack of means would ultimately lead to Catholic children attending non-Catholic schools, since Catholic schools could not compete with the former in terms of quantity, size, amenities and number of teachers. Poor Catholics would be impressed with the physical appearance and pretensions of the competition's schools and, by attending these non-Catholic institutions, would endanger their faith.[17] This belief was reinforced by Rev. Dr Thomas Graham, principal of St Mary's Training College, Hammersmith, from 1869 to 1899, who admitted that Catholic children were sometimes forced to go to such schools where a Catholic school did not exist and could not be built because of insufficient means.[18] Even as late as 1888, Cardinal Manning lamented how the poverty of the Catholic community continued to impede educational endeavours. In a pastoral letter, Manning implored the community to reach deep again to support their new missions because:

> the priests of these new and poor missions are in true poverty. Their people cannot give them the barest maintenance; and the support of the schools can only be sought from friends and the faithful beyond the bounds of their mission.[19]

John Baptist Butt, Bishop of Southwark from 1885 to 1897, lamented in 1889 the inability to secure funds for the rising number of Catholic orphans and again in 1890 the insufficient funds to support the schools needed throughout this large diocese that began at the Thames and extended south-east to the Kentish coast.[20] The lack of financial resources and growing debt concerned Bishop Cornthwaite to the point that he established for the Beverley Diocese a guide on prioritizing liabilities so that funds could be expended on 'definite and permanent' debts before all others, meaning that interest and principal payments on the buildings (schools, churches, presbyteries) would be given first priority.[21]

Lack of Qualified Teachers

Related to poverty and the inability to build enough schools was the lack of qualified teachers. In 1848, there simply were not enough Catholic teachers to meet the demand generated by increasing numbers of school-age poor children and additional school openings. The teacher deficit was recognized early on when Catholics were still solidifying their relationship with the government upon being admitted to the state education system. The October 1854 issue of the *Catholic School* contained the general report for 1853 on education in north-west Great Britain. Written by Stokes, the article noted that school accommodation remained a problem but that a more serious dilemma was a lack of teachers. He wrote: 'The manager of a school desirous to secure the services of an able master finds himself at a total loss', thereby rendering 'existing schools, as well as any additional institutions which may be founded ... crippled and ... useless'.[22] He recommended building both a male and female training college in the north-west because St Mary's, Hammersmith, could not provide enough teachers for the entire country on its own.[23] The following year with the situation no better, the *Catholic School* published 'On the Necessity of Training-Schools for Lay Teachers'. This seventeen-point tract repeated the need for improved training facilities for Catholics, beginning with the simple and rather direct realization that the absence of qualified teachers was the largest educational obstacle for the Church. It further warned of the perils of employing teachers who had not received any special training under Catholic guidance because those teachers would be expected to teach Church-required religious education to the children.[24] The Manchester area faced a shortage of qualified teachers early on as noted anxiously by Bishop Turner who urged hiring committees always to consider a candidate's qualifications rather than falling prey to political influence.[25]

The *Rambler* agreed with the *Catholic School*. In August 1855, an article titled 'The Poor-School Question' challenged the current mode of thinking on teacher qualifications, stating that 'according to popular opinion', all one has to do is 'give a man strong health, a tolerable temper, a loud voice, and a decent knowledge of reading, writing, and arithmetic, and you have the complete school master'. The article stressed the difficulty of becoming a competent master, the importance of teachers receiving rigorous training and the need for Catholic teachers to provide adequate religious instruction.[26] Implicit within this critique was an overall attack on an educational system that deemed the only necessary prerequisite for teaching was the intention to try. The worst criticism of the Catholic effort, according to this article, was that, out of 2,061 people training to become teachers at a cost of £35,000 to the government, only ten were Catholics; these ten received a total of only £193.[27]

The lack of male teachers was, perhaps, felt most profoundly. Thomas W. Allies argued that the problem of securing teachers tended to be gender specific. He noted that by 1886 Catholics had little trouble finding adequate female teachers but 'great difficulty in producing such male teachers as satisfy us' because of 'great demand upon the male sex for other things'.[28] Qualified female teachers were plentiful, due mainly to the tremendous efforts of the convent training schools, while qualified male teachers were conspicuously lacking, due mostly to the decreasing numbers of male pupil teachers matriculating to St Mary's, Hammersmith.[29] A few years later, Bishop Cornthwaite suggested that Catholics make a serious effort to remedy the lack of well-trained, male masters quickly because the new demands of the Department of Education placed an even greater burden on Catholic schools.[30] Consequently, the shortage of male teachers was such that in his pastoral letter on education in 1889 Manning selected it as the Church's most critical dilemma.[31]

No doubt the greatest deterrent to attracting boys into the teaching profession was the low salary. James Murray, headmaster of St Francis Xavier School, Liverpool, reported that, in those schools where managers supplied a sufficient number of staff, they were usually of inferior quality, since management could not afford to pay for better teachers. He blamed the Catholic community's endemic poverty and the iniquity of the elementary school system for this problem. He reported that the average annual salary of the head teacher in a Catholic school was £111 11*s*., compared to £120 3*s*. in a Church of England school, and £148 3*s*. in a state-operated board school. Murray added that although the £38 per year difference between Catholic and board school salaries was significant by itself, in reality, the discrepancy was even wider since Catholics generally taught in very large schools in metropolitan areas where the pressures and dangers were greater. He claimed that if he were teaching for the Liverpool school board, his annual salary would be £70 higher.[32] Likewise, a *Leeds Mercury* article in 1892 highlighted the low salaries offered by Catholic schools by calling attention to the average Catholic headmaster's salary being significantly lower than the national average for all schools.[33]

The higher salaries offered by non-Catholic schools often led Catholic masters to accept teaching positions with them. Understandably, the hierarchy and Catholic educationists feared and looked askance on this practice. By the

1880s, references to this problem were becoming more frequent. In response to increasing reports of this happening, in the summer of 1882 Bishop Vaughan reminded his clergy to repeat the hierarchy's prohibition of taking positions in such schools.[34] Canon James Carr, Liverpool diocesan inspector for the Church, was pleased to report in 1884 that 'the stain and scandal of a Catholic Teacher taking service in a non-religious Board School' had not occurred in his diocese. But based on reports from other dioceses, he feared that this was an approaching danger. His disgust for such teachers was palpable in the most biblical of terms:

> They have for years been educated and trained by Catholic charity and self-sacrifice; and when they are best fitted to bear fruit unto salvation, they repudiate holy engagements, and betray sacred trusts, and they devote to the devil, the world, and the flesh, talents confided to them for the cause of Christ. They may get money with Judas, but they betray their Master.[35]

Also contributing to the shortage of qualified teachers was the absence of a superannuation fund with which to provide pensions to retired teachers. With such a programme in place, Catholic educationists believed that more men and women would be willing to enter the profession. According to James Murray, 'most teachers are very desirous that a system of superannuation pensions should be established', especially for Roman Catholic teachers who 'are less able to provide for the future'. Murray believed that the teachers' contributions to such a fund should be paid from the government grant, rather than unrealistically expecting teachers to make contributions from their monthly salaries.[36] Thomas Graham noted that a pension plan would work as a great incentive for enticing more boys to enter the teaching profession.[37] Manning later added his opinion on the importance of providing pensions in his 1889 pastoral letter on education: 'Such a system of pensions', he wrote, 'could be certainly formed by the united action of managers, teachers, and Government, and it is our duty to form it without loss of time'.[38]

Frequent teacher turnover exacerbated the situation. This problem plagued most Catholic schools and stemmed from low pay to sickness and death to inefficiency or incompetency and subsequent dismissal. Primary school logbooks attest to the frequency with which Catholic school managers faced this challenge. St Joseph's School, Bury, had a total of five head teachers over the course of three academic years, three of whom were hired in a ten-month period between December 1875 and September 1876.[39] St Mary's Boys School, Manchester, fared slightly better, with four masters in nine years, three being hired between February 1868 and April 1872.[40] Such constant turnover disrupted the classroom and caused potential friction with the government, as described by the inspector's report for St Mary's: 'The sudden change of masters immediately previous to the end of the school year has proved disastrous to the examinations.

An examination conducted under such circumstances does not afford data for judging of the condition of the school.'[41] Likewise, a negative inspection report for St Mary's Girls School, Manchester, noted that the school had changed its headmistress three times in 1868, and the logbook revealed a total of six different teachers between January 1865 and June 1868.[42]

The logbooks do not include much direct information as to the reasons for such teacher turnover; however, given that many changes occurred during Christmas Break, which usually followed the annual inspection, two obvious conclusions can be drawn. First, turnover often stemmed from the manager's disappointment with the inspection; second, the teacher often succumbed to the pressure of the examination process. Nonetheless, such discontinuity in the classroom often led to inspection reports similar to that received by St Mary's School; such reports, in turn, frequently threatened the school's annual grant.

Gender Inequality

Catholic school inspection reports frequently commended well-run, efficient girls schools while criticizing inefficient and ineffective boys schools.[43] The bishops and Catholic educationists both acknowledged this disparity, attributing it to the larger number of well-educated, female religious compared with the much smaller number of male religious dedicated to education. Bishop Ullathorne referred to this problem at mid-century when he praised the excellent work of the convents in developing female teachers and proclaimed the Catholic community's greatest need was the concurrent development of male religious to improve the education of boys.[44]

One of the foremost authorities on this problem was Thomas William Marshall, the first Catholic school inspector. In his 1852 report, Marshall effusively praised the female schools he had inspected and boasted of their 'immeasurable superiority ... over those which are frequented by boys'. Marshall attributed this success to 'the special character and qualifications of the teachers', most of whom are 'under the charge of ladies who are members of educational communities ... founded with the express object of instructing and educating female children, and especially the children of the poor'.[45] In reviewing Marshall's report in July, the *Rambler* agreed with his findings and used them to impugn those in Parliament who wished to open the convents to governmental inspection.[46] As for male teachers, however, Marshall reported in 1859 that Catholics had been reluctantly forced to draw masters from the Dublin normal school, claiming that 'their training as a rule has been very incomplete and superficial, and we have found them on the whole ... an incompetent and unsatisfactory class'.[47] His obvious disdain stands in marked contrast to his high esteem for the female religious who were teaching in his district.[48]

Stokes pointed to the decade following the permission of Catholic schools to enter the government's grant system in 1847, and argued that the declining quality of boys schools relative to girls schools was because of the acceptance of government aid by most female religious communities and the steady refusal of such aid by many boys schools, notably those run by the Irish Christian Brothers. He believed that aid, coming in a variety of grants, had improved the female schools and restricted the progress of boys schools.[49] The *Dublin Review* later complained that, while girls of poor parents were receiving an education on par with the best schools in the country, the boys of those same parents suffered with uneven and often unsatisfactory education.[50] In the *Eleventh Annual Report of the Catholic Poor School Committee*, Stokes called for immediate assistance from wealthy Catholics to help remedy the situation; otherwise, the community must accept that Catholic boys would grow up uneducated or receive their education in Protestant schools.[51]

By the second half of the century, most of the girls schools were either taught by female religious or by women who had been trained by female religious in any of the three main training colleges for women: St Leonard's-on-Sea, begun by the Sisters of the Holy Child; Mt Pleasant, Liverpool, which had been run by the Sisters of Notre Dame since 1856; and the Wandsworth Training College, established by the Sacred Heart nuns in 1870. The high quality of their education and teaching standards dwarfed those of the male religious who were either too stubborn to modify their practices, as in the case of the Irish Christian Brothers, or simply too few to meet the growing demand. As more and more men were needed to undertake pupil teacher training and matriculate to St Mary's, financial restraints simultaneously thwarted their successful recruitment. Therefore, the staffs of boys schools were, necessarily, smaller, and the schools could not, with some exceptions, maintain the same high standards as their female counterparts.

Irregular Attendance

As if lack of unity, poverty and the problems of recruitment and training of teachers were not enough of a burden, another major obstacle faced by both Catholic and non-Catholic schools in urban environs came from within the classroom: irregular attendance. Poor attendance ultimately affected the financial status of a school in two ways: first, when children did not come to school, the school did not receive as much in school pence; second, poor attendance generally led to poor examination results, which could lead to reduced grants.[52] Naturally, Catholic teachers believed their attendance woes to be more profound than other denominations because of the poverty and transience of the Irish Catholic working class who comprised the majority of Catholic schoolchildren nationally.

According to logbooks and inspectors' reports, the situation was quite serious. When Stokes examined the Manchester schools in July 1853, the magnitude of the irregularity was exposed. St Wilfrid's Girls School had 133 students present at the inspection on 18 July – 23 above its average attendance. However, during the previous twelve months, an incredible 200 students had left the school, while another 295 were admitted. Similarly, St Chad's Boys School had 197 students present – 62 above its average attendance. In the previous year, 140 students left the school, while 160 were admitted.[53] Although run by the highly respected Sisters of Notre Dame, St Anne's Infants School, Liverpool, was no different than any other poor school regarding attendance. Soon after headmistress Frances Fitzgerald took control of the school in January 1864, she encountered poor attendance on a regular basis, probably due as much to the cold weather as to the presence of a new teacher.[54] Records show that attendance also tended to drop as holidays approached.[55]

The call of the factory no doubt presented the most frustrating challenge to regular school attendance. Alice Braithwaite, headmistress of St Augustine's Girls School, Manchester, was so alarmed by dwindling attendance figures that she wrote to the clerk of the Manchester School Board, Frank Ruspini, asking if there was something that could be done to prevent children under twelve from working full time. The unfortunate answer was that nothing could be done until a compulsory Act was put into place.[56] Later that summer, Miss Braithwaite discouragingly reported that a large number of her children had gone off to work during the previous week.[57] Christopher Quinn, headmaster of St Michael's Boys School, Liverpool, faced the same situation. He wrote despairingly in the school logbook on 7 August 1874, 'Active measures ... very much needed in this district as the attendance is going down without any visible cause, except that sufficient pressure is not brought to bear on parents to compel them to send their children to school'.[58] Headmistress Anne Callender frequently reported the loss of several students from St Mary's Girls School, Manchester, during 1863 and 1864.[59] Because jobs were especially scarce during these 'Cotton Famine' years (the mills stopped working as cotton imports from the United States declined during the American Civil War), the need to have additional family income was paramount. The same phenomenon was also reported in St Mary's Boys School.[60] By 1866, the mills were receiving cotton again and, ironically, the higher demand for labour now provided another reason why students were not attending school, as noted by Stokes in his annual report on St Augustine's School, Preston.[61] Charlotte Tooms, mistress of St Joseph's School, Bury, noted that the visit of her manager, Father John Fraser, on 18 August 1875 came in response to consistently low attendance figures; she explained that most had left school for full-time employment.[62] In 1868, St Mary's School, Burnley, faced a precipitous decline in its day school attendance while night school attendance actually increased, indicating a rise in the numbers of children leaving day school for full-time employment.[63] Further, it is apparent from these first-hand accounts of the daily classroom struggles that schools faced a double-edged sword. When the economy declined, parents could not afford school pence; accordingly, children did not attend school as regularly and, if they could find a job, they instead worked to earn desperately needed wages for the family.[64] When the economy improved, children could more easily find employment and, thus, temptation lured parents into sending them to the mills to supplement the family income. The bottom line was that poverty caused irregular attendance and induced parents at times to forego education for much-needed income. Cardinal Wiseman had earlier recognized part of this problem when he urged his priests to convince parents, no matter how poor, to understand their sacred duty to educate their children and to do so in a Catholic school.[65]

This was a sacred duty that parents often ignored, despite the pleas of the clergy. In a pastoral letter meant to remind parents of their religious duty and their civil right to educate their children, Bishop Cornthwaite appealed to their sense of propriety. He said to parents who sent their children to non-Catholic schools:

> You are guilty of a gross breach of duty: you are encouraging and contributing to the success of a system of education condemned by the Holy See: you are injuring your own school, established at great cost and maintained with great difficulty, by reducing its numbers, lowering its efficiency, crippling its means, and it may be risking its very existence: and who shall estimate the scandal you are giving to your children, to your fellow-Catholics, and to those outside the fold?[66]

With a decidedly desperate tone, one of Cornthwaite's clergy, Robert Lacy of St Mary's, Middlesbrough, the following year wrote to the bishop asking for advice on how to deal with obstinate parents who 'for various reasons will send their children to Board or Protestant schools ... What are we to do with such people?'[67] Never one to shy away from controversy or a good challenge, Bishop Bagshawe demanded that his Nottingham parents keep their children far away from non-Catholic schools. If they had no alternative but to send their children to one of these schools, the bishop reminded parents of the requirement to secure written approval for the removal of their children from non-Catholic religious instruction and to provide Catechism lessons at home.[68] Echoing his colleague from Nottingham, William Clifford, Bishop of Clifton from 1857 to 1893, delivered an Advent Sunday pastoral on the subject of parental responsibilities in 1882 in which he argued that the best way to show one's religious zeal was 'the care which parents ought to take for the religious education of their children' in Catholic schools. It was parental neglect of this duty, he claimed, that caused the Church to lose worshippers every year.[69] Bernard O'Reilly, Bishop of Liverpool from 1873 to 1894, noted the problem as a justification for urgent school building in the southern and northern parts of his diocese where Catholic numbers were increasing rapidly in the early 1880s.[70]

Frustration in this matter often surfaced in sermons and pastoral letters read from the pulpit. Bishop Cornthwaite asked rhetorically 'what excuse can be made in the sight of God for the conduct of those parents, who by deliberate choice, send their children where Religious teaching ... holds no place at all'. He remarked that it was only logical that these parents would find their children disobedient and disrespectful and would never learn their duty to their parents or God. Using guilt as a motivator, Cornthwaite spitefully remarked that Protestant parents took a 'stronger and better view of their duty to their children' than many Catholics.[71] Rev. Lambert, parish priest at St Austin's, Wakefield, grew so angry about this issue that he told Bishop Cornthwaite he was going to confront such parents and, if their behaviour did not improve, he would read their names from the pulpit. 'Of their exclusion from the sacraments', he continued, 'I have already informed them, but my experience amongst the Irish in this country has not led me to consider them as influenced much by principle'.[72] Bishop Bagshawe had reached the same draconian conclusion and told his diocese that recalcitrant parents would be prohibited from the sacrament of confession.[73] Bishop Ullathorne told his Birmingham diocese that such parents were committing 'a sin of neglect in a grave matter of Christian duty'.[74] Not surprisingly, the Welsh diocese experienced a similar range of problems with parents. John Cuthbert Hedley, former editor of the *Dublin Review* and then Bishop of Newport and Menevia from 1881 to 1915, often reprimanded the parents of his diocese for failing to secure an adequate Catholic education for their children. Noting the problems apparent in Cardiff, Newport and Swansea at the end of the century, Hedley chastised parents who did not send their children to Catholic schools, or sent their children to school without breakfast, or forced their children to work before and after school, and he told them that such behaviour was sinful in the eyes of God. 'Parents who do this are slave-drivers rather than parents', he exclaimed, and 'such action ... weakens the position of the Catholic School ... has the appearance of religious indifference, and ... tends to break down the strictness and firmness of Catholic faith'.[75]

Another contributing factor in poor attendance was sickness, often much worse in the slums of Manchester, Leeds and Liverpool than in remote rural villages. The logbook for St Mary's Girls School, Manchester, attests to the frequency of illness in that city during 1863 and 1864. Scarlet fever and measles tended to be the most common illnesses and the logbook entries were usually accompanied by comments about the cold, wet weather. Even when the children were not sick themselves, many were 'obliged to remain at home to carry messages, or to attend to the wants of their sick relations'.[76] A similar problem faced

Mary Frances Austin, headmistress at St Augustine's Infant School, Preston. She encountered a virtual epidemic of whooping cough, measles and scarlet fever in the summer and autumn of 1866 which she attributed to the extremely wet weather. As a result, the only consistency about the children's attendance from June through October was its inconsistency. Two years later, Austin reported that between November 1867 and January 1869, five of her students died from sickness.[77] Other frequent illnesses mentioned in the logbooks that brought illness, missed school days and sometimes even death were smallpox and typhus.[78]

Those on the front lines of elementary education struggled daily with irregular attendance, often trying to find deeper causes for the harmful phenomenon. The headmaster at St Chad's Boys School, Manchester, listed other causes of poor attendance as: '1st Carelessness of the parents. 2nd Parents at work and children taking advantage of this circumstance to play truant. 3rd Want of clothes.'[79] Constance Fox, headmistress for St Patrick's Infant School, Manchester, listed reasons for poor attendance as not having proper clothing, not having had breakfast and not having the necessary school pence. Mostly, she said, the children 'suffer from more sickness than the better class of children, because poor food and badly ventilated homes undermine their constitutions and predispose them to illnesses that are prevalent at the time'.[80] While illness was a factor with which all schools and denominations had extensive experience, the unrelenting poverty of the Catholic population created more desperate situations that exacerbated the attendance problem.

School Pence

The frustrating situation created as children were sent to work in available jobs and kept home from school when work was scarce because they had no pence to pay was compounded by the resulting lack of school income.[81] Because of irregular attendance, the collection of school pence fluctuated frequently and was seldom a reliable source of funding. The logbook for Adelphi Infant School, Salford, reveals that when factories slowed in 1869 attendance and school pence decreased rapidly.[82] Many children came to school without school pence and were sent home to collect it, causing one schoolmistress to remark: 'it is found almost impossible to get children to pay school pence'.[83] Constance Fox described this difficult situation and hinted at its negative effect on the education in the classroom:

> It is a great loss to our schools to be obliged to send the children home ... in order to get their fees. A great many children are sent home, in every school that I have ever been acquainted with, every week; Some of them return at once with their fees; others do not come until the next school meeting; others return without them on Friday

> afternoon; some not until the next week, and then perhaps without the fee; some not till the board officer or some of the managers have been to [their] house.[84]

Sometimes children were sent home for school pence so often that finally the manager would relent and allow them to attend the school for free in the hope that the child's parents might soon find enough work to afford some contribution. At times, a manager might find that over a third of his students were paying no fees at all, and two-fifths were having their fees paid by the local board of guardians.[85]

The manager of the Jesuit-run St Francis Xavier's Schools, Liverpool, summed up the effects of this kind of irregularity on the education of Catholic children:

> The result of the last examination would have been better had children brought the school-pence regularly, but when numbers of children have to be sent home week after week ... it follows that they miss their lessons, and become a drag to the rest of the class.[86]

Thus, the irregular collection of school pence increased the financial strain on Catholic schools, while repeatedly sending children home to collect the pence decreased the effectiveness of their education and could harm their examination results.

Poor Facilities and Supplies

More often than not, the lack of proper classrooms and classroom supplies further handicapped Catholic schools. In addition to the dual-use room problems, classroom deficiencies ranged from books and slates to blackboards, desks, chairs and the means for heating and fresh water. As described in Chapter 2, many early Catholic primary schools operated in less than adequate learning environments and this problem eased only as the Church built new schools. As late as 1884, the Liverpool diocese could report with some ironic humour that while the Walton mission had begun in a stable and a school had been built onto a joiner's woodworking shop, the parish desperately required better facilities. In the village of Seaforth, Bishop O'Reilly reported the same year, Catholics employed an old stable and coach-house for a church and had no school.[87] The Catholic hierarchy directed new missions and growing parishes to focus on school chapel building before incurring the cost of building a church. For example, Bishop Goss told a member of his Liverpool clergy at Bootle that if it were necessary to build a new school north of town and ultimately to create a new mission there, he would immediately license the schools for mass since the school was more vital than the church at the outset.[88] This policy, while revealing the primacy of education, also resulted in cramped quarters that were often inadequate for either education or worship and served as stopgap measures until more funding could provide separate spaces for these two basic needs of the parish. Often the schools needed expansion before a church could be contemplated.[89]

One of the earliest comprehensive lists of inspection reports was printed in the *Catholic School* in October 1853. Compiled by Thomas W. Marshall, many of the reports for individual schools remarked upon the insufficient supply of textbooks and desks or the deficient maps and slates. In many cases, he urged the schools to apply for grants to cover such expenses.[90] Francis McCarthy, headmaster of St Mary's Boys School, Manchester, complained frequently throughout 1863 about the inadequate supply of books, slates, paper and pens. Early in the year, the frustrated teacher exclaimed: 'Again, I impressed on the boys the necessity of procuring their own books and slates, etc'. Later, after one full year of fighting this battle, an exasperated McCarthy wrote: 'The children being unable in a great many cases to provide their own [supplies], their [educational] progress is retarded on this account'.[91] The headmistress of its sister school, St Mary's Girls School, echoed the same frustration: 'Some parents come to complain of poverty. [They] cannot buy books, etc., for their children.'[92] According to a history of St Joseph's parish in Preston, when the boys school received a map of the British Isles, it was considered a landmark in the school's history. It was not until two years later that each classroom finally received a separate blackboard.[93] When asked about how the poverty of the parents affected the education of the children, James Murray of St Francis Xavier, Liverpool, replied that most parents could not afford textbooks and did not take an active interest in the children's studies.[94] Ultimately, poverty severely limited the availability of classroom supplies, affecting the ability of the teachers to educate properly and, when added to the other problems encountered in the classroom, threatening the overall success of Catholic education.

Poor Lay Catholic Involvement

Catholic leaders often criticized the lack of lay involvement in the educational effort. After 1850 the hierarchy consistently emphasized the necessity of all Catholics sharing the burden and responsibility of improving educational provision.[95] Yet as of 1854, a Catholic educational report criticized the Catholic laity for their lack of interest in the effort to educate the poor.[96] In June of that same year, George Brown, Bishop of Liverpool from 1850 to 1856, admonished the upwardly mobile Catholic professional and merchant classes for their lack of support for Catholic education in his annual pastoral letter.[97] How could the Wesleyans, he wondered aloud, raise twenty-five times what the Catholics did just for their foreign missions when they had a smaller population? The answer was in greater participation by the laity, he concluded.[98] Both Bishop Ullathorne and Bishop Goss, Brown's successor, complained of similar challenges when contributions fell short of anticipated needs, Ullathorne fingering the laity who did not pay their pledged subscriptions and Goss arguing that the laity should help relieve the hierarchy's burden of school construction through greater participation, both personal and financial.[99]

The Catholic press also targeted the laity. The education battle, reminded an editorial in the *Month*, could be kindled by the clergy and aided by the Catholic press, but the fight 'is in a peculiar sense the work of the Christian laity, because education is the business, the safeguard, the honour of the Christian home and the Christian family'.[100] Writing in the same journal the following month, Thomas W. Allies urged those members of the Catholic laity not involved in the education struggle to assume their responsibility. Allies downplayed the oft-mentioned fear that the Catholic laity might try to thrust itself into the Church's realm of teaching faith and morals resulting from their material contributions. He reminded readers that 'by the very principles of [the laity's] faith, there can be no interference on their part with the teaching', which was controlled by the Church.[101] Therefore, another periodical added, the Church should not fear an increased role by the laity but should demand and welcome such activity under the broader guidance of the hierarchy.[102]

The laity was a vital link in the Church's plan to educate Catholic children but, except for a few committed laymen like members of the Duke of Norfolk's extended family, they were slow to come to the education battle. The Catholic community needed to find a way to get these men and women, ideally of the middle and upper classes, more involved in education so as to take advantage of their collective strength and wealth. One study examining the large number of lay Catholic societies that appeared in the last half of the nineteenth century lists over one hundred Catholic organizations; of interest is the lack of those relating specifically to education. Only one, the Society of the Sacred Heart for the Education of Poor Children, established in 1875, had an obvious educational purpose. Since the study's focus was on Catholic devotion rather than education, the author did not comment on the incongruity between the hierarchy's priority on education and lack of lay involvement.[103] Yet the Church needed lay Catholics to help fight the battle; it needed soldiers to march under the direction of the Church's generals, to assist in the political struggle to educate Catholic children, to contribute financially, to sign petitions, to attend meetings of educational organizations and to write letters to newspapers. Ideal lay involvement, in the minds of Catholic educationists, would be not only financial, but also spiritual and participatory.

Conclusion

Catholics often disagreed on how to address educational problems, were hampered by financial shortages that led, in turn, to a deficiency in teachers, schools and pupil teachers, and were frustrated by the irregular attendance caused by the call of the mills and a roster of the century's most devastating illnesses. Apart from the government's changing education codes, these were the most formidable obstacles facing the Roman Catholic Church in her quest to educate her children. Catholic educationists met these obstacles in *ad hoc* fashion, rather than with a finely planned, comprehensive strategy. Their *modus operandi* was reactive, rather than proactive.

The reactive nature of the Catholic Church was a reflection of its poverty; it did not have the money to plan far into the future, and, therefore, could only make broad statements about 'keeping all of their schools' or 'educating every single Catholic child in a Catholic school'. Later, Catholic attitudes began to change, not a lessening of their aggressive, defiant or confident manner, but a change in how they viewed themselves. Why remain unhappy, reluctant and quiet members of the system, they asked, when they could become active participants with an eye towards changing it? As a result of these grave challenges, it became clear that Catholics must enter the political fracas surrounding education so as to be heard and recognized.

4 ENGLISH CATHOLICS AND THE POLITICS OF EDUCATION, 1847–70: PREPARING FOR BATTLE

Much has been written on Catholic political activity in the nineteenth century and two recent works in particular have examined this subject. One argues that English Catholics were of little importance in the political world of mid- to late nineteenth-century Britain, despite their protestations to the contrary. It argues that Catholics consistently exaggerated the value of the Catholic vote and their own ability to manage it as a way to gain patronage. Overall, it calls the political experience of English Catholics in the last fifty years of the century 'one of misplaced hopes and disappointed enthusiasms', an impotent force in an age of virile political operators.[1]

More recently, another work argues that earlier portrayals of Catholic political impotence are based on a fundamental misreading of Catholic political intentions. This work asserts that English Catholic political participation was not solely to work for goals exclusive to the Catholic community but to work as individuals taking advantage of democracy to become politically engaged. This argument acknowledges greater Catholic political success than others; however, success was not always immediate, was built, in part, upon cooperation with other religious groups and achieved goals that were perhaps more broadly Christian in nature than specifically Catholic.[2]

On the subject of education, Catholics were more vocal, organized and politically active than on other issues. But this politically active Catholic community did not begin to develop until the storm of the Education Act of 1870 arrived. In fact, Catholics remained generally satisfied with elementary education from 1847 until this historic Act took effect. Happy just to have a seat at the table, Catholics made few political demands. They were free to build schools with or without state funds and were limited only by their precarious financial position.

Yet, the Roman Catholic ethos did not acquire its confidence and aggressiveness solely from the education battle of 1870. Brief flashes of this evolving identity of confidence and aggressiveness appeared in Catholic political behaviour between 1847 and 1870 on other matters important to the Catholic community, such as political squabbles over governmental intentions to inspect convents and monastic establishments, national identity problems in Italy and Ireland, oath taking, the Maynooth Grant and the appointment of Roman Catholic chaplains in workhouses and prisons. Thus, throughout this period, both English Catholics and their mostly Irish MPs slowly grew more politically active, but not necessarily more effective.

In preparation for their entrance into the state educational system, the bishops and certain laymen created the Catholic Poor School Committee to organize and focus educational efforts. It became the most important Catholic organization dedicated to education in the nineteenth century and has served the Catholic community in various roles to the present day. Thus, an examination of its founding and work in the early years of Catholic participation in the state grant system will reveal the myriad challenges the community faced from fundraising to effective communications with the government. This section also includes a look at the assistance the religious communities provided during the first years of Catholic participation in the state education system.

Mid-Century Catholic Political Alignments

Prior to the restoration of the hierarchy in 1850, Catholics leaned towards the Whigs because they looked to them as the party of Catholic Emancipation. They did not, however, in the wake of that momentous event of 1829, pursue an active role in politics. The Whigs were aligned with the Irish political giant Daniel O'Connell in the 1830s, leaving some English Catholic MPs in uncomfortably close quarters with more radical Irish. As a result, the English Catholic–Irish Catholic political alliance with the Whigs weakened and slowly, thereafter, ended with the restoration of the hierarchy in 1850 and the events that followed.[3] In response to Cardinal Wiseman's use of overly presumptuous language in his 'Out of the Flaminian Gate' pastoral that accompanied and justified the restoration, the Whig government, led by Lord John Russell and aided by allies in the press – notably *The Times* – stirred up a new and powerful anti-Catholic reaction for political purposes. Wiseman's and the Pope's effigies even burned in the streets of London on Guy Fawkes Day; soon the vitriol spread to the legislative branch as Russell brought forth the anti-Catholic Ecclesiastical Titles Bill in 1851, which was designed to keep the new Catholic bishops from taking titles already held by the Anglican episcopacy.[4]

Cut adrift by their traditional political allies, Catholics had few places to turn, since the Tories offered them little welcome. While some radicals and Peelites, such as William Gladstone, opposed the anti-Catholic Titles Bill, rising Tory leader Benjamin Disraeli supported it.[5] Stuck in the morass of political isolation, Catholics followed three mostly unsuccessful courses over the next few decades: one, they created an independent Catholic party; two, they attempted to influence whichever major party could provide what they wanted; and three, they targeted public opinion by operating outside of the party system.[6] In 1852, Catholics formed the Independent Irish party and secured over forty parliamentary seats. Created as an amalgam of Irish and English Catholics interests, the party soon suffered the loss of important leadership to the Peelite–Whig Aberdeen ministry. It lingered on for seven more unproductive years before finally dissolving in 1859.[7]

In 1859 Catholics attempted the second course: supporting the existing political party that could offer them the most in return. Thus, the political isolation of the mid-1850s soon gave way to Tory drift. One of the markers of this drift was the change in hands of the *Tablet*, the popular Catholic periodical known for its support of radical and Irish causes. Pro-Irish editor and proprietor Frederick Lucas died in 1854 while on a journey to Rome. The paper was purchased by Tory Catholic convert John Edward Wallis, a move which shifted the editorial content in the opposite direction.[8] Thus began the paper's long connection with conservatism in English politics. Similarly, many converts to Catholicism were Tories who kept their party affiliation after joining the Church. Many Catholics embraced the Tories when Russell, Viscount Palmerston and the Whigs, in general, supported the national unification movement in Italy which threatened the temporal power of Pope Pius IX. Tories were less sanguine about Italian unification, especially given Italian nationalist Giuseppe Garibaldi's republican background, and, as a result, Catholics and Tories formed an unlikely alliance in 1858, with Disraeli promising Cardinal Wiseman that the Tory government would not intervene in Italy. From this alliance Catholics also received the right to have their own army chaplains of equal rank and salary as Protestants.[9] Wiseman even openly supported the Tories in the parliamentary election of 1859. However, the Tories were not returned to office – Palmerston and the Whigs were. Wiseman's active political involvement in 1859 stood in marked contrast to his statement to a colleague in 1851 that he would not officially sanction the formation of the Association for the Defence and Increase of Catholic Liberty because he always wished to restrict his activity to 'ecclesiastical and spiritual duties'.[10] His change of mind eight years later serves as an early example of the increasing political awareness and involvement of Catholics.

The Catholic–Tory alliance ended briefly in 1864–5 because Catholics were viewed as an expendable constituency.[11] The Earl of Derby, Disraeli's party superior, angered Catholics first by receiving Garibaldi on his visit to England and then by making derogatory comments about Catholics in 1865 in an effort to rouse his ultra-Tory base. Disraeli re-cultivated the alliance a year later, with the assistance of Tory Catholic MPs John Pope Hennessy and Edward Ryley, but the alliance dissolved again in 1868 when the Irish bloc wished to resume cordial relations with the Whigs because of their more liberal stance towards Ireland. From 1859 forward, Catholics drifted between backing the Whigs (and later the Liberals) because of their Irish policy and the Tories because of their Italian policy, a situation aptly described by a letter to the editor of the *Manchester Guardian* on 3 April 1862, in which Irish MP Charles O'Neill wrote that English Catholics had deserted the Liberals because the 'three most distinguished members of the present Government, Lords Palmerston and Russell and Mr. Gladstone, have each made themselves personally offensive to every sensitive Catholic'. He cited the Italian issue as the most pressing cause for Roman Catholic dislike of the current ministry but prophesied that, once that issue was gone, all Catholics would return to the Liberal fold.[12] Thus, Tory drift did not indicate an active adoption of Tory policy, but rather a reaction to specific current events and issues.

The death of Wiseman, and with him his Tory sympathies, brought a more pro-Liberal Henry Edward Manning to the archepiscopacy. Even so, during Prime Minister Derby's third ministry, Manning and Disraeli initiated a dialogue on political matters important to Catholics, including ideas on how to pacify Ireland and Fenianism. By the time Disraeli became prime minister, following Derby's resignation in February 1868, Manning had convinced him that a charter for the Catholic University in Dublin would do much to bring Catholic support behind the Tories and quell the unrest across the Irish Sea. Unfortunately, Disraeli's plan backfired when Gladstone unexpectedly announced plans in March 1868 to disestablish the Church of Ireland. This announcement trumped the prime minister's much more modest initiative, shifting Irish Catholic hopes and the political momentum to Gladstone and effectively destroying Disraeli's administration. Gladstone assumed office later that year, after which Manning abruptly discontinued his correspondence with Disraeli, leaving the former prime minister with the justifiable belief that the Catholics had stabbed him in the back.[13]

Mid-Century Catholic Political Action

The question of religion and politics in Ireland was just one of the issues that brought Catholics into the political arena in the mid-Victorian period. Although national education remained a relatively quiet issue, the hierarchy, lay Catholics and Catholic MPs considered other issues of enough importance to engage actively in parliamentary politics, or, in some instances, in extra-parliamentary action. Although it cannot be argued until much later in the century that this gradual political awakening successfully influenced public policy initiatives, it reflected a rejection of their quiescent *status quo*, increasing Catholic confidence and the willingness to begin playing offence rather than defence.

At mid-century Catholic parliamentary representation was virtually non-existent except for the Irish Catholics elected to the Commons and a few English Catholic peers in the Lords. Out of thirty-seven Catholic MPs, only four were from England; the rest hailed from Ireland. Fourteen Catholics served in the House of Lords.[14] Thus, English Catholics understood that their political power rested in Ireland, and, therefore, their voice came from members representing Irish constituencies; although Irish MPs often extended constituent care to Irish Catholics living in England and Wales, the very same group to whom the hierarchy was tending in educational and spiritual affairs.[15] The inability of Catholics to stand for and win English constituencies can be explained by the correlation between a strong Catholic (read: Irish) presence in areas such as Liverpool and Manchester and a stronger, reactionary, anti-Catholic movement that arose in those same areas and effectively prevented the election of Catholics to Parliament. Additionally, until the franchise-extending Reform Act of 1867, the majority of Catholics in England could not vote. For these reasons, Irish Catholic MPs looked after the political fortunes of Catholics in England and Wales, although Irish affairs came first.

As indicated, one of the earliest issues that captured the attention of Roman Catholics was the question of Italian unification that surfaced in the late 1850s, a topic on which Catholic MPs Sir George Bowyer and John Pope Hennessy proved indefatigable in the Commons. Bowyer was one of the few examples of an English Catholic serving an Irish constituency. A native of Berkshire, he converted to Catholicism in 1850 and represented Dundalk as a Liberal from 1852 until 1868. Hennessy, a native Irishman, served Westmeath from 1859 until 1865 and had the distinction of being the first Catholic Tory to sit in Commons since Catholic Emancipation. Despite their party differences, both consistently argued the 'Catholic' side during debates on Italian unification. They defended the interests of the Pope, warned of the dangers of ultra-nationalist republican Giuseppe Garibaldi and generally opposed the Italian designs of the Liberal ministry.[16] In subsequent years, Catholics held general meetings in support of Pius IX and the temporal power, neither of which was a popular subject in England at the time.[17] Although Catholic pronouncements on Italian affairs made little difference in altering the foreign policy of England towards Italy, prominent Catholics were, at least, finally engaged in politics.

In 1857, Catholic MPs took umbrage at a parliamentary proposal to rid British Jews of any political restrictions based on their religion. Catholics naturally desired to have the remaining oath from the 1829 emancipation settlement – which required Catholic MPs officially to deny the Pope any right to interfere in British domestic affairs – removed as part of the Jewish bill. By doing so, the one remaining political disability based upon religion could be erased. A scathing editorial in *The Times* claimed that, 'whenever there is anything ill-judged, unseasonable or in bad taste to be said or done, [Catholics] are sure to do it'. Prominent Catholic politician Charles Langdale, however, defended the Catholic position on this bill in a letter to the editor, arguing for true equality for all religious denominations, which this bill, as written, would not bring: 'When a measure is introduced giving relief to every other class of the community, I cannot quite understand that it is ... unreasonable for the sole one excluded to complain and beg to share in this general remedial Act'. He also stated that the extant oath which Catholics MPs must take was 'a fertile source of insulting observations to Catholic members' and not an innocent test, as *The Times* had argued, that Catholics happily accepted as the price for the right to sit in Parliament.[18] The bill ultimately failed.

A year later, when a revised Jewish bill was brought before Parliament, Irish MPs similarly defended the Catholic position. George Bowyer argued that the retention of the Catholic oath was anathema to the liberal political legacy in England. If all paid the same taxes,

> all owed the same allegiance of the crown, and in time of war they equally shed their blood for their country, and bore the burdens imposed ... [then] they all had an equal right to participate in the government of their country.

The Catholic oath, he asserted, prevented this ideal situation in Parliament. John Francis Maguire, Irish MP, followed his fellow countryman with a speech that again aggressively asserted equality. This bill excluded Catholics from the political equality awarded to others, an equality justified, he believed, by 'their numbers, by their contributions to the public taxes, by their services in every department of the State, and by the blood shed by their co-religionists in the wars of Great Britain'. Maguire concluded by demanding 'this badge of inferiority ... be abolished'.[19]

The emerging political confidence and assertiveness of the Catholic community was also revealed in the annual debate over the Maynooth Grant.[20] In the 1850s, Tory MPs Richard Spooner and Charles Newdegate consistently argued for the repeal of this yearly parliamentary grant. In the spring of 1852, Thomas Chisholm Anstey, English MP and Catholic convert, provided the initial Catholic defence to Spooner's motion of inquiry into the state of affairs of Maynooth. Instead of simply attacking the motion, which Anstey believed was a disguised attempt to repeal the annual grant, he upped the ante by threatening to add an amendment to Spooner's measure which would not only repeal the Maynooth grant but also every other Act that had given state funds to support religious endowments.[21] When the debate on the measure opened in May, a full-scale Catholic defence was presented by the Catholic MPs, led by Anstey and eagerly supported by the Irish Catholic bloc. No less than seven Catholic MPs attacked Spooner's measure; one told Commons it had been introduced in a 'speech of unadulterated, malignant bigotry, base in manner of delivery, as in matter it was extremely offensive'. Taking a different approach, Francis Stack Murphy welcomed any inquiry into the practices at Maynooth, boldly asserting that any governmental inquiry into Maynooth would only boost the seminary's credibility.[22] When Spooner and his colleagues complained about the length of speeches by Catholics on this matter, William Keogh, Irish MP for Athlone, defiantly protested that such was not the case, especially since Mr Spooner himself spoke for almost three hours.[23] The successful defence of Maynooth against these inquiries and initiatives for repeal of the grant was hardly timid and reserved.

Debates over convents and monasteries, which first came under fire when Henry C. Lacy and Richard Spooner introduced a measure in 1851 to require inspection of convents much like the government did of asylums, provoked perhaps the angriest Catholic response and provided a further example of a nascent confidence and aggressive spirit of the Catholic community in England.[24] Francis Stack Murphy derided the bill as one whose 'object [was] to insult and degrade religious females of the Roman Catholic persuasion', and to allow for unprovoked inspection of convents when the laws likewise prevented the entering of a house in search of the vilest of criminals without a warrant. Such 'wanton' legislation was unfortunate, he argued, as was the proclivity of young MPs to try their 'prentice hand' by attacking the Catholics of the country.[25] Bishop Ullathorne penned a pamphlet that defended the convents and attacked the bill's supporters, while arguing that the bill violated English liberties and decorum.[26] In the context of the hierarchical restoration crisis and the passage of the Ecclesiastical Titles Bill, Ullathorne's words exemplified the reflexively defensive attitude of Catholics and their willingness to battle over an issue in the public forum. Lacy's and Spooner's bill eventually failed, but Dr Thomas Chambers, MP for Marylebone, introduced a similar measure two years later. George Bowyer, Lord Howard and Francis Stack Murphy all engaged in the debate over this Inspection of Nunneries bill. Bowyer told the Commons that the gentlemen behind this bill were entirely ignorant of the nature of convents; he highlighted the important role that convents played in the education of both middle- and upper-class Catholic girls, as well as the poor. Murphy reiterated the danger to the education of poor Catholics if female religious orders were treated as this bill intended, and appealed to Home Secretary Palmerston not to sanction a bill 'that would rankle in the breast of every Roman Catholic in the kingdom'.[27] In the midst of the parliamentary debate, Langdale criticized *The Times* for the multitude of letters printed in favour of the bill. His own letter to the editor of 1 June inveighed against Chambers and his supporters:

> Let the promoters of this atrocious invasion on the decencies of Catholic ladies have at least the manliness to avow that their bigoted hatred of the Catholic religion thus seeks a vent against these helpless and harmless members of its faith, because they have not the courage to adopt a more bold course of persecution against those who would have power to repel their insults.[28]

Irish MP Mr Fagan later called upon all Irish members to unite in a 'serrated front' against this 'most insulting inquiry'.[29] Chambers's bill failed, as did other attempts by the state to intervene in the affairs of convents in 1853 and 1854.

Unfortunately, the issue reappeared with even more fury over a decade later when Charles Newdegate asked the Commons in 1865 to appoint a select committee to enquire into the convents of the country. Rising in defence of the female religious, John Pope Hennessy recalled their courageous services rendered in the Crimean War and their extensive value to the education of poor Catholics and to the training of future Catholic teachers. He denounced Newdegate's motion as one aimed to 'raise the popular indignation ... against those ladies who passed their lives in educating the poor, attending the sick, and performing acts of charity'. Ten days later, Hennessy's anger drove him to question Newdegate's character, stating that 'it did not need a very courageous heart to strike a blow at those whose sex or sacerdotal character rendered them incapable of self-defence'.[30] Later in the month, Daniel O'Donoghue, another Irish Catholic MP, asked Newdegate if he really believed all of the lewd stories about Jesuits and convents he had presented to the Commons. And if, when he had finished relating such stories in a serious manner before Parliament, did he 'rush into some lonely place, and enjoy a hearty laugh?' O'Donoghue also told his fellow MPs that Bishop Ullathorne had opened his convents in the Diocese of Birmingham to Newdegate's inspectors, but that 'the honorable Member had refused the inquiry which had been offered him'. That, O'Donoghue said, should have revealed the false intentions behind this bill and any future efforts on the part of Newdegate.[31] Hennessey's stout leadership combined with Newdegate's failure to enlist support from his own party leader – Disraeli – and the Liberal ministry's general disapproval killed the bill, which fell 109 to 79 on the Commons floor.[32]

Five years later Newdegate was at it again, appealing for another select committee. This time, Catholic agitation outside Parliament complemented the work of the MPs. In the midst of the debate on the important education bill in the spring of 1870, a number of petitions arrived at Parliament during the first week of April arguing against the appointment of Newdegate's committee. A testament to the organizing skills of the Catholic community, 75 MPs presented more than 150 petitions from England, Scotland and Ireland on 6 April. Eighteen more MPs presented additional Catholic petitions three days later.[33] Also, *The Times* reported that one of the largest meetings of Catholics ever in London was held on 8 April at the Stafford Club, Piccadilly. With the bishops in Rome attending the Vatican Council, the meeting primarily included laity, lower clergy and male religious. At this meeting those in attendance heard that, on the night Newdegate's motion carried, the Duke of Norfolk and Sir Charles Clifford created a petition, which was subsequently forwarded to every parish in England: hence, the impressive number of petitions received in Commons. Clifford also explained that they sent a delegation to Prime Minister Gladstone to discuss the matter. Since it appeared that Newdegate's committee might still be appointed, Clifford asked those gathered to do all they could to resist such an unconstitutional procedure and, if Newdegate should succeed, to 'demand that it should be full and impartial, and in the face of open day, [and] before a court where the law of evidence was respected'.[34]

Two days after the meeting, an anonymous Catholic wrote a critical letter to the editor of *The Times* proposing the following scenario:

> Picture to yourself, sir, the howl of rage and indignation that would resound through the land, the monster petitions, the indignation meetings that would be got up were some member of Commons to rise and move that a committee be appointed to ... inquire into the morals of the ministers of the Establishment, and inspect all vicarages and parsonages and bishops' palaces, on the grounds that such a committee was necessary because a certain number of ministers have of late figured in the Divorce Court.

The writer warned members of Parliament that if the government passed this resolution, 'every Catholic voter will at the next election not forget every member, be he Conservative, Liberal, or Radical, who votes with Mr. Newdegate'.[35] In the end, Catholic opposition and Newdegate's overzealousness convinced Prime Minister Gladstone to offer a compromise that declawed the measure enough to satisfy Catholics that the approved select committee would not be harmful.

Clearly, from 1847 to 1869 Catholic political activity abounded despite the relative silence on the issue of education. In some instances, political activity was centrally guided, defensively aggressive and verbally astute. Spirited political engagement ranged from concern for the Pope's security in the face of Italian unification to what Catholics viewed as a sectarian attack on their religion and their right to practise it unfettered. At a time when anti-Catholicism still periodically boiled over into physical violence, Roman Catholics justifiably feared a further degradation of their place in society and loss of civil rights.

Although much of this political activity was performed by their Irish co-religionists, the effect on the Roman Catholic community was paramount. These issues provided opportunities for Catholics to test their political mettle, like using atrophied muscles that had lain dormant since before the penal era. This was a period of political maturation when the methods were more significant than the results, when playing in the game mattered more than actually winning. With ever-increasing political confidence and a growing tenacious spirit, Catholics equipped themselves to tackle each new opportunity more effectively and, ultimately, to face the most vital issue yet. This issue would require more political organization, militancy and action than the other issues combined. Moreover, it would bring Catholics into greater conflict with the state and shift them closer to the Tories in political alignment. That issue was education of the poor.

The Catholic Poor School Committee

The most important organization created by the English Catholic Church in the struggle for the schools was the Catholic Poor School Committee. Begun in 1847, the same year that Catholics received official notice that they could enter the government's education system the following year, the committee's creation was, in part, a response to that monumental decision. One of the few studies of this organization has notably emphasized its early struggles and relationships with the hierarchy and the religious orders.[36]

The state system of primary education with which the Catholic Poor School Committee would work originated in 1833 when the failure of an exorbitant education bill in Parliament convinced legislators at least to offer modest school construction grants not to exceed £20,000 per year. Communities could request these monies as long as they raised half of the proposed sum in advance. The government restricted the distribution of the grants to the two pre-eminent education organizations: the Anglican National Society and the nonconformist British and Foreign School Society. The string attached to the grants came in the form of government inspection; however, the government allowed religious communities to employ inspectors of their own faith. The Whig government of Prime Minister Melbourne created the Committee of the Privy Council on Education six years later in 1839 to administer what was, by then, becoming a popular measure, the budget for which would balloon up to £100,000 by 1846. Under the direction of James Kay-Shuttleworth, first secretary of the Committee of the Privy Council, the grants programme developed into a rudimentary education system, with a national pupil-teacher training programme, teacher training colleges and increasing standards that had to be met by schools to secure future funding.

The Catholic hierarchy established the Poor School Committee, comprised of one priest and two laymen from each diocese, in order to centralize and unify Catholic educational efforts, as well as to liaise with the Committee of Council on Education.[37] Despite the mixed composition of the committee, it reported to and was controlled by the Catholic hierarchy. The Poor School Committee was designed to serve the Catholics just as the National Society served the Anglicans and the British and Foreign Schools Society served nonconformists in receiving and dispensing state grant money to their respective schools. No longer content simply to sit on the sidelines while other denominations received state grants for education, Catholics finally staked a claim to their share of governmental assistance in education.

The Poor School Committee had its origin in earlier Catholic organizations, most recently the Catholic Institute, a lay organization formed in 1838 to publish and distribute cheap tracts to answer anti-Catholic propaganda, as well as to take an active interest in the education of the Catholic poor.[38] In 1847, the Institute recognized the importance of the cause of education, noting in its *Second Annual Report*, 'the great evil that threatens the Catholics of this realm, is the ignorance and consequent irreligion of 40,000 Catholic children'.[39] A year earlier, in 1846, Charles Langdale had approached Robert Peel's ministry with a request to allow Catholics a share of the Privy Council grants that had been going to Anglican and nonconformist schools since 1833. Before he answered the Catholics, Peel's ministry fell; thus Langdale had to start again, this time writing to Prime Minister John Russell in August with the same request. After further communication between the Institute and the government, Langdale received a letter from Kay-Shuttleworth informing him that the Committee of Council on Education would consider a properly completed application for any type of denominational school, Catholic or Protestant.[40] Meanwhile, Langdale contacted the vicars apostolic in early 1847 about his idea that, if Catholics were to enter the state system, education should be removed from the purview of the Institute and a new organization created to oversee education under Church direction.[41] John Briggs, vicar apostolic of Yorkshire District from 1840 to 1850 before becoming Bishop of Beverley from 1850 to 1860, replied to Langdale that the hierarchy cautiously supported this suggestion but wanted answers to questions about whether Catholics could receive grants for teaching schools, whether Protestant children could attend, whether they could have a Catholic inspector and whether Catholic children in workhouses would be included in the scheme.[42] An important step in the process of joining the state system occurred when Thomas Griffiths, vicar apostolic of the London district from 1836 to 1847, secured a meeting with Prime Minister Russell and pressed upon him the desire Catholics had for their own schools to be state-assisted and that 'Catholics should enjoy as much benefit as any denomination distinct from the Established Church'. According to the letter Griffiths sent to Langdale, the prime minister was amenable to Catholic inclusion and had asked if there was an organization his government could contact to move the process forward. The Catholic Institute was still that organization.[43]

The Catholic Institute submitted an application for a Catholic school in industrial Blackburn, and, after the hierarchy convinced the government that the school would not exclude Protestant children or force them to attend religious instruction, the government agreed to allow Catholics access to education grants beginning in 1848.[44] After this successful effort, the hierarchy returned to Langdale's idea that an organization totally dedicated to education, which the Institute was not, should be established, consisting of both laymen and clergy.[45] Thus, the Catholic Poor School Committee was born. The vicars apostolic considered naming one of their own to chair the new committee but decided against the idea due to the prevalent religious animosity towards Catholics at the time. Charles Langdale, the acknowledged leader of the lay Catholics, assumed the chairmanship and began what one historian has termed his invaluable efforts to bring the recusant tradition to life on education.[46] Wary that past attempts to coordinate a unified educational effort in the Institute had failed, Langdale asked the hierarchy bluntly for a public declaration that they were behind this new organization and that they would use their authority to ensure local clergy cooperated with the organization's efforts.[47]

The hierarchy's joint letter of response to Langdale and to the new Poor School Committee explained their intention behind the organization. It also foreshadowed the proprietary and defensive outlook they developed during the next fifty years:

> We recognise your committee as the organ sanctioned by us of communication with the government; and we have every confidence that your committee ... will be fully aware of our determination not to yield to the Ministers of the day any portion, however small, either of our ecclesiastical liberty, or of our episcopal control over religious education of the children of the poorer members of our flock.[48]

Elementary education and the training of teachers emerged as the committee's two priorities and Catholics began improving existing and building new schools over the next few years with the caveat that state grant aid required annual state inspections.[49]

In its negotiations with the government, the committee secured the right to have Catholics perform the inspections, although the inspectors would be employed by the Committee of Council on Education. Pleased to have achieved this concession from the government, the committee carefully and reassuringly explained to anxious school managers what inspection entailed and how it benefited the school:

> By inspection is meant a friendly visit of sympathy, support, and advice, from one who, by experience, ability and tact, is admirably qualified to render assistance to the managers of schools; one who, while he knows what a good school ought to be, and how to make it so, is not incapable of appreciating difficulties.[50]

Shortly after being approved for government grants, the committee initiated its communicative responsibility by circulating to all of the missions in England and

Wales instructions and suggestions on the best way to qualify for government aid and to found new schools. This effort to ease the schools into the system was well received in the Catholic press.[51]

No matter what ambitious intentions the committee had about increasing educational provision, its horizons were limited by the internal funding it could secure. Obviously, applying for and dispensing state grants did not require much money. However, the committee wanted to generate its own system of grants by creating a general education fund. The most promising source of funding came from the annual Catholic Poor School Committee collection. The vicars apostolic established the collection soon after the committee's creation, and a joint pastoral letter released on 15 February 1848 instructed that the collection be made an annual event upon which 'the eternal salvation of thousands does depend'.[52] In an effort to connect the annual collection to an existing and regular part of the Church calendar, the hierarchy moved the annual collection to the Feast of the Sacred Heart of Jesus in 1852.[53] A further fundraising stimulus arrived in late 1849 when Pope Pius IX granted a plenary indulgence to anyone who subscribed to the Poor School Committee's general fund, something the hierarchy had requested from the Holy See.[54]

Despite the papal seal of approval, the hierarchy and the Catholic press had to promote avidly the activities and benefits of the committee to generate enough interest for the collection. Bishop Turner was reminding the Salford diocese as early as 1851 about the need for 'liberal and hearty co-operation' to support these efforts to educate the poor. Further north, William Hogarth, Bishop of Hexham, urgently asked his growing diocese in 1852 to 'stem the torrent of moral desolation' by supporting the Church's efforts to educate the poor. A week later and perhaps in conjunction with Hogarth's letter, Thomas Joseph Brown, Bishop of Newport and Menevia (Wales) from 1850 to 1880, addressed the Poor School Committee's need for greater funding by calling the 'education of the our poor children' the very first duty of Catholics.[55] Later in the year, both Bishop George Brown of Liverpool and Thomas Grant, Bishop of Southwark from 1851 to 1870, highlighted the work being done by the Poor School Committee and the urgency of making financial sacrifices to support its work. Grant noted that without a greater effort at that year's collection, his diocese would have to close three to five missions and their respective schools.[56] No doubt, the emphasis on education of the poor from the first Synod of Westminster that summer provided inspiration for these episcopal directives.[57]

Too often, the Poor School Committee found that its funding came from the same small group of wealthy Catholic families who bore the heaviest burden of financial support for education while middle-class Catholics remained absent from the subscriber lists.[58] Such was the slow work of raising the public awareness of the Poor School Committee that Langdale wrote to Bishop Ullathorne on behalf of the committee requesting that all the bishops issue a pastoral letter just prior to the annual collection the first week of June as a reminder for the following week.[59] Faced with decreasing collections, Bishop Brown of Liverpool reminded his clergy in 1854 to tell their congregations about the papal sanction and the indulgences available for contributors so as to generate more interest and a greater collection.[60] Even Cardinal Wiseman, faced with a similar situation in his own diocese of Westminster, was not above employing base guilt in his appeal. He said that, although the Church did not know each person's contribution, 'God sees what drops from each one's hand, and sees too what remains in his coffers; He knows exactly in what proportion to your powers, you respectively give'.[61]

The press could be just as persuasive. An editorial in the *Catholic Standard* from 20 April 1850 implored Catholics to come to the aid of Catholic schoolchildren.[62] A month and a half later the same paper increased its editorial pressure:

> The best organized body that religion has seen in this country since England was cajoled and cursed with the Reformation is at our disposal. [The Poor School Committee] depends on the quantity of life we pour into it ... [And its] work has grown faster ... than its funds.[63]

The creation of the Poor School Committee certainly did not help the overall financial situation of the Catholic community, but it did generate money specifically targeted for schools which, even if it was never enough, was still organizational progress.

While fundraising was an internal problem, inexperience in dealing with the government was another, and one whose root cause could not be reduced to Catholic poverty. Generally speaking, since the seventeenth century, Catholics had gone out of their way not to be noticed by or have official relations with the government. Now, education brought these two mutually suspicious parties together. The Poor School Committee's first secretary, Scott N. Stokes, spent much of his first few years writing to the Council with questions about regulations and policy. Perhaps due to the committee's lack of experience working within the system or due to its defensive nature and native distrust of the government, its correspondence in the early years often reflected outright suspicion of the state's intentions. In May 1849, Stokes wrote to the Council to ask why four of his schools had not yet received word on the findings of Inspector Thomas W. Marshall with regard to the apprenticeship of pupil teachers when other Catholic schools had received their results: 'I am desired to mention these circumstances and to allude to the very serious difficulties which may be expected to arise from further delay in dealing with these cases', he concluded with some amount of impatience.[64] Later that summer, Stokes began correspondence on the possibility of receiving grant aid for the creation of a Catholic training college. After his initial request was rejected because the Council required new buildings specifically designated as colleges, Stokes wrote a more detailed and contentious letter in which he related his awareness of several Protestant training colleges 'not erected for [that] specific purpose [which] nevertheless enjoy a full participation in their Lordships grants'. He demanded an immediate explanation why Catholic interests were being treated differently. In a final bit of creative complaining that tapped into the fear of Irish radicalism so prevalent at the time, Stokes said it was a shame that Catholic schools had to rely upon teachers trained in Ireland who 'may be expected to produce almost unconsciously in the minds of their scholars some degree of that alienation in feeling and sentiment, which ... can scarcely prove beneficial to the state'.[65] Coming in the year following the failed Irish uprising of 1848, this comment purposely intended to alarm the Committee of Council on Education.

Later that same year, Stokes protested what the Poor School Committee believed were school inspection examination questions designed to perpetuate Victorian prejudice against Catholicism. One question read, 'In what points is the assimilation of Paganism and Popery apparent?' Stokes also objected to the Council's change in the number of students required before a school could obtain a pupil teacher; the requirement had been one pupil teacher for every twenty-five students but had been recently raised to one in sixty, a change that would seriously injure Catholic schools, some of which 'can never expect an attendance of from 120 to 140 students'. In both examples, Stokes appealed to 'that religious impartiality and freedom from bigotry' that the government displayed towards other denominations.[66] Just three months later, in January 1850, Stokes was again lecturing the Council on the necessity of equal treatment for all denominations and that the appointment of teachers should be 'open to general competition and awarded with reference to attainments alone'.[67] Stokes's communication with the state, while laced with obvious insecurity, has all of the trademarks of the newly aggressive, increasingly bold and tenacious spirit just beginning to transform Catholic identity at mid-century.

When Stokes left the Poor School Committee in 1853 to become the second Catholic inspector of schools, his successor, Thomas W. Allies, continued Stokes's propensity for expressing his agitation with the Council. After the Council's Minutes of June 1856 called for the use of 'Her Majesty's Inspectors' for the inspection of workhouse schools, Allies wrote to R. R. W. Lingen, Council Secretary, with his guard up, reminding the Council that inspectors for Catholic industrial schools must be Catholic.[68] When a Protestant inspector showed up to inspect the Catholic industrial school at Hartlepool the following month, Langdale sent a curt letter to Lingen stating succinctly that this action would abrogate the deal put in place in 1847 whereby state inspectors of Catholic schools would be Catholic and approved by the Poor School Committee.[69]

Since Catholics were new to the system it was only natural that the committee required a few years to get operations running smoothly. The prevalence of anti-Catholicism dating from the Maynooth controversy in 1845 to the massive outbreak surrounding the restoration of the hierarchy in 1850 and Prime Minister Russell's inflammatory Ecclesiastical Titles bill in 1851 explain the committee's defensive, persecution complex. The religious bigotry was not imaginary; thus the defensive posturing was a natural response by the Poor School Committee to prevent violations of its agreement with the government. Stokes and Allies were simply relaying the questions, complaints and attitudes of those they served, primarily the Catholic school managers and the bishops. Take, for example, Bishop Goss of Liverpool. He expressed his rising anger and frustration at the anti-Catholic resentment building in his diocese as it struggled to erect schools: 'We are building churches and schools, and meanwhile our poor, young and old, are being denounced'. Likewise, the bishop supported state assistance for larger and isolated Catholic primary schools but remained wary of too much government interference in the operations of smaller schools closely tied to Church property.[70] Therefore, one can surmise that this defensive and sometimes contentious nature pervaded the thoughts of most Catholic educationists.

A second important function of the committee was teacher training, and the establishment and support of Catholic training colleges can be argued to have been its greatest achievement. In its first annual report, the committee complained about the constant frustration of not locating enough qualified teachers.[71] That first year, the committee placed five female teachers-in-training with the Sisters of the Holy Child Jesus in Sussex, an action it hoped would form the nucleus of a much-needed, domestic female training college. Likewise, the committee settled on the French Brothers of Christian Instruction for males and sent five young men to the town of Ploermel in Brittany to be trained under the care of this religious order with the hope of later establishing a training facility in England.[72]

When the students who had been training at Ploermel finished their training and returned in 1850, the committee established the first Catholic teacher training college for males in England: St Mary's, Hammersmith. The cost of the buildings in 1850 totalled £9,089 19*s*. 9*d*., but only £618 16*s*. 9*d*. came from the coffers of the Poor School Committee because, along with other donations, four members of the committee personally contributed over £1,000 each.[73] With the rapidly increasing need for male teachers, however, Catholics realized that the college would not produce enough male religious to meet the demand, an opinion expressed in the March 1855 issue of the *Catholic School*. The committee reasoned logically why a lay training school was also necessary:

> The training-school at [Hammersmith] has been in operation about three years. It has had ... under its care about six-and-twenty subjects. It has sent out about seven teachers. About 280 schools ... are now under the care of secular teachers. The number of Catholic schools is increasing every year ... At this moment, therefore, the secular teachers are continually outstripping the religious in number, and are entering on the most important of all works next to that of the priesthood, without training or preparation, intellectual, moral, or spiritual.[74]

Although the committee preferred the use of religious in the classroom, they had to face the reality of the situation. Thus, in December 1854, St Mary's opened up a lay department, which took advantage of the fresh supply of male pupil teachers who were finishing their apprenticeships in Catholic primary schools.[75] The cost of the new construction to open a lay department was £7,000, of which £2,500 came through a grant from the Council and £2,475 8*s.* came from private subscriptions, leaving over £2,000 to be made up by the Catholic community at large.[76]

In the late 1850s, however, St Mary's began experiencing a decrease in numbers, mainly from the inadequacy of the pupil-teacher system in providing acceptable candidates. Due to this situation, the school opened a preparatory class in 1861 to boost enrolments, but it was not until 1871 that almost every place at the college was filled.[77] Thomas Graham, principal of St Mary's, summed up the purpose of this training experience and its value to the Catholic education effort when, testifying before a parliamentary commission in 1886, he stated:

> I take [the chief purpose] to be to fit a man who enters it, with the capabilities for it, to become a teacher thoroughly efficient to train the children in all subjects prescribed for a good common education, and in good morals, and in their duties to their fellow man.

When pressed if this Catholic college was to be a place where the mind was stocked with knowledge or rather a place where the art of teaching was developed, Graham answered: 'Both, but particularly the latter, because the first could be done independently of a training college'.[78]

Much to the relief of the Catholic community, the burden of providing female training colleges was much lighter, thanks to the generosity of the female religious orders at work in England.[79] In 1853, Stokes described the situation in which there was a male training school but none for female religious:

> Every nun cannot expect to be born a good Teacher, nor will every Order be found equally successful in school. For this ... we must anxiously look forward to the selection by the Bishops ... of one Community, specially charged with the care of an institution, similar in character to that at Hammersmith for the general supply of trained Teachers.[80]

Two years later two separate female religious orders established training colleges at no cost to the Poor School Committee.

Founded by Cornelia Connelly, a formerly married, ex-Protestant American with three children, the Sisters of the Holy Child Jesus opened the first female training college in 1855. Cardinal Wiseman saw in her the piety, charisma and determination to bring a new female religious order committed to education into England. He also realized that this order would be the perfect place for female converts who could bring their educational training to the schools. Mother Connelly opened the training college on the premises of their boarding school in St Leonard's-on-Sea, Sussex. A handful of her nuns sat for the public examinations and obtained teacher's certificates, and, by the following spring, the training school was in operation with nine students attending on state scholarships.[81] St Leonard's-on-Sea training college operated for eight years, producing close to 100 trained female teachers. It closed, however, due to administrative and financial problems in 1863.[82] Fortunately for English Catholic educationists, another female training college had opened in Liverpool the same year as St Leonard's-on-Sea.

The Sisters of Notre Dame de Namur established their first house at Penryn in Cornwall in 1845 and moved to Clapham, in south London, three years later. After establishing a reputation for excellent instruction and subsequently opening more communities throughout England, the order was approached by the Poor School Committee in 1855 about the possibility of opening a training college. So desperate did the committee view the situation that Thomas W. Allies actually visited the Rev. Mother General in Belgium to make the request in person. As recorded in the annals of the Notre Dame nuns,

> the prospect of benefitting [*sic*] many thousands of poor girls and infants by furnishing a supply of virtuous efficient school mistresses induced the Rev. Mother not only to listen favorably, but to offer to the Committee for the purposes of a Normal College a large house and gardens in Mount Pleasant, Liverpool.[83]

Like the Sisters of the Holy Child Jesus, a small group of Notre Dame sisters sat and passed the required examinations. The training college opened in early 1856 with twenty-one students, again at no cost to the Poor School Committee. The committee's only financial commitment was to defer some of the annual maintenance costs. Unlike St Leonard's-on-Sea, Mount Pleasant Training College survived the financial hardships of the early 1860s, due primarily to the financial windfall brought to the order by Sister Mary of Saint Francis, known before her entrance into the religious life as Mrs Edward Petre.[84] It remained in operation as the premier female training college through the remainder of the century and far into the next.

The teaching colleges succeeded as an ambitious venture for such a poor community, but one that was necessary to overcome the lack of certified teachers. Although financial trouble constantly burdened St Mary's, the emphasis here should be on the intentions rather than ends. The Catholic community would not have been able to support St Mary's without financial support from the Committee of Council on Education. As for the female training colleges, the Catholic community was simply lucky to have female orders willing to build and operate them. The community could not have supported both St Mary's and a female training college. According to estimates provided by the secretary, Allies, the Catholic community had saved £56,000 by not having to build female training colleges that the female orders financed themselves.[85] Yet, it was the confidence to ask for assistance to create the men's institution, much like the other richer denominations were doing, that indicates again the transformation beginning within the community. Roman Catholicism was showing that it was not afraid to take its place alongside the other denominations providing educational training, even when that effort was as financially and physically daunting as beginning and running a teacher training college.

While successful in building St Mary's College and implementing the religious inspections, the Poor School Committee often stumbled and received its share of criticism. Most focused not on the goals of the committee but on its lack of meetings and action, its use of funds for questionable activities or its lack of a sense of urgency. Enough criticism mounted in the mid-1850s over the slow resolution of the trust-deed settlement, a resolution that finally enabled Catholic schools to receive building grants, that the bishops decided to write to Charles Langdale to reassure him of their 'complete confidence in [the committee's] activity, zeal, generosity, and usefulness'.[86] Yet despite the occasional mistake or slow reaction time of the Poor School Committee and the often frustrating efforts of the bishops to get the Catholic laity more involved in supporting education, the Poor School Committee remained the vital link between the Catholic community and the state for the remainder of the century and beyond, albeit with some structural changes.

Conclusion

By the late 1860s, a growing percentage of dissenters remained dissatisfied with the educational system, especially because state funds supported the Anglican schools to which they often had to send their children because it was the only elementary school nearby. These dissenters believed it would be better to sever religious instruction from elementary schools altogether and leave it for their Sunday schools where they could control it. Further, a smaller, more extreme minority clamoured for secular education purely on ideological grounds as they believed that a modern liberal state should not have religious ties. These secularists, however, knew that education had hitherto been the preserve of religious bodies in Great Britain because the system that existed in the 1860s was the creation of the churches. To the Anglicans, Catholics and some dissenters, the idea of educational reform that excluded religion from a system that had been built by the churches was unthinkable. In 1868, as pressure was mounting to provide a free, compulsory, nondenominational and, for some, a secular system of education, William Ewart Gladstone became prime minister, bringing a reform-minded Liberal ministry to power. Educational reform was on the short list of tasks for the new government and one that would be attempted in the late winter of 1870 when a landmark education bill was introduced to Parliament by Gladstone's vice president of the Education Department, W. E. Forster. This would be the spark to greater action that the Catholic community needed.

5 ENGLISH CATHOLICS AND THE POLITICS OF EDUCATION, 1870: THE BATTLE BEGINS

In the minds of Catholic leaders, the state overreached itself with the Education Act of 1870. It was that fateful year, as Manning later told a crowd of Catholics in 1885, that the 'children in English schools [became] children of the State'.[1] Prior to 1870, all education was provided by voluntary schools of various denominations supported by internal subscriptions and state education grants. The Act, however, established nondenominational board schools, supported by rates paid by all property owners, in direct competition with the denominational schools. This event forced Manning and the rest of the hierarchy to re-evaluate their political stance; they realized that an aloof position outside the political arena rendered them ineffective. With the 1870 Act we see Catholic political action for education, both inside and outside of Parliament, expand far beyond what it had been previously. In Manning's eyes, when the state discarded the system that provided all elementary education and forcibly thrust itself wholly on education instead, then 'the clergy had a right to enter into practical politics'.[2] A culmination of increasing Catholic political activity in 1870 combined with a debate over a significantly altered education system that, in Catholic minds, led to an injustice against which they would aggressively fight for years to come.

Education Enters the Catholic Political Landscape

The issue of elementary education permanently entered the political agenda of Catholics in 1870 and shared prominence with Irish affairs until the end of the century. During this period, Irish affairs tended to align Catholics with the Liberals, while education brought Catholics and Conservatives together. W. E. Forster's education bill in 1870 placed education at the top of the Catholic agenda, although, as will be shown, various Catholics and Catholic organs reacted differently to the bill. More importantly, the subsequent passage of the bill set in motion a process by which Catholics from all walks of life and to varying degrees actively became engaged in the effort to safeguard and expand Catholic education. Further, due to the unforeseen consequences that emerged soon after the new education system began in 1871, Catholic attitudes shifted from contentment at receiving some educational assistance, as witnessed from 1847 to 1870, to demanding that the system be improved and made equitable to all participants.

As already indicated, the 1850s revealed a Catholic community still warming to its role as a participant in the government's education system and finding the transition challenging. Of note, this decade witnessed disagreement among the sometimes cantankerous bishops regarding their fledgling educational network. Notorious even among this group of headstrong bishops was Yorkshire-born Bishop Ullathorne who declared in 1857, after nearly a decade of participation in the state grant system, that control over their Catholic schools was now threatened by an overly intrusive government. Alarmed that Catholics had given up too much liberty in joining the education system, Ullathorne warned in his widely distributed pamphlet *Notes on the Education Question*:

> If we slacken our efforts on the plea that Government will help our schools ... if we allow the main support of our schools to come from the Government, if we let inspection become direction, if we bind our schools to conditions implying a perpetual right of Government interference ... our freedom is gone.[3]

While Ullathorne did not advocate disassociation with the grant system, he let it be known that he was keeping a watchful and sceptical eye on the educational relationship between Catholics and the state. However, his publication annoyed his fellow bishops. Bishop Turner wrote to Bishop Briggs in Leeds complaining of Ullathorne's inflammatory grandstanding because if all of the bishops agreed to enter the system the previous decade, then 'how is he authorized to disapprove of [it] now?' He should have kept his opinion to himself, grumbled the Salford bishop.[4] Only two months later at the annual bishops' meeting and because of Ullathorne's pamphlet, the bishops were reassured by the Poor School Committee that no harm would come to Catholic schools. Interestingly, all bishops were present when they issued a unanimous resolution that approved of their decision to enter the 'sufficiently safe' educational system.[5] Two years later, Ullathorne himself admitted that the Catholic acceptance of government aid was a prudent decision.[6]

In 1859, the *Rambler* publicly attacked the Poor School Committee for its inactivity on important educational matters occurring at the national level. The government had recently created a royal commission – the Newcastle Commission – to investigate the efficacy and rising cost of elementary education. The *Rambler*'s editors were furious that the committee had not even held a meeting to discuss the proposed commission, let alone petitioned the government to include a Catholic on the commission.[7] 'For many months', the editorial complained, 'we have regretted that the Poor-School Committee communicated so rarely with its supporters and the public, and finds so few opportunities to rouse and inform the Catholic body upon educational questions'.[8]

Initially, the Poor School Committee was simply planning not to participate by refusing commissioners access to Catholic schools, justifying its decision not to get involved by arguing that it was adhering to the original agreement that secured Catholics as the only permissible inspectors of Catholic schools. The Newcastle Commission had no Catholic members; therefore, the committee refused to participate. Langdale explained the committee's logic in a letter to the bishops in October 1858, who met the following month to consider the proposal and declined to participate. Cardinal Wiseman explained the hierarchy's decision in a pastoral letter to the Westminster Diocese: 'the Bishops have felt that a sacred and religious principle was at issue, and that the concession demanded was equivalent to a surrender of the very ground on which Catholic Inspectors had been demanded and obtained'.[9] Bishop Turner warned his clergy not to allow any inspector into their schools, other than the usual Catholic one, and Bishop Ullathorne concluded that allowing Protestant inspectors from the Newcastle Commission into Catholic schools would result in a slippery slope leading to their loss of religious freedom.[10]

Unfortunately, the Poor School Committee and the bishops misunderstood the purpose of the commissioners, who were only to gather data and make inquiries rather than perform inspections. Catholic leaders were allowing lingering historical mistrust of the government to become an obstacle in the improvement of their schools. Once the committee actually convened and the members realized they had misunderstood the purpose of the Newcastle Commission, and after receiving the stinging criticism from the *Rambler*, Langdale sheepishly wrote to the Education Department to offer to collect the statistical information for the commission. The Education Department accepted the compromise offer and the matter, for the time being, was settled.[11] Subsequently, the bishops wrote to their deans and clergy, instructing them to complete the royal commission's forms with great care to show the commission that Catholic school managers 'understand and appreciate the work contracted to them'.[12] Letting go of the past with its attendant mistrust and suspicion was not an easily accomplished task; thus Catholics learned from this experience and moved on.

In 1862 Parliament debated Education Department Vice President Robert Lowe's Revised Code, changes to the education code that followed from the Newcastle Commission report's recommendations. Leading politicians hoped to push the school–government relationship in an economical direction because Liberal ministers, especially Prime Minister Palmerston's Chancellor of the Exchequer William E. Gladstone, were concerned about the escalating national education budget. Upon the bill's passage into law, the Education Department began basing school funding on average attendance and an annual examination by a government inspector, who visited the schools, checked the attendance books and examined the children's reading, writing and mathematics skills. Because the annual examination only covered those three subjects, education would soon devolve into a process of rote memorization and teaching to the exams. Lowe's revised educational system earned the pejorative description 'payment by results' and lasted until 1897. The result of Lowe's changes was a system emphasizing thrift rather than effective elementary education. While critics warned of the dire consequences that could result from such a retreat in educational provision, the budget minders rejoiced, especially when the education budget was reduced by £200,000 in four years.

The first petitions against the new code that arrived at Westminster in mid-February 1862 largely represented Anglican schools. Petitions continued to arrive from around the country for three weeks, as the debate on the code dragged on. Yet, seemingly oblivious to the pending educational legislation, Catholic MPs such as the O'Conor Don and John Pope Hennessy brought forth petitions relating to grievances in Ireland and not education.[13] An intense debate on the proposed code occurred on 1 March; not one Catholic MP participated but several brought in petitions requesting Poor Law reform in Ireland.[14] Finally, on 6 March, a Catholic MP, Sir R. Clifton, presented a petition against the proposed code from St Barnabas Catholic School, Nottingham, the first on this subject from Catholics. Four days later, the O'Conor Don presented a similar petition from St Augustine's School, Liverpool. Further petitions from Catholics trickled in over the next two weeks, including one signed by the Catholic Poor School Committee and two each from the teacher training colleges at St Mary's, Hammersmith; Mount Pleasant, Liverpool; and St Leonard's-on-Sea. In all, twenty-three Catholic parishes or schools sent petitions to Parliament against the Revised Code, compared with hundreds from Anglican national schools and nonconformist British schools. Remarkably, not one Catholic MP entered the parliamentary debate to express the views of the Church on the matter.[15] When the bishops met during Low Week in late April, they agreed that the new code was highly objectionable but in an atmosphere of resignation they believed there was little they could do beyond what had been accomplished already.[16] Because thirty-one of the thirty-two Catholic MPs represented Irish constituencies in 1862, Irish Catholic affairs took precedence over English Catholic ones; thus the Revised Code took a back seat to more pressing Irish concerns, such as the reform of the Irish Poor Law and the Irish education system. This dilemma of English Catholic concerns being periodically marginalized by Irish Catholic politicians remained problematic for English Catholic leaders until the 1890s.

By the late 1860s, as Catholics slowly expanded their educational system with state assistance, a healthy fear of growing state power began to surface in Catholic publications and pronouncements. Reflecting dissatisfaction with the

Revised Code as well as a gnawing fear that the political tide was shifting away from a Church-controlled elementary school system towards something more secular and perhaps compulsory, doubtful Catholics feared for their schools. At a meeting of the Liverpool Catholic Reformatory Association in February 1867, Bishop Goss articulated Catholic alarm when he reminded the crowd that they could not allow the state to trample upon the rights of parents by assuming the right of educating the child. The popular Father James Nugent added that once the state assumed full financial responsibility for elementary education, it would fold the management of Catholic schools into its own hands, leaving Catholics on the outside looking in.[17] Later in the year, Goss warned Manning that with increasing rumours about Parliament revisiting the educational system, Catholics should be sceptical about any new proposal that may harm the current denominational system because the state would certainly abuse any increased power it attained.[18] In 1869, Bishop Cornthwaite explained to his diocese that the rising importance of the secular educational party and the concurrent increase in state power were not coincidental. The latter was enabling the former and the secular party was 'advocating, not the extension or modification of the present system, but its abolition' in the near future.[19]

When exactly the changes would come no one knew, but the conventional wisdom among Catholics was that a comprehensive bill that might drastically alter the educational landscape was lurking and, thus, there was a need to be prepared, especially on the Poor School Committee.[20] Lord Howard, current chairman of the Committee, believed that with falling numbers at the training college for boys at Hammersmith and decreasing funds being raised for all of its efforts, the Poor School Committee was not in a position of strength to weather any national education changes.[21] The amount collected in the annual Catholic Poor School Committee collection had dropped in the 1860s, causing consternation among the bishops. As early as 1862, the Poor School Committee was asking bishops for missing collections such as the request sent to Bishop Cornthwaite for the missing collections from Bradford, Bramley, Halifax and Keighley for 1861. By 1868, the situation had not improved much in and around Leeds. A disappointed Bishop Cornthwaite wrote to his diocesan clergy in July asking for their help in increasing collections and remitting those collections to the committee because 'we ... in this diocese have not done all that we might and ought to have done' in the cause of raising funds. Ashamed of the fact that twenty missions had not sent any collections the previous year and nine had not sent funds for two years, Cornthwaite pleaded for assistance and renewed zeal in the effort.[22] The bishop blamed the falling collections on two problems: the urgent demands of other Catholic charitable needs; and the lack of appreciation among lay Catholics on the 'importance of the whole question of the education of the poor', especially considering the rise of the 'strong, energetic, and influential' secular education party.[23] Anticipating the impending educational changes and the increasing challenges of raising funds for the Poor School Committee, Manning wrote to Lord Howard to communicate the desire of the bishops to stimulate the effectiveness of the committee by tightening its administrative design. Such changes included sending small teams of Poor School Committee members throughout the country to hold public meetings to increase the awareness of the committee's efforts, charging local diocesan members of the national committee with personally collecting and remitting subscriptions to the London office, and directing the focus of the committee's external efforts on the administration and examination of the teacher training schools, while leaving the operation of the local elementary schools to each diocese. These changes, they hoped, would provide a 'great impulse' in the committee's effort to educate the Catholic poor.[24]

As rumours began circulating in 1868 that the new Gladstone ministry might call for an official examination and possible reform of the elementary education system later that year or early the following year, a decision stemming from the expanded franchise of 1867 and the perceived need for a better-educated electorate, most publicly minded Catholics occupied Liberal political ground due to Gladstone's bill that year for the disestablishment of the Church of Ireland.[25] However, Liberal leaders did not necessarily count the Catholics as stable allies, especially considering Pius IX's *Syllabus of Errors*, which denounced such modern movements as liberalism, and the recently convoked Vatican Council, where doctrinal ideas such as papal infallibility would be debated and eventually adopted. The Tories were certainly no repository of good will for Catholics either, and the isolation that had stymied past Catholic political efforts enveloped them again. The *Tablet* openly declared on December 1868: 'We belong to neither of the rival political parties'.[26] However, this was a position that Bishop Goss believed was advantageous for Catholics because it allowed more flexibility for Church leaders to push for the good of the Church.[27]

Sensing educational changes on the horizon and that those changes might reflect the rising tide of secularism, the *Dublin Review* urged Catholics to take action in the upcoming storm:

> When the time shall come (and it is at hand) for a trial ... of the great question of popular education, the Catholics of this kingdom will know how to act. We are confident that they will be found active in general and local meetings, in canvassing for members of Parliament, in elections at the hustings, petitioning Parliament, writing pamphlets, constantly recurring to the use of the press, and, above all, by wisely and heartily co-operating with all the denominations who will work with them.[28]

These exhortations projected great confidence but also included a bit of wishful thinking as to the political acumen and influence of the Catholic body. The *Tab-*

let joined in a similar line of advice in January 1869, asking Catholics to work ecumenically with like-minded Anglicans:

> We shall do well to look at once to the real interests of religious education throughout the country, and to form a strong league with members of the National Society in England, who are equally with ourselves in favour of denominational education.[29]

Three weeks later the *Tablet* addressed the rumoured parliamentary examination of the educational system. Holding true to its more conservative line, the paper warned the Gladstone ministry that 'if there be any question upon which the Catholics of these realms are capable of breaking with the Government, to which they have given in the past election so unusual a measure of support, it is upon this very question of Education'.[30] These implied warnings to the Gladstone administration, however, while reflecting growing confidence were simply bluster because the Catholic vote was too small to make or break a ministry; no doubt, if even noticed, the Catholic statements only reinforced the perception of Catholic political unreliability. The *Tablet* was now in the hands of Herbert Alfred Vaughan, Bishop of Salford from 1872 to 1892.[31] He believed that, despite differences on other issues, the Catholic community was 'thoroughly united in their demand for Denominational Education'.[32] Both journals also believed, perhaps wishfully, that Catholic support for Irish causes would eventually take second place to education.

The effort to create a free, state-supported, secular system of elementary education advanced in 1869 with the formation of the radical National Education League; those who opposed such a system created the reactionary National Education Union to counter the Education League and keep elementary education in the hands of the religious denominations where it had always been. Responding to these partisan developments, the government again decided to enquire into the health of elementary education, this time only focusing on four industrial towns: Liverpool, Manchester, Birmingham and Leeds. As with the Newcastle Commission eleven years earlier, each denomination was asked to cooperate with the state's educational inquiries. The reaction of the Catholic community, now under the skilful and more determined guidance of Henry Edward Manning, reveals an extraordinarily changed outlook. Instead of stubbornly refusing to cooperate out of fear and mistrust as it had a decade earlier, the Poor School Committee recommended full cooperation. By participating, the Poor School Committee argued that 'Catholics will take their place as citizens, and will entitle themselves to be heard in the settlement of future policy'.[33] Such a radically different response indicates a changing Catholic ethos, a maturation and growing confidence that a decade of lectures and sermons on the importance of education had leavened. With Manning leading the way, the Catholic community, from London to the parishes, was slowly realizing the need to become active 'citizens' participating in the public policy process if they wished to ensure the survival and continued expansion of their schools. This realization forced some Catholic leaders into organizing, lobbying, petitioning, editorializing – in a word, politicking – during a time when their nonconformist educational opponents, who wanted a state-supported secular system, were gradually gaining the ear of Parliament.

The Education Act of 1870

A turning point for the Catholic community occurred in 1870, the year of the controversial Education Act that significantly altered the educational landscape. The initial bill proposed by Gladstone's head of the Education Department W. E. Forster intended to create a rival system of rate-supported, nondenominational schools administered by publicly elected school boards. The long struggle over this bill inspired various Catholic clerics and laity to engage actively in the education struggle. When Catholics, like the Anglicans, realized the damage this new system with its unlimited funding from the rates (local property taxes) could inflict on the denominational school system, the political tocsin sounded. Even before the bill was even introduced, Manning had warned that 'the preservation of our Christianity, of our public morality and of liberty of conscience' was at stake.[34]

At the outset, Catholic public opinion on the education question appeared synchronized with the bishops: any shift of the education system in the direction of secularism required resistance. As early as January 1869, a large meeting of Birmingham Catholics led by Bishop Ullathorne revealed a Catholic community ready for the national debate. That evening Canon Sullivan expressed his fear that Catholic freedom was being threatened by recent educational developments and warned the audience that they must improve internal funding to defend their freedoms *vis-a-vis* education. The Poor School Committee's Lord Howard praised the recent work of the Catholic community on educational affairs, especially in the construction of churches and schools, but forewarned that a great crisis was looming, one in which they would have to fight to preserve religious education. Nothing, he concluded, was more important to Catholics.[35] The following month large outdoor rallies in the East and West Ends of London brought several thousand Catholics together to support the denominational system and condemn any movement towards state-sponsored and compulsory secular education.[36] By autumn, Catholics feared the growing influence of the National Education League at Whitehall and, at a crowded meeting of Catholics at the Birmingham Town Hall, Bishop Ullathorne fanned the flames by asking his listeners:

> Are you willing that your Catholic schools should have less support from the public funds than the unreligious schools ... (Loud cries of 'No, no'). Is it your wish that the

> tax-gatherer should come to your door to demand by law a part of your money, all which money is to go to these Godless schools, whilst your own schools are to have no part of that money? (Renewed cries of 'No, no')

Thus, without even knowing what scheme the government was going to unveil, one of the tetchiest bishops was already declaring the Catholic rejection of it, and, in no uncertain terms, demanding that Catholics receive an equitable share of the rates for their own schools.[37] This was the first public mention of this oft-repeated Catholic claim over the next three decades.

The real work began the following year. Speaking at a National Education Union meeting at the Town Hall in Manchester early in the new year Thomas W. Allies, secretary of the Poor School Committee, voiced the Catholic desire to see the present denominational system continued. The *Tablet* editorial page agreed and asked that the entire Catholic population of England and Wales be stirred into action.[38] The same issue included a lengthy letter to the editor from Lord Howard, chairman of the Poor School Committee, who revealed his frustration that Catholics were not better organized to meet the imminent challenge like the Anglicans and the Wesleyans, and which served as veiled criticism of the hierarchy and, notably, Manning for not being better prepared.[39] On 12 February the *Tablet* sensed the legislation was near and called for more action: 'A little more public life would do us all good'. The editorial recalled the laudable work of some clergy who had attended and spoken to Union meetings and praised Rev. D. Canty for bravely venturing into the 'lion's den' by attending a League assembly where he publicly declared that he 'was ashamed of the meeting for having hissed the sentiment that the Bible should be read in schools'. The criticism of a lack of 'direction, information, suggestion, encouragement, and general stimulus' was articulated without a specific target but, reading between the lines, was partially aimed at the hierarchy, which was currently in Rome at the Vatican Council, and partially aimed at the Poor School Committee.[40] Two days after the bill was read in the Commons, the first Catholic response came from the *Tablet*, which described the bill as 'an odious form of persecution' and the editors immediately called for the creation of local versions of the Poor School Committee to begin the defence of Catholic education.[41]

After the Queen had announced that an education bill would soon be unveiled in February 1870, Catholic leaders organized plans for public demonstrations. Meeting at the Catholic Club in Liverpool, Canon (and future bishop) Bernard O'Reilly and Father James Nugent created a rather ecumenical watchdog committee comprised of prominent Catholics of all political stripes: Liberal, Conservative and Home Rule. At this committee's instigation, Catholics held a large demonstration on St Patrick's Day in Williamson Square, Liverpool, a few weeks after W. E. Forster brought his education bill into Parliament. The crowded and boisterous meeting adopted the following resolution to be sent to Parliament: 'Religion being the basis of all true education, this meeting holds that any system which would tend to secularize education cannot be acceptable to the Catholics of this country'. Further, Father Nugent made a motion to send a Catholic deputation to explain to Forster how prejudicial the Catholics found his bill. Quickly seconded, Nugent's motion brought thunderous cheers.[42]

A letter to the editor of the *Tablet* in February called for more popular action on the part of Catholics. The anonymous writer asked the journal to 'stir up such an agitation' as will show the country that the Catholic community 'will not tamely and without a struggle submit to the tyranny of an irreligious majority'.[43] Catholic anger and fear were in response to the bill's initial plan to establish board schools, which could, in a nod to secularist pressure, opt out of religious education altogether. After considerable debate over the next few months, a later controversial clause – the Cowper–Temple clause – required the board schools to teach religion, albeit of a non-doctrinal kind. Catholics rightly feared that, given the gaps in their still-expanding and rather inchoate school network, Catholic children might attend a nearby board school and be harmed spiritually, whether that school included non-doctrinal religious education or no religious education at all. Perhaps stung by the criticism in the press, the Poor School Committee quickly convened in London, meeting for three days to create a petition to be signed throughout the country and presented to Parliament.[44]

This Catholic petition campaign in response to the proposed education bill resulted in petitions to Parliament beginning in early March and continuing into April. The difference between the number of petitions received from Catholics on the Revised Code eight years earlier and the number received in 1870 is extensive, as the latter numbered close to two hundred. An early petition from the clergy and teachers of St Augustine's School, Manchester, set the tone for much of the subsequent communication; it criticized the bill for not extending denominational education and, fearing the worst from the National Education League lobby, asked that religious freedom in the classroom be protected.[45] Other petitions drew upon the basic concepts of equal rights and asked that Parliament not pass a bill compelling Catholic children 'to attend schools where the course of instruction would be a violation of their consciences'.[46] For six weeks petitions arrived from Catholic parishes and communities throughout England, Wales and even Ireland, despite the fact that Irish education would not be affected by this legislation.[47]

With the English hierarchy in Rome for the Vatican Council, the engineering of such a determined political effort is a credit to the lower Catholic clergy, the Catholic laity and organizations such as the Catholic Poor School Committee. Yet, the fact that the bishops were otherwise occupied weakened the overall Catholic campaign. Manning was not surprised by the introduction of the education bill. In a letter dated 24 February, he told Gladstone that he anxiously awaited his copy of the bill – introduced into Parliament on 17 February – and related his reservations concerning the local school boards rumoured to be established by the bill.[48] His Lenten pastoral, released in England on 28 February, made an oblique reference to the bill, encouraging Catholics to 'not cease to labour to multiply our schools till not one Catholic child shall lack a sound Catholic education'.[49] Back in London, Allies's patience with the bill's provisions had worn thin. He reacted with another letter to the editor:

> And to help us ... the State offers us as a contribution, a fourth towards building, and third towards maintenance, under very strict conditions. But the State adds, if all this be not completed in a year's time, I will come with a dragnet, such as I have never enabled you to use ... and I will sweep your children by the thousands out of the bye-streets, alleys, and courts of the vast cities ... I will place them in schools, for the whole building and maintenance of which I will provide by an unfailing fund out of the rates which you will pay; and wherein they shall be taught, either no religion at all, or such a religion as the managers may choose. And the religion ... to be taught in these schools is one, which ... will certainly be in deadly opposition to that faith which the parents of these poor children brought to my shores.

'Is this', Allies asked in obvious attack on Gladstone, 'the justice which the Ireland that is in England has to expect from that statesman, the glory of whose life we thought it would be to redress the wrongs of the most wretched people on earth?'[50]

After the second parliamentary reading of the bill in mid-March, the *Tablet* was incredulous on the continued silence of the Catholic MPs. The paper blamed Liberal extremism and Tory intolerance for not allowing the one Catholic member, Myles O'Reilly, who had been agreed upon by all Catholic MPs beforehand, to speak on the floor of the Commons, despite his several attempts to catch the speaker's eye. However, the paper also suggested that a better strategy should have been employed for the second reading of such important legislation.[51] When the editors of the *Dublin Review* expressed their editorial opinion on the provisions contained in the education bill in April, they noted with lukewarm approval: 'We must be thankful that the Bill is no worse than it is ... [because] the principle of the present Bill is to maintain the educational system which is already in operation'.[52] By July, even the humour of the *Dublin Review* was wearing thin, as it noted that all of the concessions made that summer by the government during the extended debate favoured secular education, not denominational.[53]

Manning preferred to rely upon his own personal political influence in observing and responding to the impending legislation. His correspondence with Gladstone while in Rome is well documented and imparts the sense that the archbishop believed his personal relationship with the prime minister would bring more Catholic interests to fruition than would public and parliamentary protests. It must be remembered that the first draft of the bill did not completely rule out rate-aid for voluntary schools, so while Manning did reluctantly acquiesce to the proposed legislation, he certainly did not know what radical turns it would take once it became fodder for compromise in Parliament.[54]

Earlier, in November 1869 and prior to his departure for Rome, Manning had discussed with the Lord de Grey, the future Marquess of Ripon and Catholic convert, the precedent set by the Reformatory Schools Act of 1866, which allowed children to attend a school of their parents' religious persuasion at the expense of the local authority.[55] Wanting to apply the same principle to the general education system, Manning had written to Gladstone and referred to the argument he had posed to de Grey four months prior: 'The Reformatory Schools Act gives a basis on which we can unite with Government. It secures our teaching and management: It gives full guarantee to the Govt. in the secular part of education.'[56] Knowing that the Liberal de Grey would be instrumental in the passage of the current bill through Parliament, Manning believed his suggestion would be seriously considered and that Catholic interests would be protected even if the bill reflected some of the ascendant demands of the radical National Education League. Manning's blind spot was that he did not appreciate the pressure facing Gladstone from his more radical constituencies pushing the bill towards a secular solution.[57] Finally, on 20 March, Manning informed Gladstone of his objections to the bill. First, the archbishop complained of the paltry twelve months granted to denominational schools to address educational deficiencies before local boards could legally establish new schools. Second, he feared that local boards would inflict upon Catholics the kind of hostility that Manning witnessed in his dealings with Poor Law Guardians, the type that periodically broke through the calm veneer of Victorian society into anti-Catholic prejudice and violence. He wrote: 'If left to the will of the Local Boards I have no hope for our Schools'.[58] By April, Manning had learned of the proposed compulsory attendance clause and wrote to the prime minister, complaining: 'No compulsory education can be just unless the faith and conscience of the people be respected'. He concluded, based on Gladstone's account of the debate, that English Catholics, like those in America, would be forced to create their own schools outside of the state system.[59] Gladstone's letters to Manning highlight the prime minister's quandary. Clearly, the events in Rome – of which Gladstone was well apprised by the liberal Catholic and anti-ultramontanist Lord Acton and which led to the eventual acceptance of the contentious doctrine of papal infallibility – lessened the effectiveness of Manning's pleas to his old friend on behalf of Catholic schools. Gladstone wrote on 26 March 1870 to Manning: 'I need not say that the R.C. position in relation to all [education] demands is much damaged by what is going on in Rome'. The negative effects of the Vatican Council in promoting doctrine considered anathema to European liberals, Gladstone argued, were not a matter of speculation: 'I know it by actual and daily touch'. Gladstone was sympathetic but told Manning his hands were tied.[60]

The bishops met in Rome in late February, perhaps unofficially, to discuss the bill and expressed their suspicion and disapproval of the idea of school boards to the Poor School Committee. They believed that the current system (which the school boards would partially supplant) showed equity and fairness to Catholics.[61] Ironically, when Gladstone capitulated to radical demands and struck from the bill the possibility of voluntary schools receiving rate-aid, Manning recognized a small silver lining; naturally, he believed that Catholic and other denominational schools would subsequently receive a larger Privy Council grant. With the cumulative vote for school board elections added to the bill in its committee stage, Manning realized that minority groups such as Catholics would have better chances of placing representatives on the actual boards.[62] This change still did not alleviate fears of the actual school boards and the schools they would build. Ultimately and reluctantly, Manning accepted the new system as the best Catholics could expect. Manning's thoughts on the bill as he returned from Rome can be gleaned from a letter to Canon Michael O'Sullivan found in the Birmingham diocesan archive. Writing from Brighton on his way back to London, Manning clarified his thinking on the bill. His initial course of action upon returning now was to complete the collection of statistical information on children in Westminster diocese, create new schools as quickly as possible to block board school construction, increase school efficiency and move all Catholic schools under the state grant system to benefit from the government aid. He hoped that Birmingham and the other large cities could follow suit. Manning said that he would approach the London School Board with a willingness to work cooperatively and added, 'I believe that with straight forwardness we shall get them to make terms with us'.[63] Some scholars maintain this acceptance lasted until the beginning of the next decade.[64] However, there is evidence that Manning's anxiety on the subject began almost immediately upon implementation of the Act. The archbishop's 1872 treatise, *National Education and Parental Rights*, laid a firm foundation for the rights of parents in the face of a secularized, state-supported education system and foreshadowed later arguments on rate sharing by arguing that 'Parliament has no course to pursue but to make grants of the public money for education, on equal conditions, to all subjects of the Crown'.[65] This discourse anticipates his more conspicuous and openly quarrelsome tracts from the 1880s when equality and the protection of Catholic schools from unfair competition became his battle cry, and yet these arguments appeared less than a year after the new changes went into effect.

While Manning pursued high-level correspondence with Gladstone, Catholics at home sought other extra-parliamentary routes. The most influential lay Catholics in England, including Lord Howard of Glossop and his nephew, the fifteenth Duke of Norfolk, assembled in Leeds in mid-May to discuss the bill, now in its third month of debate. Together, they drafted a critical petition, which they ultimately sent to Parliament, asking Commons not to pass a bill that would violate the conscience and liberties of Catholics by forcing them to attend schools in which the discipline and course of instruction were anathema to them.[66] A few days after the meeting, Lord Howard wrote to Bishop Cornthwaite in Rome with an update on the situation. He argued that without improved and unified action, Catholics might lose all that they had gained since 1847. Frustrated with the bishops being removed from the present crisis, he pleaded for their guidance; he even hinted that he might resign from the committee if the hierarchy would not approach the crisis 'without thorough and business like action'. Attached to this letter, Howard included a copy of two resolutions approved at the April meeting of the Committee: one directing clergy and laymen to form local subcommittees to collect funds for and report local educational statistics to the Poor School Committee; the other asking the bishops to sanction the first resolution and inform the committee by 1 August of their plan to 'meet the impending educational crisis'.[67]

Many of the same persons again convened the following month at the home of the Duke of Norfolk to discuss further political strategies for combating the bill, which was slowly but steadily progressing forward. Norfolk explained that he and others had been in regular contact with the bishops on the status of the bill and that discouraging developments had led them to call this emergency meeting with the purpose of writing directly to the prime minister. Those in attendance that evening decided they would not adjourn 'without signifying to the Administration [their] conviction that nothing would satisfy the Catholics of England but the permission to go on as they had done with denominational education'. They made a final decision to initiate a Catholic Education Crisis Fund for the bishops to use in fighting the consequences of the bill once it became law.[68] Norfolk requested that *The Times* print the circular approved at this 13 June meeting. Published on 5 July, it clearly described the threat to Catholic education included in the proposed legislation, revealing a contentious and confrontational attitude and lamenting the possible discontinuation of building grants for denominational schools:

> Such is the gratitude shown by the State to the religious zeal which alone has hitherto educated its people; and such the encouragement given to that secular spirit which has hitherto raised a great clamour, but built no schools.[69]

Therein lies the essence of the more assertive and combative stance that Catholics used for the next thirty years in subsequent education debates: education must remain the offspring of the churches. For his part, Lord Howard entered the July debate on the bill in the House of Lords, arguing that the voluntary system was worth saving, that rate-supported secular schools would damage the overall Christianity of England, and that the American system served as an example of the danger to come from such proposed changes.[70]

In late summer, *The Times* surprisingly praised the remarkable response on the part of English Catholics to the education bill that year. By the end of August, most of the bishops had returned from Rome to direct local diocesan steps to counter what would soon become educational law. For example, Liverpool Catholics created a local education crisis fund committee to supplement the centralized committee founded in London earlier that summer. Because existing Catholic schools accommodated only 15,646 students and there were nearly 24,000 Catholic children between the ages of five and fourteen in Liverpool, the primary goal of this local committee was to raise money to build schools, lest a board school be established there to 'fill up the gap'.[71] The next month, Liverpool Catholics held a large meeting in the Theatre Royal to discuss the education problem. Bishop Goss, whose pastoral letter the previous month had railed against the Education Act by complaining that 'despotism does not cease to be despotism simply because it is exercised by a Liberal government', presided at the meeting.[72] Goss criticized the recent Act and the government for allowing non-sectarian religious education in board schools, which he called a 'sop [thrown] to the ... Nonconformists'. He further criticized the conscience clause that restricted religious teaching in denominational schools to certain times of the day. Referring to the implicit pact between the Church and state on education, Goss argued that, by adopting the Education Act, the government 'had thrown it overboard' – a sentiment that Manning would echo some fifteen years later.[73]

In Leeds, Bishop Cornthwaite got to work on the diocesan crisis fund committee. Norfolk wrote to him in mid October urging him not to lose any time in establishing a local board that could work with the national Crisis Fund Committee, of which Norfolk was chairman. The rules for dispensing funds stated that monies would be based on local need and local efforts among all of the dioceses. However, as late as 13 October, Cornthwaite had not yet returned the necessary forms with the required statistics to merit receipt of crisis funds and Norfolk gave him until 15 November to forward the information.[74] The following week, the bishop addressed a lengthy pastoral letter to the diocese, stressing what he said was the 'religious persecution' of the new Education Act, emphasizing the need to act quickly to relieve their educational deficiencies and declaiming the next Sunday to be the date of collection. He announced that the diocese needed additional school room for 5,448 children, which would demand a serious effort by the clergy and laity, and if they wanted a healthy disbursement from the national crisis fund committee, they first required a substantial collection.[75] In Birmingham, Bishop Ullathorne created a similar crisis fund committee in response to what he called the great crisis facing English Catholics.[76]

A sense of panic can be detected in a letter from Norfolk to the bishops when he reminded them that applications for the school building grants to meet any educational deficiencies were due by 31 December; in the meantime, he asked them to hire rooms until the new schools could be built to meet the educational needs of the estimated 90,000–100,000 Catholic children not attending Catholic elementary schools.[77] The first Crisis Fund disbursements to the dioceses came in December, although as Thomas W. Allies announced, these amounts were far below what the committee wished to provide, as it amounted to less than 9*s.* per student.[78]

Conclusion

The debate over the 1870 Education Act, both before and after its passage, revealed several political shortcomings within the English Catholic community. First, it was not united; not even the hierarchy agreed on this new system of education. Led by Bishop Ullathorne, a vocal minority of bishops in Rome and some lay leaders in England resisted Manning's recommendations on the bill, especially his apparent willingness to surrender the right to have Catholic inspectors. Manning, more astute in reading the temper of the education reform movement, recognized certain political inevitabilities and sought to avoid battles he knew could not be won.[79] Although Manning received criticism in some Catholic quarters for 'selling out' to the government, he was, in fact, reading the political and educational climate and readjusting Catholic claims based on that interpretation.[80] No doubt, the initial lack of unity from the top weakened the Catholic position in this momentous debate at a time when they needed their political strength.

Second, Catholic political influence was not as persuasive as some of them believed. Manning was not successful in convincing the prime minister, whom he had known for many years, to come to the aid of Catholics. Although one analysis presents Gladstone's late changes on the bill as a reflection of Manning's moderately successful influence, this interpretation ignores the probability that Gladstone's concessions resulted from pressure brought to bear by radically minded nonconformists.[81] The fact that some of the changes actually pleased Manning does not prove that Manning or the Catholics provided the catalyst to force them. More troubling, the Catholic presence in Parliament failed to contribute a significant voice to the rigorous debates that surrounded the education bill. Irish MPs, while bringing petitions from their home constituencies – petitions which were undoubtedly a collaborative effort between the politicians and the Irish bishops – did not enter the floor debate on the bill at all. This lack of direct involvement on the part of the Irish MPs was linked to Gladstone's introduction of an important land bill for Ireland at the same time that Forster brought in his education bill. In the month of March, no less than six different Irish MPs vigorously debated the land bill on the Commons floor, while none participated in the educational debates. Even on 22 July when both issues were debated in succession, both J. P. Maguire and Edward Synan spoke on the land bill but not the education bill.[82] As in 1862, legislative matters involving Ireland trumped those regarding education in England, the Irish Catholic petitions notwithstanding. This lack of parliamentary voice, due in part to the Irish bloc's natural preoccupation with Irish affairs, later contributed to the hierarchy's decision to become more personally involved in the politics of education over the next two decades. Further, a great deal of time and energy was expended in April 1870 defending against Newdegate's latest bill to enquire into convents. Perhaps it was just bad timing that the Vatican Council was still in session when three major bills that affected and involved Catholics (two English, one Irish) came before Parliament in the spring of 1870.

The third revelation made apparent by the education bill episode was that Manning and company were unable to see that events at the Vatican Council were forcing Gladstone into a position in which he could not honour Manning's entreaties.[83] Catholics generally possessed a compartmentalized outlook, one that easily separated domestic educational affairs from universal ecclesiastical affairs, leaving Catholic leadership blind to the fact that earnest Protestants, like Gladstone, could not view the two affairs separately. The proclamation of papal infallibility, interpreted by liberals like Gladstone as a further hardening of the Church's anti-liberal stance first pronounced in 1864's *Syllabus of Errors*, negatively affected their domestic political influence with a Liberal ministry and it appears that Catholics did not fully realize that fact.

With the enactment of the Education Act in 1870, denominationalists now faced the onerous task of making their schools efficient and ridding their parishes of educational deficiencies within a six-month grace period or watching the newly empowered school boards come in and build schools where the existing problems could not be so quickly remedied. This race against the clock would prove formidable enough for the relatively wealthier Anglican Church, let alone for the poorest Christian community in Britain. As the reality of the Education Act sank in, Catholics needed to devise an effective strategy to survive in the new education system, as well as to become practised players in the public policy arena. To that end, over the next two decades, a single contentious issue, one determined archbishop and a few tough bishops came to dominate the political agenda and efforts of Catholics in England and Wales.

6 ENGLISH CATHOLICS AND THE POLITICS OF EDUCATION, 1871–90: ENGAGING WITH THE ENEMY

Only three years after the Education Act of 1870, Archbishop Manning decided to make education the most important issue of the remainder of his archepiscopate. Determined not to do it alone, Manning knew that his singular voice could not bring about an equitable solution for Catholics. The effort would require agitation from other members of the hierarchy, as well as the laity. It would require an energized Catholic Poor School Committee, as well as new organizations to provide the corporate leadership necessary to make Catholic opinions heard in the press and in Parliament. In a letter to Cardinal Paul Cullen, Archbishop of Dublin, Manning chose to employ a military analogy as the appropriate description of the battle they faced on education: 'It is the field on which I should most wish to fight a general action'.[1] Education was the issue that built the most consensus among the Catholic community. It was also an issue that gave them common ground with their Anglican neighbours, with whom they would ally in the battle over the schools. First, however, they needed to recruit their soldiers and marshal their munitions.

In the Wake of Education Act

Festering within the Catholic community in the 1870s and 1880s was a growing distrust of the school board system and disgust with the increasing financial inequality that accompanied its growth. The Catholic press reflected these beliefs frequently. A survey of articles on education provides some indication of the Catholic political drift in the post-1870 Education Act era. It also provides a platform for discussing how the Irish question soon came to complicate further the education debate. Importantly, the press soon reflected the growing confidence and militancy that was becoming part of the community's identity as they pursued an educational solution that satiated their temporal hunger and spiritual thirst.

In 1871, the *Tablet* emphatically denounced the Education Act in an article that focused on a recent pamphlet which had argued that the Act was as good as the Catholics could expect from the government and that Catholics should be content with what they had received. The editors responded by calling the Act a revolutionary measure upholding principles of revolution that are divorced from religion and society. Their editorial viewed the recent education debate as simply a part of the larger cultural war that was raging around them. They urged their readers to uphold their political duty to fight against such revolutionary principles, especially regarding education. Success could only be accomplished in 'calm and determined conflict with the social and political difficulties which encompass us'.[2] Three weeks later the *Tablet* addressed the education issue again when the latest Poor School Committee report was released. The paper's tone verged on panic: 'We have never been in greater peril than we are in to-day or needed more combined and speedier action'. This time, instead of harping on the dangers of the Act, the article suggested Catholics make every effort necessary to secure as much new grant money as possible so that no Catholic child would have to attend a board school, where their religious liberties would be harmed.[3]

The *Month* first responded to the educational reforms in January 1872. The writer sympathized with the government's desire to legislate on the subject of elementary education but believed that the process had been diverted from the question, 'shall the best primary education be secured for every child' to 'shall the cry for education be wrested by the Nonconformists ... into a weapon of offence against the denominational bodies?' The writer argued that the Act fell short of providing the optimal solution and that the nonconformists were to blame because they allied themselves with the secularists.[4] The *Dublin Review* registered its general opinions on the Act in 1872. Its tone implied hopeful dissatisfaction: 'doubtless the Act of 1870 has inflicted on Catholics severe mischief, and has dealt with them very unjustly'. But the writer argued that the Act was not anti-Catholic *per se*. A proper Catholic education could be provided under the requirements of the new law, he wrote, but the effort had been made more difficult. The article argued that the worst aspect of the Act of 1870 was the removal of government building grants for voluntary schools, but saw cooperation with other supporters of the voluntary denominational system as a way to change this policy and defend against the secularists.[5]

That tepid optimism in making the system work to their advantage had all but vanished by 1875 when the *Dublin Review* expanded on the theme of educational inequality. In an article titled 'Secularism in Elementary Education', Catholic anger finally boiled over. The writer claimed that the journal's earlier optimism had dissipated, especially after the changes brought by the Education Act of 1873, which furthered the secularist cause.[6] He argued that when voluntary school students did not meet the standards of the examinations, the schools lost grant money. But when board school students failed, thus causing a decrease of the Privy Council grant, '[the amount] is, *ipso facto*, made up by the rates, and the inconvenience to the [board school] managers is therefore almost nil'. All voluntary schools could do in this situation was to ask their supporters for even more contributions. Finally, this writer pleaded with the Catholic laity to get more involved in the political process:

> [Our] voices should be heard by all those whose duty or privilege it is to prepare Bills, and Codes ... so that our objections may receive due consideration, before statesmen are publicly committed to any course affecting the interests of our schools.[7]

Catholic sympathy with the Liberal party, galvanized by the disestablishment of the Church of Ireland in 1868, began to erode following the Education Act of 1870. Simultaneously, Prime Minister Gladstone's openness to Catholics and tolerance of their political self-importance likewise declined due, in part, to the papal infallibility decree, but also due to the internal bickering that he witnessed between the liberal Catholics, whom he favoured, and the ultramontanes, whom he distrusted.[8] Gladstone interpreted papal infallibility as an example of the Church always preceding party and policy because by adhering to the decree, he thought, Catholics undermined their civil allegiance to Great Britain. Therefore, Catholics were not to be trusted.

Although Catholics had not been satisfied with and began to attack the principles contained in the Education Act of 1870, it was criticism of the Act by nonconformists which eventually caused fissures within the Liberal party and contributed to its defeat in the general election of 1874. Nonconformists faulted the Act for supporting denominational education, especially the clauses which allowed school boards to send children to voluntary schools on the rates or compel children to attend the local school, which in rural areas tended to be Anglican. Ironically, Catholics began to align with the Anglicans who, for the most part, supported the Act for the very same reasons the nonconformists did not. This placed Catholics in the precarious position of having to support or, at least restrain, their criticism of an Act which many of them believed went against the educational principles of their faith. Thus, the initial strategy was to accept the Act as irreversible and try to improve the denominational schools within the system. As Anglicans generally supported the Education Act and the subsequent task of ameliorating its harmful effects to denominational schools, that meant Catholics and Anglicans could begin to share an educational goal; also, this meant a return of the Catholic drift towards the Tories on education, as the Conservative Party was much more supportive of denominational education.

Roused during the debate in 1870, Catholic activity increased in the next few years, revealing that the event had energized the community. The Crisis Fund, begun the previous summer in the midst of the education bill debate, emerged as the community's top priority. With only six months to fill their own education gaps before building grants ended, school boards could be created and board schools erected, Catholics embarked on an aggressive school-building agenda. The Crisis Fund Committee wrote a code of rules to guide the disbursement of the monies and distributed these to the bishops. To prevent dioceses from adding to already adequate school provision, the Committee directed that monies could only be used to build new schools or enlarge existing ones where the demand existed but not to build new schools to replace old ones. Second, the Committee would only send funds to dioceses that created their own diocesan education councils to serve as their local agents and that each council first had to report to the central committee on which schools they wished to help in advance. No grants could be used for schools on which construction had begun prior to 13 June 1870, a provision sure to anger those missions that had proactively started work on schools before the debate on the education bill had begun. Finally, as an incentive towards success, the committee would grant monies in relation to the amounts raised locally.[9] To assist the Crisis Fund's efforts, the hierarchy next released a lengthy joint pastoral letter read in all Catholic churches on 20 April 1871 asking for 'doubled vigilance ... to supply promptly' elementary schools for the Catholic poor. Reiterating the Catholic philosophy that education without religion was simply not education, but merely instruction, the bishops invited all Catholics, especially calling out the clergy, laity and parents, to give more time and money than they had given before to prevent the possibility that Catholics would soon be forced out of necessity to attend newly built board schools.[10]

It is clear the bishops were consulted on the code of rules in a meeting on 20 March 1871 with the committee, as one surviving set of rules in the Birmingham diocesan archive has the notes of Bishop Ullathorne in the margins as he worked out what this meant for his diocese.[11] Revealing a still potentially discordant Catholic community committed to education but sometimes disagreeing on the minutiae of achieving those ends, an unpleasant disagreement broke out between Bishop Cornthwaite and the Crisis Fund Committee in July over the wording of the rules. Despite the acceptance of the rules by Manning and the rest of the bishops, Cornthwaite had reservations about rule IX, which required the local report on schools before funds were sent. He viewed this as an infringement on his rights as bishop. A series of increasingly testy letters between Cornthwaite and Thomas W. Allies, member of the Crisis Fund and secretary of the Poor School Committee, reveals a community still in the throes of transformation between the complacent Catholicism of early Victorian Britain and the active Catholicism of later Victorian Britain. In this case, the authority of the bishop was, in his mind, questioned, leading to his request that the code of rules be rewritten for his diocese. This prompted an impertinent letter from Allies who emphasized the 'generosity and confidingness' of the

Crisis Fund Committee run by laymen compared to the 'severity and strictness' of the Poor School Committee maintained by the bishops. At an impasse, the committee planned to interpret Cornthwaite's insistence on the change of wording in the code of rules as a rejection of funds, to which the bishop was angrily incredulous. Cooler heads prevailed when the Crisis Fund Committee offered a compromise that was acceptable to the bishop and the matter was settled so that Catholic schools in the diocese of Beverley could finally receive crisis funds.[12] What was surfacing here was a residual bitterness felt by the lay Catholics who had to and did orchestrate much of the Catholic defence of education, including the creation of the Crisis Fund Committee, the previous summer without much help from the bishops, who were in Rome. While the bishops appreciated that effort, Cornthwaite here was trying to take back the initiative he believed was his right with regards to education.

For the diocese of Birmingham, Crisis Fund monies meant beginning the construction of fifteen new schools, four of them in Birmingham alone, and the enlargement of three existing schools all in 1871. In pounds and pence, the disbursement from the committee amounted to £2,000 towards construction costing nearly £11,000 to accommodate just under 3,000 children. Clearly, the funds were helpful, but in this case, the diocese would still have to raise £9,000 to meet the expense of such educational expansion.[13] The dispute with the committee now ended, Bishop Cornthwaite took an exceedingly active role as chair in organizing the local council activities in the Beverley diocese. His pastoral letter on 6 October 1871 emphasized the duty of giving towards this united effort 'to save the faith of our children' in what he already was calling an unequal system. Using a militaristic metaphor, he wrote, 'it is hard to have to fight a battle, and one of such grave importance, and be compelled also to contribute to the arming of our enemy'. Of the twenty-four missions in the diocese, Cornthwaite estimated 6,520 Catholic children without school provision, which using the Birmingham figures as a guide, would probably cost the diocese over £22,000 towards which they were promised £2,557 from the Crisis Fund.[14] The bishop had to be pleased a year later when he reported that fundraising efforts combined with the Crisis Fund monies had not only met the deficiency of 6,520 places but had added an additional 8,434 places in the diocese. To this confident bishop, however, the battle was just beginning because 'the men who now-a-days call themselves liberals, but who are intolerant of every opinion but their own' would be continuing their quest to exclude religion from education.[15] On its second anniversary the Crisis Fund Committee could successfully report on the 144 new or enlarged schools that its £23,180 19*s.* had assisted to meet the needs of 36,092 Catholic children not previously accommodated with school places. The five dioceses of Liverpool (£3,575), East Scotland (£2,660), Salford (Manchester, £2,353), Southwark (London south of the Thames River, £2,350), and Westminster (London north of the Thames River, £2,175) received nearly 60 per cent of the Fund's monies. This success was tempered by the necessity of having to raise slightly over £119,000 for the remaining expense of this expansion effort from private and government grants sources.[16]

Another form of agitation occurred in the newly formed local school boards. Many dioceses permitted and encouraged Catholics to run for school board seats, even if they did not agree with the premise of the school board system. An early question concerned how those Catholics should vote when the boards were considering building schools. The ruling from the hierarchy demanded that Catholics vote against any schools having religious education other than Catholic and, to prevent being seen as offering approval of secular education, Catholics were to abstain from voting on schools from which religion would be excluded.[17] During early deliberations on the London school board, Catholic members petitioned for the reading of the Douai version of the Bible in board schools where no less than forty students were Catholics. Charles Langdale and others spoke on behalf of this measure, including Catholic school board member Mr Hutchins, who spiritedly remarked that on the issue of having Catholic teachers instruct their children on the faith, 'they would nail their colours to the mast' and not back down.[18] A similar motion on Bible choice was made by a Catholic member of the Liverpool school board, where it was also defeated. The Catholics present told the rest of the board that they saw no prospect of reaching common ground on this issue.[19] So important was ensuring Catholics were elected, Bishop Bernard O'Reilly called for Liverpool Catholics to make sure they went to the polls to vote for the Catholic candidates even if it meant a loss of a half-day's wages. Three years later, O'Reilly extolled the successful effort of working-class Catholics in electing Catholic candidates to the Liverpool school board in 1873 and asked them to do it again with a new slate of candidates due to a death and retirements.[20]

Catholic activity also took place inside Parliament. During a debate on education in March 1872, Lord Robert Montagu, a convert to Catholicism in 1870, attacked the 1870 Act for its support of secular education and raised the spectre of radical politics. He argued that 'while the different religious bodies were spending money to build schools and to spread education, those who called themselves secularists had not built a single school'. Montagu pleaded that 'only by providing ... a religious education' could they prevent the working classes from 'joining in a struggle between capital and labour, and electing a *proletaire* and Socialist House of Commons, which would work its own ruin'.[21]

As the Gladstone ministry prepared the 1873 Education Bill, there occurred a similar experience to what happened in 1862 and 1870. Since the details of the bill were not made public until summer, denominationalists could only offer general petitions in favour of religious education soon after the Queen's speech announced that changes to the education code would be forthcoming. Catholic petitions expressing support for denominational education first arrived on 1 March and continued throughout the month, much as we saw in 1862 and 1870, although there were not nearly as many as had opposed Forster's bill three years earlier.[22] The decrease in petitions can be attributed to Forster's decision not to make public the details of his new bill until early summer; therefore potential opponents had nothing specific upon which to focus their attack. Second, more Irish legislation, Gladstone's university bill, occupied much of the time and efforts of both Irish and English Catholic MPs and Catholic dignitaries, like Manning, during the spring of 1873. This was the issue that eventually caused Gladstone's ministry to fall.[23] Gladstone announced in early March that the amendments on the education code would have to wait until the Irish university bill was settled.[24] Despite the prime minister's efforts, the bill failed, due, in part, to opposition from Catholic MPs, thus effectively bringing an end to Gladstone's second ministry.[25] In response to the row over the university bill and the talk of impending changes in the elementary education code, Manning addressed education in a speech at the Liverpool Catholic Club on 21 March. The archbishop showed just how politically motivated Catholics had become when he told the crowd that he (and the Catholic community) had been content to exist outside of politics until the state violated its educational agreement with Catholics in 1870. As such, he told them education was now the question of the day and he hoped that the issue would dominate the next election. He called upon 'every Catholic, be he layman, priest, or bishop ... to exercise his power at the next general Election in the matter of Christian education'.[26] When the relatively minor alterations to the education code were finally announced in late summer, Catholic politicians were engaged in another issue that diverted their full attention away from education: supporting the new Prison Ministers bill then before the Commons.[27] The bishops emerged from their provincial council in August one week after the education bill became law and only announced a general invitation for Catholics to continue their progress on the elementary schools. Their joint pastoral letter did not mention the education bill specifically because the changes in the code were comparatively minor.[28]

By 1874, Catholic support of Liberals had withered further. In Manchester, Salford and Wigan, Catholics began to rally behind Conservatives because of the education question or because they wanted to show Liberals that ignoring the new Irish Home Rule faction would be at their peril.[29] Herbert Vaughan, Bishop of Salford, urged his parishioners to use the education issue to guide their votes. In no uncertain terms, he told Catholics of the Manchester metropolitan area: 'no Catholic can vote for any candidate who proposes to saddle the country with a secular and godless system of education'.[30] This shot was aimed directly at the Liberal party, which was rife with discord because of internal disagreements over education – its radical members wanted a complete secular system of education – Home Rule, disestablishment of the Anglican Church and temperance.[31]

A local example of Catholic involvement with the fissures within the Liberal party bears examination in Liverpool. In a city where support for the newly articulated concept of Irish Home Rule was strong, the political intrigues of Irish Catholics in the election of 1874 led to further Liberal discord. Having proven their electoral might in a local election in 1873, the Home Rule faction wanted to make a bolder statement during the general election. At a meeting of the Catholic Club, the Irish party suggested running a Catholic candidate against the two familiar Liberal candidates, William Rathbone and W. S. Caine. Radicals in the Liberal party were pressuring Rathbone and Caine to support the repeal of clause 25 of the 1870 Education Act, a clause acceptable to both Anglicans and Catholics.[32] After the Catholic Club settled on a Liberal Home Rule candidate, James Samuelson, they soon discovered that Samuelson had already accepted an invitation to sit for nearby Birkenhead; then they decided not to put forward another Liberal Home Rule candidate. Meanwhile, Caine angered Irish Catholic voters when he publicly criticized the popular Father James Nugent, widely known for his tireless efforts on behalf of the Catholic poor of Liverpool. The Home Rule Association next asked their supporters not to vote in the election, an appeal that caused 37 per cent of the Scotland Ward district, which was heavily Irish Catholic, to stay home on Election Day. As a result, Caine was not elected; Rathbone and two Conservatives were. The final act to this drama was that the Catholic Club split between those who voted, and later joined the local Liberal party, and those who followed the Home Rule Association's directions, and broke off their alliance with the Liberals. The departure of the moderates to the Liberals left the leadership of the Home Rule Association open to more radical Irish Nationalists, which further distanced them from the Liberals in Liverpool.[33]

Disraeli's Conservative party captured the election; whether they based their choice on the education or Irish question, a high percentage of Catholics voted for the Tories. Wary of the Catholic vote, radical Liberal MP John Bright had noted the danger to Gladstone while the election was still in progress. Catholics, he wrote, 'vote as the Priests tell them, and the priests are for public money for Catholic schools, and they have no politics apart from the Church'.[34] The political inclination of Bishop Vaughan can be inferred from a letter written while in Burnley to Lady Herbert of Lea, a friend with notable political connections:

> Gladstone is thrown out by the Radicals. I hope you will try and persuade him of that. The Radical creed was precisely three condemned propositions in the Syllabus on popular Education. How could Catholics vote for that? ... Better suffer a little tyranny from the Tories than vote for the radical programme in Education. The Catholics would have supported Gladstone but they could not support his Radicals.[35]

Gladstone, much like Disraeli in 1868, was brought down in part by the Catholic defection after he had introduced a bill trying to please them.[36] It is no wonder that the pens of both men drew Catholic blood in the form of Disraeli's novel *Lothair* in 1870 and Gladstone's *The Vatican Decrees in their Bearing on Civil Allegiance: A Political Expostulation* in 1874. Yet, despite their bad experiences with the Catholics, both men would be receptive to Catholic advances in the future on both education and Ireland.

During Disraeli's second ministry, Manning again played the role of advisor on Catholic and Irish affairs, as he had done for Gladstone. He and the prime minister cultivated an amicable relationship as the archbishop provided periodic counsel, and Manning later wrote that when he and Disraeli resumed their relations, the prime minister did not recall the political duplicity that he had attributed to Manning regarding the Irish university bill in 1868. The prime minister also told him that he had heard, understood and accepted the archbishop's reasons for ceasing their correspondence on that subject.[37] This rapprochement, combined with Gladstone's vicious attack on the loyalty of Catholics in his *Vatican Decrees* pamphlet, furthered the drift of Catholics away from the Liberal party. Even the Old Catholic families were cutting their ties with the Whig/Liberal tradition. The Duke of Norfolk's first vote in the House of Lords in 1879 was in support of a Tory measure, and Lord Talbot, the Duke's brother-in-law, stood as a Conservative in 1880.[38] Finally, Catholics were inclined to support the Tories' pro-Turkish stance on the Eastern Question, despite the atrocities committed by Turkish soldiers in Bulgaria in 1876. Prime Minister Disraeli believed that keeping the Ottoman Empire, the 'sick man of Europe', alive was in the best interests of keeping a balance of power in Europe. For Tories, this belief trumped the Turkish horrors perpetrated against the Christian Bulgarians, a striking example of Disraeli's *Realpolitik* that stood in marked contrast to Gladstone's widely celebrated condemnation of the Turks and Disraeli's foreign policy. When the Liberals appealed for Christian autonomy from the Turks, the Conservatives countered that this would simply replace the domination of the sultan with that of the czar. Clearly, Disraeli feared the Russian bear more than the Turk. This was the position taken by Manning and the Catholics, as well.[39] A final indication of the Catholic drift to Conservatism was that those Catholics who had reached the middle and upper-middle classes were more inclined to prefer the policies of the Tories, while, simultaneously, the Liberals were losing poorer Irish Catholic voters to the Home Rule party.[40]

In 1876, Lord Sandon introduced a bill with further amendments to the education code. He intended to improve attendance by establishing attendance committees in areas where there were no school boards. The language of the bill placed the onus on parents to ensure their children's attendance under threat of penalty.[41] While compulsory attendance was not yet a reality, the system was moving towards that end. Catholics held an important meeting on 21 June at St James Hall, London, to discuss the topic of education and the impending debate on Sandon's bill. Because the concept of compulsory education had been received favourably in the Commons on the previous night, the Marquess of Ripon, now a practising Catholic convert, warned that this issue would most likely dominate the educational debate and the new bill. If compulsion was on its way, he moved that the liberty of parents to select the school of their choice 'be preserved inviolate' in the upcoming battle.[42] This demand developed into a popular Catholic battle cry in the subsequent parliamentary debates.

Furthering Catholic preparation for the impending legislation, the Poor School Committee met on 12 July just as debate on the bill was beginning in Parliament. In attendance were the leaders of the Catholic laity, Norfolk, Howard and Ripon, and members of the hierarchy, including Manning and Vaughan. Since the details of the bill were still unavailable, the Committee simply passed resolutions to continue their support for denominational education and to keep their schools as efficient as possible to hold off the board school threat.[43] As in 1870, the Poor School Committee was preparing proactively for whatever changes might result from the bill. In contrast to the debates of 1870 and 1873, however, numerous Catholic MPs participated in this parliamentary debate.[44] When a member of Commons proposed an amendment to dissolve school boards that were inactive because sufficient voluntary action had been taken, a fierce debate raged for several days, during which both Lord Montagu and Irish MP the O'Conor Don argued in support of the motion. The O'Conor Don pointed out that one of the Protestant members opposed to this amendment represented Manchester and had been returned with a large Catholic vote. He drily asked all members in similar positions 'whether, after the course they had taken on this occasion, [could] they expect to obtain such a majority again?'[45] With poor Catholics in mind, Lord Montagu proposed his own amendment asking the Poor Law Guardians to pay school pence for those children for whom the school board had failed to implement clause 25 of the 1870 Act. When Montagu's amendment was attacked, another Catholic MP, Mr O'Shaughnessy, came to his defence and asked all members present to keep in mind that the board school system was not originally intended to 'supplant but only supplement denominational schools'.[46] This statement emerged as a popular Catholic *mantra* over the next two decades. In the end, the amendment was not attached to the bill. Manning wrote to Ripon in June while the bill was being debated to say he thought Montagu's amendment was poorly timed because it might give the wrongful impression that Catholics were against the bill in general and this could be used by the secularists as a way to attack the entire bill with the apparent support of Catholics, which was not the case. Cardinal Manning argued that their focus should remain on two points: preserving the governmental grant system to denominational schools and freedom of choice for parents on choosing schools for their children. 'The present system may not be all that we may wish', he wrote, 'but it gives us the two objects ... upon which we may fight for their preservation'.[47]

Upon the bill's passage, Catholics met to discuss the changes to the education system and to propose resolutions in light of those changes. Believing that much of the bill was a victory for secular education, Manning advised a large crowd in the Mechanic's Hall at Nottingham that it was their duty to prevent the continued spread of the board school system by building as many of their own schools as possible in areas of need.[48] Great cheers followed Manning's humorous announcement that they should change the secularists' educational slogan from 'education universal, compulsory, and secular' to 'education universal, voluntary, and Christian'. Reflecting the coalescent effect of education on Catholic leadership, the Duke of Norfolk and the Marquis of Ripon, members of opposite parties, joined Manning on stage and proposed their own resolutions to the same effect, calling on Catholics to make the necessary sacrifices for education and declaring that education without their faith could not be 'conscientiously' accepted.[49]

The significant Catholic political response in 1876 reveals the growing urgency to protect education in the board school era. Unlike 1862, 1870 and 1873, there was no significant Irish legislation occupying the efforts of the Irish Catholic MPs. Interestingly, Catholics distributed fewer petitions in response to this bill than they had on past bills; in fact, the total number of petitions received from all denominations and constituencies was considerably lower than in 1870 and 1873. Those Catholic petitions that arrived expressed support for the education bill with certain amendments only. None supported the bill as it stood.[50] Perhaps knowing that the Irish Catholics MPs would have more time to devote to this cause, the hierarchy decided that there was less need to expend the effort to circulate a petition to the local parishes. Nonetheless, the Catholic effort was noteworthy, especially for a bill whose purpose was only to amend further the 1870 Act. Reflecting the increasing sense of Catholic urgency spreading through the dioceses, Bishop Bagshawe noted from Nottingham a few months before and after the Cardinal's visit that Catholics saw secular education as a genuine threat to the nation, something the community would have to resist with all of its strength, even when enticed by the glamour and fine amenities of the rapidly expanding board schools. In revelatory and militaristic language, Bagshawe described the education battle as one of many waging on earth: 'everywhere the army of Christ is in conflict with the powers of darkness, and to-day we call on you to arise and fight for ... that army'.[51]

As for electoral politics, the 1880 general election was the first in which both parties solicited the Catholic vote and where the now colder embers of anti-Catholicism were not rekindled for the event.[52] However, just prior to the election, Disraeli angered the Home Rule party by stating that Home Rule was 'a danger, in its ultimate results, scarcely less disastrous than pestilence and famine'. In response the Home Rule party accused the Conservative leader of trying to stir up ethnic tensions for the election. They urged the faithful to 'vote against Benjamin Disraeli as you should against the mortal enemy of your country and your race'.[53] Lord Ripon, the most well-known and politically experienced Catholic since his conversion in 1874, had remained an ardent Liberal despite his exchange of Canterbury for Rome. He wrote a letter in March 1880 to the *Tablet* explaining the merits of supporting the Liberal party and, referring to Disraeli's Irish comments, tried to drive a wedge between the Catholics and the Conservatives over Home Rule. Since the Home Rule movement was first launched in May 1870 by Irish MP and Protestant lawyer Isaac Butt, it had emerged as the second important political issue behind land reform with much of the Irish constituency. After the fiasco over Gladstone's university bill in 1873 and with the secret ballot in place, the Home Rule party had grown quickly. It subsequently captured fifty-nine seats in 1874, over half the number of Irish representatives. For much of the remainder of the 1870s, Home Rulers played the obstructionist card in the Commons to clog up the legislative process since neither political party had shown much interest in acquiescing to the Home Rule demand of a subordinate but separate parliament for Ireland.

Many Catholic Tories responded to Ripon's political appeal in kind, including the Undersecretary for War, Lord Bury, who questioned Ripon's claim that the Catholics owed a debt to the party of Emancipation because, he noted, that was also the party of Gladstone, who had been rather antipathetic towards Catholics the previous six years. As a final rebuff to Ripon, Bury stated that Catholics and Tories had more in common because 'they [both] dread the complete secularization of education'.[54]

Ripon tried to calm Catholic fears that the Tories were raising about education by replying that a Liberal ministry would not touch the Education Act of 1870, and he used his position as chairman of the Catholic Poor School Committee as political collateral. He also suggested, rather unbelievably and perhaps untruthfully, that Catholics needed 'to keep everything connected with our schools out of the battlefield of politics'.[55] This was naivety, disingenuousness or wishful thinking on his part because, since the Education Act of 1870, the hierarchy had believed and acted as if it was impossible to separate education from politics. The bishops might say publicly that they supported neither party but a closer examination of their statements usually indicated something else, such as Manning's call to political action in March 1873 and Vaughan's election-year statements to his diocese in 1874. What emerged was a situation in which Liberals were trying to reassure Catholics that education was safe with them, despite their radical, secular wing, while Conservatives were hoping to further the Catholic drift in their direction despite their historical suspicion of Catholicism and their anti-Irish stance. Meanwhile, the Home Rule party was proving formidable not only in Ireland but in Irish communities in England and Scotland where neither party was earning Irish Catholic support.

The result of the 1880 election was a Liberal victory, although the party's success with Catholics was not robust. Fifty-five Catholics were elected to Parliament, but all were from Ireland and all but four were Home Rulers. The political strength of Catholics throughout Britain now resided solely in the Home Rule party, whereas the other parties could only court Catholics at the risk of offending their base constituencies.[56] At this point, the Irish in Britain were becoming more committed to Home Rule than to educational interests, despite strenuous efforts by the hierarchy to keep education a priority.[57] Notwithstanding 1876, this point surfaced in 1870 and 1873 when the Irish Catholic MPs spent more time and effort on Irish affairs than on the education issue at hand. This occurred despite Manning's tireless efforts on promoting education and the annual Catholic Poor School Committee collections that also targeted the poor Irish in Manchester, Liverpool and London. However, the portent of this election was the increasing strength of the Irish party and, if the Roman Catholic hierarchy wished to secure the education settlement they desired, they would have to gain the committed support of the Home Rulers or pursue extra-parliamentary strategies in an even greater degree than before. Eventually, Manning rose to this challenge in the 1880s, most notably with his work on the Cross Commission, and Vaughan succeeded Manning in this effort as archbishop in the 1890s.

How Catholics responded to the passage of the Education Act of 1870 adds more colour to the story of their education battle. Once the Act passed, the clock began ticking as denominational schools had to acknowledge and address school deficiencies quickly before board schools could be established nearby. When the Act went into effect in 1871, there were 383 Catholic schools with 797 departments, 654 certified teachers, and 73,111 children in average attendance. These schools received £1 0*s.* 11*d.* in average income per student in attendance, and cumulative totals for the year of £25,881 and £19,709 in voluntary contributions and school pence respectively. By the end of 1872, Catholics operated 464 schools with 914 departments, 805 certified teachers, and 80,155 children in average attendance. Average income per student in attendance rose nearly three shillings to £1 3*s.* 3¾*d.*, and totals for voluntary contributions and school pence were £31,197 and £23,695. The 21 per cent increase in schools, 14.6 per cent increase in departments, 9.6 per cent increase in average attendance, 23 per cent increase in teachers, 20.5 per cent increase in voluntary contributions and 20.2 per cent increase in school pence compare favourably to the same figures as reported for Anglican schools during the same period: 9 per cent increase in schools, 2.7 per cent increase in departments, 9.4 per cent increase in certified teachers, 6.6 per cent increase in average attendance, 10 per cent increase in voluntary contributions and 8.8 per cent increase in school pence. Average income per student for Anglican schools rose just under 2 shillings from £1 5*s.* 7½*d.* to £1 7*s.* 5¾*d.*

More impressively, after ten years of effort against the proliferation of board schools, there were 789 Catholic schools, 1,319 departments, 1,697 certified teachers, with an average attendance of 152,641, up 106, 66, 159 and 108 per cent respectively. For comparison, Anglican increases in those four categories were 72, 34, 79 and 67 per cent. While the compulsory attendance law in 1880 boosted attendance somewhat, one has to marvel at how the poorest Christian community in Great Britain opened 406 schools and 522 departments in ten years.[58] The diocese of Liverpool, which reported in 1870 a deficiency of school places for children at 24,059, built or enlarged 66 schools by March 1877, thus increasing accommodation for 21,216 students.[59] The diocese of Salford's deficiency of school accommodation was not as dire as Liverpool's, but Bishops Turner and Vaughan directed an intense school expansion programme to meet their accommodation needs. After assessing an estimated deficiency of 6,077 school places for children in 1870, the Diocese built or enlarged 29 schools by the end of 1877 and 49 by 1881.[60]

The 1880s: The Education Question Intensifies

Catholic prelates played a weightier role in the politics of education during the 1880s. Cardinal Manning on a national level and Bishops Bagshawe, Cornthwaite, O'Reilly, Vaughan and others on a local diocesan level continued the trend of prioritizing the education of the poor, but did so in a much more conspicuous way than simply issuing pastoral letters on the subject and calling for increased contributions to the Poor School Committee. The action taken by these leading Catholics, along with other like-minded denominational school supporters, helped lay the groundwork for the next monumental education Act in 1902. As early as 1872, Manning had recognized and began warning about the imminent danger that voluntary schools faced in competition with the board schools, which had been in operation for just over a year. By the end of the decade, board schools had shown signs that they could outpace voluntary schools with their unlimited draw upon local funds. Manning's pastoral letter read in the churches of the Westminster diocese on 30 July 1878 stated the unintended consequences of the 1870 Act:

> unless the efficiency of our voluntary Christian schools can be maintained, the school board system, which is brought in as a supplement, will become the National system of England; and the Christian ... schools will cease to be the system, and become the supplement.[61]

Despite the Act's increased grant to voluntary schools, they could simply not keep up with the better-funded board schools. By 1880, board schools were spending £2 1*s*. 11¾*d*. per student while the Anglicans and Catholics spent £1 14*s*. 10¼*d*. and £1 10*s*. 6*d*. respectively.[62]

The Education Act of 1880 moderately altered the education system by making attendance compulsory in all elementary schools; all school boards and school attendance committees were required to have by-laws in place requiring compulsory attendance from the age of five to ten. This Act finalized what Lord Sandon's Education Act of 1876 had begun. Compulsion was now the law. A month after the passage of the new Act, Manning addressed a large crowd in Nottingham on the subject of denominational schools. In reference to the recent legislation, he concluded it had made ensuring a Catholic education even more difficult, and he reiterated that education must be accomplished by the voluntary efforts of parents and Church, with supplemental assistance from the state. He told his audience that, since all members of society paid taxes, all should reap equal benefits. Such was not the case since 1870, he said. The government was subsidizing one religious sect over another, albeit a secular sect, and this he angrily claimed was 'State tyranny'.[63] By June 1881, prior to the introduction of a new educational code by Secretary of Education A. J. Mundella, Manning was arguing that the recent Education Acts had irreparably damaged the religious ethos of England. He called for a governmental inquiry into the education system, because it was growing unjust and unequal due to the recent Education Acts.[64] This represented the first of several calls for such a governmental inquiry.

Mundella announced his new code in August 1881 with little fanfare. The major changes included the following: the examination grants would be paid based on the percentage of children who passed; a new merit grant would be paid to teachers who excelled above their peers; teaching college graduates could earn certification after only one year of probation; and all children on the school registers for twenty-two weeks required examination.[65] The effects of this new code were not lost on the Catholic community. Bishop Vaughan felt compelled to call all of the diocesan school managers for a special meeting to discuss the code. What specifically worried Vaughan with regard to poor Catholics was the percentage grant process and the twenty-two-week stipulation for examinations because Catholic children's attendance, like that of most poor, remained at the mercy of economic fluctuations, which led to unpredictable attendance patterns. He also suggested that the new merit grant for teaching would work to the disadvantage of smaller schools in poorer districts which could not keep up with the well-financed and larger urban schools. Lastly, Vaughan feared that overall working expenses of their primary schools would be increased.[66] And they were. Total expenditures rose £31,179 between 1879 and 1882, but, due to the increased attendance from the 1880 Act, expenditures per student in attendance dropped slightly from £1 10*s.* 10¾*d.* in 1879 to £1 10*s.* 6½*d.* in 1882.[67]

Given the poverty of the Catholic community, the increasing requirements found within the successive education codes and the often apathetic Irish MPs, Manning knew it was time to act outside and beyond the Catholic population. As a prelude to any overt politicking but with latent political intent, Manning wrote a series of articles for the journal *Nineteenth Century* that appeared in late 1882 and early 1883. Bringing his argument to the national press was a more efficient way to spread his ideas on the subject than trying to influence the Gladstone ministry through personal contact, as the two long-time acquaintances never totally repaired the rupture in their relationship from the mid-1870s. This media exposure extended beyond those London Catholics who usually heard his diocesan pastorals and reached a much broader, national, interdenominational audience. In these articles, Manning reiterated his demand that the country re-examine the Education Act of 1870.[68] After their publication, Manning contacted the prominent Tory Sir Richard Cross about the urgency of examining the education system to 'avert the national disaster of the gradual extinction of our Christian education', and suggested how the battle-lines should be drawn up:

> The Church of England, the Catholic Church, and the Dissenters, who still care for religious Education, if they act together might rouse the country. And next I should wish to see a Royal Commission appointed to review the whole course of legislation since 1838.[69]

After a second letter from Manning, Cross contacted Tory leader Lord Salisbury, who was initially receptive to Manning's suggestion because he had hopes of securing the Irish vote in the upcoming election.[70]

With Manning contacting the leader of the opposition about a national re-examination of the Education Act of 1870 and beginning his agitation through the national press, Bishop Vaughan expressed his own thoughts on the new code to the local Manchester-Salford Catholic community, thus marking the beginning of an educational crusade that occupied his efforts for the next twenty years as bishop and archbishop. On the first Sunday of Lent in 1882, Vaughan told those assembled at the cathedral that the national system of education, as established by the Education Act of 1870, was threatening Christianity. 'The logical result of such a system', he argued in what was later published as *A Letter on the Educational Peril to Christianity*, 'must be to foster and spread the spirit of religious indifference, to favour the growth of rationalism and unbelief'. Revealing the increasingly militant Catholic spirit, the bishop, not unlike his archbishop, concluded with a military metaphor: 'we must resolve to fight to the last for our parental rights, and for the Christian and Catholic education of our youth. No sacrifice can be too great to win this victory. We fight for the cause of God.'[71]

The hierarchy met again at Archbishop's House on 18 April 1882 to discuss the status of their schools and how best to work within the confines established by the education code changes.[72] The result of this meeting was overtly political and would be visible within a month. Beginning in May 1882, the Catholic community began sending education petitions, drawn up at the meeting in April, to both houses of Parliament. Prepared within each parish with as many signatures as possible before being sent to their MP, the petitions listed their two grievances as the inequality of the dual system to those who supported denominational education and the extravagance of the board schools to which the poor had to contribute. Due to their contributions to their own schools, Catholics asked to be relieved of the local education rate. They also demanded that provisions be made to keep the board schools from using their unlimited funds to create middle-class schools for children whose parents could afford their education but used the board schools as a cheaper alternative.[73] This petition campaign was unlike any other by Roman Catholics in this period. Bishops like Bagshawe in Nottingham wrote to their clergy with clear instructions to urge their parishes to join this 'unanimous protest against the injustice of the present system of public education'.[74] Beginning in mid-May and lasting for three months, over 250 petitions to both houses of Parliament arrived from Catholic parishes around the country.[75] This effort made the petition drive of 1870 pale in comparison, and this time the Catholic members in the Lords were as busy presenting the petitions as those in the Commons. This effort continued the legacy of petitioning that we witnessed in the 1860s and 1870s, but on a much grander scale. Even some Anglican petitions began to trickle in on the same subject.[76] Concurrently, the Catholic bishops sent the Gladstone ministry a list of resolutions agreed upon at their Low Week meeting in April, the point of which was to remind the government that the rights of parents and Church to educate were sacred and to remind Catholics not to attend board schools.[77] While the petition campaign was a success in terms of organization and inspiration, there was no governmental response to either the petitions or the resolutions, as Gladstone's ministry spent much of the summer concerned with Irish affairs after Chief Secretary for Ireland Lord Frederick Cavendish and Thomas Burke, his under-secretary, were murdered in Dublin in early May. The subsequent debate on the Prevention of Crime Bill for Ireland monopolized the Commons floor into July, drawing considerable input from Irish Catholic MPs O'Connor, Nolan, Henry, Synan, O'Donnell and Dillon. The political response that Catholics had wanted – ultimately a royal commission on elementary education – did not materialize, but further talk of a commission surfaced a couple years later as Lord Salisbury was preparing for the general election of 1885. Due to the enormity of the petition drive three years earlier, Salisbury and his party were no doubt clear on the importance of education to the Catholic electorate, an electorate which had expanded in 1884.[78]

Despite the organization shown by the 1882 petition drive, Vaughan concluded that the Catholic effort was lacking in centralization and consensus. This had become evident with the problems they had experienced in the 1870s and the uneven Catholic political responses since. While Manning laboured on a national level and the Poor School Committee raised money and distributed grants, Vaughan still sensed something was missing. After the Duke of Norfolk stated at a Catholic Union meeting in April 1884 that 'we are all dissatisfied with the condition of [educational] affairs; but in no body of Catholics ... would you find a unanimous opinion as to a certain course of action which it would be right to take', the Bishop of Salford came up with an idea to help remedy this state of uncertainty.[79] He began the Voluntary Schools Association (VSA) in 1884 to serve the Salford diocese with the intention of expanding it to every diocese in the country. Its initial purpose was to generate enough agitation so as to ask for a 25 per cent increase in the government grant. Further, the VSA wished the government to fix four problems. First, Vaughan wanted to abolish the system that limited the grant to 17*s.* 6*d.* per unit of average attendance. This system punished poverty because, even if the school warranted more money, unless it showed an independent income of 17*s.* 6*d.* per student, it could not receive more. The second grievance concerned the requirement that parents apply in person to the Board of Guardians to have school pence paid due to poverty. Not only did this mean time away from work, but the poor considered it a demeaning and humiliating experience. It did not seem fair to Catholics and other voluntary school supporters that parents whose children attended board schools and who needed remission of their fees did not have to appear before guardians but could apply through their child's teacher. The third grievance addressed what the Education Department called 'unnecessary schools'; these were voluntary schools built in locations where board schools were deemed to have provided enough accommodation for all of the children. Thus, even if Catholics built a school out of their own funds, they might not receive grants because the government could rule that their school was unnecessary since the local board school had plenty of room. Vaughan believed this violated their religious liberty. Finally, the organization believed denominational schools should be relieved of paying rates to support the board schools.[80]

By early February, Vaughan had secured the approval of Cardinal Manning and Bishops Cornthwaite and Bagshawe. He next wrote to Bishop Ullathorne explaining how the VSA would operate and stressing the unity needed among Catholics to make the association a success in Birmingham and the rest of the country. On the invitation of the ill Ullathorne, Vaughan travelled to the Midlands the following week to present the VSA plan at the Birmingham Catholic reunion meeting. Ullathorne asked Vaughan to highlight the board school system's attack on the core principles of the British Constitution – liberty of conscience and equal rights for all before the law – in his address. Ullathorne's exasperation with the present system boiled over in his letter as he railed against board schools 'who can purchase any amount of land they think fit for their purposes, build any amount of school accommodation in a costly style, and devote any amount of the people's money to support' their education, while the Church schools received 'no help whatsoever from the education rates to which they equally contribute'. He wished Vaughan luck in using the VSA to bring these matters of injustice to the attention of Parliament.[81] Some local VSAs quickly set upon the challenge of producing a document for political lobbying purposes, as shown by the list of resolutions approved by the London association which Manning sent to the other bishops as an example for their own dioceses. Not surprisingly it asked for more than any ministry at the time would consider, including: an increased grant to Catholic schools, payment by school boards for Catholic children in Catholic schools, guaranteed grants for Catholic schools with a year-long average attendance of thirty scholars, grants not to be affected by low local subscriptions and a separately levied school rate that would support both board and denominational schools.[82]

After receiving Cardinal Manning's approval, the organization assisted his continuing campaign to have the education system re-examined by royal commission. Vaughan circularized his priests in July 1884 with a list of the resolutions passed at the first annual meeting of the VSA and asked them to conduct their own meetings to instruct Catholics on how actively to support the Church in educational matters. With an acute eye towards the political landscape, the bishop also asked his priests to ensure that as many Catholics as possible register to vote in the next general election. Then he added with didactic political guidance: 'I refer to this with a view to strengthening our Educational demands, which must be enforced as far as possible at the next general Elections'.[83] Vaughan's creation of the VSA and the implementation of its agenda marked a new step in political activity. Whereas political activity had been limited to speeches at Catholic rallies, articles in the Catholic and national press and parliamentary petitions, the VSA was an organization with national objectives attainable through political agitation and influence. Catholics now employed both personal lobbying, in the person of Manning, and organizational lobbying. Additionally, the VSA was to be built from the parishes up. Consider these instructions found in the Lancashire diocesan archive from 1884:

> That in each diocese ... an organization be formed for the purpose of spreading information among the people on the Education question, by distributing fly-leaves and tracts, and by holding public meetings, petitioning Parliament, and in other ways

> helping to form public opinion as to the fairness and justice of our Educational claims.[84]

While the VSAs enjoyed widespread Catholic support, not all Catholic leaders were of the same mind on this effort. Bishop Cornthwaite asked prominent Catholic Lord Ripon to be president of the Leeds VSA and Ripon refused, replying that while Catholics certainly had legitimate complaints about the current educational system he feared that political agitation would endanger what healthy benefits they now enjoyed, which included some £120,000 to £150,000 annually for their elementary schools and training colleges. Even if the VSA agenda was somehow miraculously implemented, he argued it would only cause a stronger reaction from their enemies which would result in not only the loss of the new provisions but the elimination of those benefits the Education Act of 1870 had secured for them. As a result, the bishop took the reins as president.[85] This late example of Catholic division on an educational subject reveals some of the paranoia and lack of confidence still haunting Catholic leaders, although Ripon's importance in the Liberal party, personal investment in the Education Bill of 1870 and his recent return from India where he served as Gladstone's viceroy placed him somewhat out of step with the Catholic majority.

In the VSAs, Catholics were constructing a grass-roots political action association on a national scale; this indicates that it was not just going to be Manning and Vaughan in the trenches but lower members of the clergy and the laity. Thus, the war would be waged in local parishes, as well as London.

The Election of 1885

The general election of 1885 brought the education issue and the Irish question into full view and Catholic leaders tried to swing both Catholic and popular opinion behind the Tories, whom they believed offered the best hope of helping those denominational schools losing ground in the dual system. As such, this election marked the culmination of the Catholic drift towards Toryism. Early on, Catholics made clear that 1885 would be a year in which they would be vocal and active in the pursuit of a just education system. Firing the first salvo was Father John Kershaw, who attacked the elementary education system in a January 1885 *Dublin Review* article. In an aggressive diatribe, Kershaw repeated the Catholic claim that the existing system was unjust towards denominational schools. He alleged that the notion of the 1870 Act helping the poorest students was a fallacy, since 'the poorer children have in many cases been left to be dealt with by the charity of the religious bodies, whilst the School Boards have adopted an ambitious programme, enabling them to compete with the higher and privately conducted schools'. He concluded by admitting the mistakes Catholics had made in not waging a fiercer battle to ensure the fairness of the dual system in debates on the Education Acts of 1870, 1873 and 1876, and he then asked for an energetic and ambitious effort on the part of all Catholics to fight for their schools.[86] The more militant tone of this article may be attributed to Herbert Vaughan's increased involvement as editor of the journal in 1884.[87]

In February, Vaughan penned a pastoral letter, later published as *Pastoral Letter on the Parental Right and Church Guidance in Education*, which was read during Lent at all the diocesan churches and outlined the bishop's emerging philosophy on education, beginning with his firm stance on the rights of parents. Vaughan told his fellow Catholics that it was not too late to restrain the progress of secular education. 'We recommend', he concluded, 'you to exercise all your political and civil rights in this cause, and to support the action of the Voluntary School Association'.[88] Late February found Vaughan polling his school managers, no doubt with the intention of gathering the most damning information he could on the inequality of the dual system directly from those most affected by it.[89] This information could then be used to further the cause of the VSA in its pursuit of educational reform. Vaughan later took another step forward in the Catholic political evolution of the 1880s by explicitly asking his clergy to join in the political battle over education:

> The Public Elementary Schools question is one of deep religious interest. It is a question of life and death to the souls of millions. You will therefore be strictly within the sphere of your pastoral duties if, both in church and out of church, you do everything in your power to rouse your people to a sense of the vital importance of this question, and to induce them to use their civil and political rights wisely and firmly in its behalf.[90]

Remarkably, the Bishop of Salford was actively urging his clergy to use the pulpit to influence Catholic voters. Not only does this say something about the increasing politicization of the Catholic community but also of the bishops' confidence that this could actually make a difference in the political arena, especially with the Irish question taking centre stage in contemporary politics.

Discontent reached beyond Manchester. Bishop Cornthwaite used sarcasm in his Lenten pastoral letter to illustrate the rapid ascension of the board schools once they took hold of the unlimited public purse and could tax others for their own expansion. Particularly galling to the Bishop of Leeds was the refusal of government grants to newly built Catholic schools deemed too close to existing board schools for financial assistance, a situation which had occurred in his own and other dioceses.[91] Liverpool's Bishop O'Reilly told his clergy to preach to their parishioners on the unreasonable clause of the education code that limited the grant awarded to a school if the school manager could not raise a certain proportion of the funding. This clause, he argued, caused excessive harm to voluntary schools in poor locations where poverty forced school managers to work with smaller budgets, a situation which could lead to lower efficiency, negative inspection reports and even a further reduction in grant money.[92] It is interesting that this letter to the clergy, which would usually be a private matter of communication between the bishop and parish, was released to the local press in a publicly and politically motivated action.[93]

Later that year, as the election loomed large in the mind of Manning, he continued to guide Catholic educational and political opinions into place. Whereas Vaughan had the advantage of speaking to a single diocese, the cardinal's position necessitated him spreading his ideas to all of English and Welsh Catholicism. While on his late summer holiday to northern England, Manning gave a rousing speech on education to a Catholic crowd near Newcastle. He stated his two central objections to the current system: one, the children were considered wards of the state rather than wards of their parents, who should direct and control their education; two, the system was 'unequal and unjust' to supporters of denominational education. Manning echoed one of the VSA's four grievances by referring to the problem of a transient working-class population and how, hypothetically, a newly emerging Catholic centre of population could be denied assistance for a school because a board school already happened to be there. Manning also repeated his call for extending the laws regarding reformatory and industrial schools to elementary education as a whole and thereby providing local monies for all schools based on the parents' choice. At the end of his speech, Manning demanded that all Catholics exercise their civil duties: 'At the coming Elections, we must ask something in return for our votes. (Hear, hear) We must ask Parliamentary Candidates what are their intentions, and accordingly as they answer, so must we give our votes. (Loud applause.)'[94] That the Catholic archbishop was telling the faithful to weigh their votes carefully with regards to the candidates' education policy was yet another step forward in the Catholic political maturation of the 1880s.

Manning's speech at Newcastle coincided with his article in the October issue of the *Dublin Review*, which was also published in several Catholic periodicals and later republished as a pamphlet. Using a didactic approach to political guidance, Manning titled his article 'How Shall Catholics Vote at the Coming Parliamentary Election?' The archbishop named five areas of concern to Catholics, including disestablishment of the Church of England, housing of the poor, land ownership, intemperance and education; it was only on the final issue that Manning gave outright instructions to Catholics. He recommended Catholic voters ask each candidate two questions: 'Will you do your utmost to place Voluntary schools on an equal footing with Board schools?' and 'Will you do your utmost to obtain a Royal Commission to review the present state of education in England and Wales, and especially the Act of 1870 and its administration by the School Boards?' Manning concluded that only those who answered yes to both questions should be supported.[95] Following his lead, other bishops addressed their faithful. Bishop O'Reilly of Liverpool and Bishop Ullathorne of Birmingham obediently instructed Catholics to base their votes upon the candidates' answers to Manning's two questions.[96] O'Reilly also reassured Liverpool Catholic voters that not supporting the Liberals was sanctioned by the Church. 'To many of you', he stated,

> it may be painful to vote against the political party with which you have been long associated. Still as the calls of conscience are above those of party, we hope you will look upon it as a duty to obey your conscience and not count the cost.[97]

In Nottingham, even Bishop Bagshawe chose to temper his pro-radical, pro-Irish impulses to encourage Catholic voters to use their votes for the 'defence of Christian doctrinal education against the attacks of its enemies'.[98] Furthering the obvious political guidance, a joint bishop pastoral letter and list of resolutions announced on the eve of the election their support for candidates who would do their best to protect Christian liberty against 'intellectual despotism', allow for the growth of denominational schools and work to address the inequalities in the educational system, one of the most glaring of which was the fact that board schools received twice as much government support in the form of rates and grants for teaching secular education as voluntary schools received in grants.[99] This hierarchical agreement on education is even more surprising because it is tantamount to a political declaration of support for one party over another and the hierarchy contained both Tory- and Liberal-leaning members.

While Manning and the others had not mentioned either party by name, it was understood that the Conservatives would benefit from this political guidance, especially since the radical wing of the Liberal party, influenced by Gladstone's former Board of Trade president Joseph Chamberlain, had revealed its plan to offer free education in all board schools, by abolishing all fees and providing a greater grant from the state. They had not mentioned helping the denominational schools.[100] In fact, Chamberlain saw no need to change the voluntary school arrangement, other than placing them under popular control, which was the last thing these schools would want.[101] When the press stung the bishops for their 'partisan attitude', they responded defiantly. If support for candidates who endorsed Christian education made them sound like partisans, then, they argued, 'it is the partisanship of the Christian world against the anti-Christian and pseudo-Liberal world'.[102] The *Tablet* subsequently sent Manning's two questions to all parliamentary candidates in London. The results were interesting. Only three Conservatives provided inadequate responses, while nearly 60 per cent of all the Liberal candidates failed this test. Similar results came from other towns as well.[103]

As noted, the other factor in this election was the Irish question. After the enfranchisement in England and Wales of more Irish voters, Gladstone decided not to make clear his intention on Home Rule until after the election when those new voters had spoken. As a result of Gladstone's evasiveness, Charles Stewart Parnell, leader of the Home Rule party, asked Thomas Power O'Connor, president of the Irish National League of Great Britain and MP for the Scotland Ward district of Liverpool, to release a statement urging all Catholics to throw their votes against the Liberals, the party which had been most receptive to Home Rule hitherto. What happened was a convergence of the education and Irish questions on the same side of the political divide for the first time. The results proved that Parnell's power and influence were not as mighty as the Catholic clergy. Catholic voters only obeyed Parnell when his instructions agreed with what the priests were telling them, and as we know, the hierarchy, from Manning to the bishops, had made education the priority in this election year. Home Rule was not a major concern of the hierarchy; in fact, Manning would not be converted to Home Rule until the following year, and Vaughan would never accept it.[104]

When Richard Cross announced just prior to the election that a continued Salisbury government would, in fact, initiate a royal commission along the lines of Manning's recommendations, it seemed as if, perhaps, Catholic influence had made a difference on the national level. Manning quickly wrote to Cross:

> I have read your announcement with the greatest joy and hope. In 1870 the whole matter of Education was in the hands of the adversaries ... of voluntary schools. In 1885 it is in the hands of those who have been friends and fellow-workers in education for half a century.[105]

It remains to be uncovered whether the Conservatives' offer was genuine or engineered for gaining votes. We do know that Manning had planted the seed in the minds of Cross and Salisbury in 1882 and 1883, and that Vaughan and the VSA had been running a nationwide publicity campaign to that effect for over a year. Yet, despite the strategy of Parnell and the Conservatives' promise of a royal commission on education, the election went to the Liberals by a margin of 335 to 249, with the Home Rule party holding the difference of 86 seats. Salisbury remained as a caretaker prime minister until January when he was defeated on an unrelated resolution and resigned office. Prior to the ministry's defeat, however, the long-awaited royal commission was publicly announced.[106]

Manning remained keenly aware that Catholic political influence in Parliament depended upon the Irish Catholic members, who, by the mid-1880s, had committed themselves to Home Rule. During 1885 and 1886, Manning faced the unenviable challenge of trying to appease Ireland, the Irish hierarchy and the Home Rulers, while at the same time attempting to manage Catholic educational interests in England and Wales. The first obstacle to those ends was his personal objection to Home Rule as it had been typically expressed prior to Gladstone's announcement in 1886 in favour of the measure. Since it was considered axiomatic that Home Rule meant a separate Irish Parliament, Manning was rightly concerned about Catholic interests, since such a resolution could lead to the removal of Irish MPs from the Westminster Parliament. This meant that the small and often irregular voice that Irish Catholic MPs had provided at Westminster for the English Catholic community would be lost altogether, with very little chance of getting a Catholic elected for an English constituency.[107] With education at the top of his domestic agenda, Manning feared such a development. The second obstacle was that the Irish Catholic bishops were beginning to come around to Home Rule as a political solution for Ireland. His third problem came from his own backyard, as some members of the English hierarchy were less than receptive to Irish interests, especially Home Rule. This applied particularly to Vaughan, who was still the owner and editor of the anti-Home Rule *Tablet*.

At the end of December 1885 William J. Walsh, Archbishop of Dublin, questioned Manning about the scathing criticism of Irish MPs and Irish bishops appearing in a certain English Catholic periodical. Why, he demanded, had Irish MPs been asked to support the educational interests of the English Catholic community while setting aside their Irish goals for the time being, when at the same time 'we have the most scurrilous attacks made on those same Irish members and on the Irish Bishops'. Walsh was obviously referring to Vaughan's *Tablet*.[108] Those English Catholics to which he referred, like Vaughan and the Duke of Norfolk, consisted of the old Catholic stock and saw any break with Ireland as a threat to Catholic interests in general; thus, they wished to keep the *status quo*. But Walsh gave Manning a counter-argument made easier by his perspective from Dublin. Perhaps if the Irish question were settled, Walsh asserted, then 'would not the Parliamentary force of English Catholicity become far more available than it is now even when it is aided by the somewhat irregular help given by the Irish MPs in the House of Commons?'[109] Basically, the sooner the Irish gained Home Rule, the sooner Irish MPs could attend to English Catholic educational interests. Walsh even admitted that Irish political assistance on education had been uneven over the years due to the primacy of Irish affairs. This argument appealed to Manning, but he could not agree as long as the Home Rule proposal included a separate Parliament, which it did when Gladstone officially brought his Home Rule bill into Parliament on 8 April 1886. Manning was, however, in favour of 'giving to Ireland a power of self-administration in all matters affecting Ireland alone'.[110] Yet, Manning kept his views to himself during the subsequent debate over Gladstone's bill for fear of offending the Irish populace, bishops and MPs, the latter of whom Manning was witnessed greeting in the Commons after one of Gladstone's Home Rule speeches and declaring 'we cannot spare one of you'.[111] He also communicated to Vaughan his strategy for the Catholic Church. Echoing Archbishop Walsh, Manning told Vaughan on 11 June in no uncertain terms that

> we cannot put education before [Home Rule]. The Irish vote in England would be lost by doing so. We should seem to oppose Ireland. We should hopelessly divide our own people. The Education Question would not be listened to apart from Ireland. We can speak on both, but not on Education alone.

Since Catholic political power went through Ireland, then the alienation and loss of Irish support would be devastating to the education question in England and Wales. The shrewd political move then was temporarily to place the Irish situation before the education question, because, in the long run, that would ensure the best opportunity for keeping the Irish politicians on board in the ongoing education battle. Manning also told Vaughan that he would soon announce his views prior to the upcoming election, and he added, 'Education cannot be helped at this election, nor do I think it can be hindered'.[112] Despite a plea from Bishop Ullathorne not to weigh in on the question of Home Rule because it might divide the English hierarchy and Catholic population, in July Manning publicly expressed his support for a federal solution where Home Rule for England, Scotland and Ireland should be allowed in all matters that were not Imperial in nature, while still stating the necessity of keeping an Imperial Parliament.[113] Although the election results revealed the unpopularity of Gladstone's bill, as Liberals lost 136 seats, the Tories returned to power and Home Rule was postponed for the time being, Manning had accomplished much with his timely endorsement. The English archbishop had come through for the Irish and gained their appreciation both at home and in Ireland and that was important to Manning's long-term educational scheme.

The Royal Commission

Manning's politicking continued as he took his place on the royal commission – the Cross Commission – which began its work later that year.[114] He sent a pamphlet to Salisbury immediately after the election urging the Conservative prime minister to 'use this unprecedented condition of Parliamentary balance … to redress the inequalities created by the Act of 1870, and to place the Voluntary Schools on the broad basis of a law common to the whole people of the country'. Within this pamphlet, Manning again recommended using the precedent of the Industrial and Reformatory Schools Acts to offer rate-aid to all schools, an idea he had first floated to Lord de Grey (now Lord Ripon) in November 1869 when the country was preparing for W. E. Forster's education bill.[115] The prime minister did not adopt Manning's suggestion, but the commission continued its review of the elementary education system. Meanwhile, the bishops prepared for the commission by collecting statistical information from their clergy and preparing their respective lists of grievances and disadvantages under which their schools operated.[116] In Liverpool Bishop O'Reilly actually circularized his clergy with suggested and rather specific answers to the commission's enquiries to present a uniform face; yet he warned them to answer in their own words, implying that similar, exactly worded answers would not be taken seriously.[117]

In order to sway Catholic, public and commission opinion, Manning kept up his informational assault during the commission's two-year examination. In 1887 he published 'Suggestions for a Common System of National Education' to clarify his views. He acknowledged that the Education Act of 1870 could not be repealed, but also refreshed his readers' memories that the inclusion of the principle that 'all who pay [the rate] should share [it]' had been included in Forster's original draft of the bill that was eventually dropped during the debate.[118] He blamed clause 14 of the 1870 Act as the one that precluded voluntary schools from receiving the rate.[119] Therefore, he demanded that clause 14 be abolished and that the elementary education system be made equitable, universal and supported by the education rate.[120]

By late 1887, Manning was advocating the adoption of that part of the Newcastle Commission report of 1861 in which voluntary schools would receive local rates administered, not by school boards, but by local education boards or councils, a recommendation that had been dismissed at the time. The essence of Manning's recommendation was included within fellow commissioner Lord Sandford's 'Memorandum as to the mode of Bringing Education within the Scope of the Local Government Bill', a pamphlet which played a major role in educational development in England and Wales until 1902. Sandford recommended the abolition of school boards and use of newly formulated county councils to oversee the education system. In addition, he advised putting voluntary schools on the rates and, in return, giving to county councils the power to examine each school's books and participate in their management. Given that they were working so closely together on the commission and the numerous similarities that existed between Manning's publications of 1886 and 1887 and Sandford's 'Memorandum', it is likely that Manning represented an important influence on Sandford's thoughts on the subject.[121] Manning's joy at a possible solution and the hierarchy's willingness to compromise was evident when all the bishops voted in the spring of 1888 to accept rate-aid under county councils and also, as a compromise, some measure of taxpayer control in the management of their schools.[122]

The eventual ideological division of the Cross Commission and its submission of majority and minority reports prevented any significant reforms following the end of its charge in 1888. The majority report, reflecting Anglican and Catholic interests, recommended in part sharing the rates along the lines of Sandford's 'Memorandum', while the minority report, reflecting nonconformist opinion, disagreed. Manning, however, would not be deterred. After the commission finished its work, he immediately began a campaign to keep the reform agitation going; this entailed a three-pronged strategy: one, to fight the minority challenges in the public eye; two, to secure Anglican support for universal rate-aid, which had wavered in the last months of the commission; and three, openly to lobby the Salisbury ministry that the time was right for reform along the lines of Sandford's proposal.[123] Unfortunately, Prime Minister Salisbury had to please all of his constituents, and rate-aid for denominational schools would have angered the Liberal Unionists who had left the Liberal party over Home Rule and coalesced with the Tories.[124] Unfortunately, this inconvenient reality remained a blind spot in the vision of the Catholic leadership, thus rendering their immediate influence at Whitehall unwelcome.

Out of frustration that his and Sanford's plan would not be realized, Manning fingered his Anglican counterparts as the culprits and highlighted Salisbury's schemes in a letter to Bishop Ullathorne on 20 December 1888:

> Here are fifty stripes for the backs of those cowardly Anglican Bishops for deserting their own principles and showing their uselessness ... I had hoped the Tories would remain in office to carry the proper measures, but they are in the hands of the Liberal Unionists, and as cowardly as to their adhering to their principles as the Anglican Bishops. Politically, what a state we are in! There is nothing for it but downright agitation and teasing the Ministry with endless petitions from all classes. We sadly want a good Catholic leader in the House.[125]

Perhaps his final words rang truer than the others. Despite the increased and matured political activity on the part of Catholics for educational reform during the decade, they had only made some small inroads towards their ultimate goals. And even though Britain had a Catholic home secretary, Henry Matthews, Catholic influence in the Commons, and generally speaking in the political arena, was deficient.

Conclusion

Catholics still had to rely upon Irish MPs for their political voice in Parliament. Despite Manning's support for Home Rule and his good turn for Ireland during the 1886 election, Irish politicians and the Irish hierarchy quickly became embroiled in another land reform fight in Parliament. In a related matter, Salisbury's ministry used heightened coercion during this period to crack Irish resolve and calm Irish unrest. However, their strategy failed and Irish resolve increased.[126] Further, embedded in this Irish question was another attempt to solve the higher education problem in Ireland for Catholics, a solution which, if it ended in a Catholic university, could then split the Home Rule party between its Catholic-Nationalist and its Liberal nonconformist supporters in England.[127]

Irish Catholic MPs, as in previous years, remained occupied with their Irish priorities, and, from 1888 until Parnell's disastrous fall in 1890, these issues were central not only to Irish affairs but also to parliamentary affairs. That and the ministry's refusal to pursue the education issue further meant that, for the time being, the Catholics would have to wait until the Irish situation was less volatile and the government more willing to inch closer to a resolution such as that endorsed by Manning and the majority of the Cross Commission. That opportunity would not come until well into the next decade.

7 ENGLISH CATHOLICS AND THE POLITICS OF EDUCATION, 1891–1902: A STRATEGY FOR SUCCESS

Although much of the political analysis of Catholics in the late nineteenth century has focused on Cardinal Manning, this chapter contends that Bishop, and later Archbishop and Cardinal, Vaughan was, at the very least, equal to the efforts of his predecessor in the political arena, especially after he moved to Westminster in 1892. Prolific in authoring pamphlets, petitions, articles and letters to the editors of several newspapers, Vaughan also travelled the country industriously to speak on behalf of denominational education. Along with the new archbishop's increased lobbying efforts was the heightened political effort of Catholics in Parliament. Whereas not one Catholic spoke in the Commons during the initial debate on the 1870 Education Act, the education debates of the 1890s featured much greater Catholic input. Part of the explanation for this change can be found in the fall of Irish leader Charles Parnell and the subsequent split in the Home Rule party that weakened the Irish cause. After Gladstone's second Irish Home Rule bill fell to defeat in the Lords in 1893, the issue faded from the political stage for nearly a decade, allowing Catholic MPs to refocus their efforts on an acceptable education settlement.

A few months before the 1892 general election returned a minority Liberal government to power under Prime Minister's Gladstone's fourth ministry, English Catholicism experienced the death of the long-time Gladstone confidant, Oxford convert and socially-radical-leaning Manning and his subsequent replacement by the old Catholic, conservative-leaning Vaughan. Despite their differences over social and political issues, including Home Rule, they remained friends for over forty years and shared the same perspective on education. Vaughan would not have the same level of political access that had given Manning the ear of Gladstone and Disraeli, but the last eight years of Vaughan's time at Westminster happened to coincide with an incredible run at the helm by the Conservatives. That concurrence may have had more to do with the success of the education policy that Catholics preferred and pursued than any other factor. It did not hurt that Conservative Prime Minister Salisbury and his ministry were committed to bringing more aid to denominational schools, which made them more receptive to Vaughan's and other Catholics' pleas, resolutions and petitions.[1] Finally, since Vaughan remained opposed to Home Rule, his views did not bring the immediate censure that a more pro-Irish archbishop's would have from a Conservative government.[2]

The 1890s: A Political Awakening

The election of 1886 had returned the Tories to power after the fiasco of Gladstone's first Irish Home Rule bill split the Liberal party and forced anti-Home Rule Liberals like radical Joseph Chamberlain to create the Liberal Unionist party, which allied with the Conservatives. Capitalizing on the opposition's split, the ascendant Tories and Liberal Unionists governed Britain, with the exception of a three-year interval from 1892 to 1895, until 1905.

It is no surprise that denominational education's status improved during this time of conservative hegemony. Free education again became a topic *du jour* when Salisbury's ministry proposed an elementary education bill, known as the Fee Grant Bill, in 1891 to abolish school fees. Catholic opposition to the bill emanated from two premises. First, most Catholics opposed the underlying principle of the bill – free education – because of their staunch belief in the right and obligation of parents to provide their children's education. Acceptance of free education seemed to undermine that Catholic philosophy. The Catholic School Committee, whose name was changed in 1889 to reflect a broader educational outlook to include secondary education, lobbied Parliament with resolutions against free education.[3] Manning initially revealed an ambivalent attitude about the impending legislation because he believed denominational schools were strong enough to withstand any coming changes, including the idea of popular control, which he believed would be safeguarded by Catholic parents.[4] By June, however, his ambivalence had hardened into opposition and he wrote to tell his Cross Commission partner Lord Sandford, 'the more I think of this Fee Grant Bill, the less I like it'. The archbishop believed that this reform should be part of a complete overhaul of the system which he and Sandford had recommended since the end of the Cross Commission three years before.[5] Thus, the legislation did not go far enough for him. The second objection went beyond the problem of simply accepting free education, or, as it was called at the time, fee grant aid. It was the fear that ratepayers would subsequently want increased control over all schools that accepted the aid; hence the phrase 'popular control' entered the political lexicon on education. With that in mind, Manning wrote rather hyperbolically that Catholics were 'in a crisis the gravest we have ever known, and in all probability, the last'.[6] The bishops, as a whole, remained united on the second fear, believing that giving a taxpayer control over school management simply because he lives in the district was 'singularly impudent'.[7] However, the *Tablet* supported the bill, which meant that Vaughan as owner of the Catholic periodical since 1868 saw less harm in the bill than Manning.[8] The disagreement between Manning and the Catholic School Committee on one hand in opposition to the bill, and the *Tablet* and Vaughan in support of it represented the last of the major Catholic divisions over education in the century. Clearly, an important part of Vaughan's legacy was his ability to usher in greater Catholic unity on the subject of education; although he was, no doubt, helped by the fact that most of the obstinate first-generation bishops, and Catholic controversialists, were dead by the 1890s.[9] Dissension over free education later dissipated when attendance numbers actually rose in the two weeks leading up to Act's implementation on 1 September and parental donations and subscriptions remained at an adequate level.[10]

Irish Catholic MPs took a more realistic approach to the bill. They recognized the great financial benefits of the bill, and they set out to accept it, albeit without the concessions towards popular control that some nonconformists were demanding. Colonel John Philip Nolan, representing Galway and speaking for the Home Rulers, argued in the Commons debate on 29 June 1891 that popular control would be dangerous to Catholic schools. He cited as evidence the fact that over one hundred Catholic schools had been denied funding because of local school boards, and he believed that local popular control would eventually lead to the closure of Catholic schools and the requirement that Catholic children attend board schools. He also added that the Irish members would be committed to denominational education despite their having been 'returned to vote upon most questions with the Liberal Party'.[11] Clearly, Nolan was chosen to speak on behalf of the Irish MPs on the Fee Grant bill since he entered every debate and was the only Irish MP to do so. But, not unlike other years in which an education bill was on the table, an important Irish measure, the Land Purchase Bill, was simultaneously being debated in the Commons and occupying the time and effort of Irish MPs.[12] In the House of Lords, the Marquess of Ripon, the veteran Liberal and convert who had actually introduced the Education Bill of 1870 on the floor of Commons, expressed his agreement with the principle of free education and acknowledged that the 'tendency of public feeling' was directed towards 'some greater public supervision' since a greater amount of public money was to be given to denominational schools. Yet, he rued the fact that the bill did not clarify how public supervision would be implemented and he feared for the religious nature of denominational schools under popular control.[13] Thus, he occupied a middle compromissary ground between his political and religious compasses.

Once the bill had passed and schools who entered the new scheme were scheduled to receive a grant of 10 shillings per student, the bishops informed their school managers that they had permission to declare their schools free but also had the obligation to tell their parishes that they were still required to support the schools financially. In Wales, Bishop of Newport and Menevia John Cuthbert Hedley expressed the fear that many of the bishops felt: 'if the freeing of the schools is to mean the failure of Christian charity, we had better have remained as we were'. Thus, it remained necessary for Catholic parents who could afford school pence to continue to contribute that amount for books, desks, repairs and subsidies for teacher salaries, because they also had to expect that contributions from the working class would disappear with the new Act in place.[14] Bishop William Gordon, who replaced the stalwart educational defender Robert Cornthwaite in June 1890 and was Bishop of Leeds until 1911, repeated a similar message to his clergy in Yorkshire and added that even with the 10 shilling grant, they could now expect increased school expenses due to expanded Education Department requirements.[15] Long-time Bishop of Clifton William Clifford echoed both Bishop Hedley and Gordon in his message to the diocese for Advent that year. He hoped all Catholic parents, including the working class, would not cease their obligatory contributions to support Catholic education by substituting regular subscriptions for the now unnecessary school pence as expenses would surely rise.[16] Catholics rightly believed that there was a never-ending and incremental expansion of operating expenses that schools must adopt to continue receiving state funding, the board schools, of course, being easily able to cover those expenses with an increased rate.

A few months before Manning's death and after the Fee Grant Act had passed, Vaughan added his thoughts on free education in an unsigned editorial printed in the *Dublin Review*. Revealing a shift in hierarchical opinion, Vaughan noted that free education had increased attendance in some Catholic districts and that it was a 'blessing', which had rendered considerable aid to both poor parents and poor schools. His claim that Catholic attendance had increased was corroborated by other dioceses.[17] Perhaps one can view the imposition of Vaughan's view replacing the earlier opposition of Manning as symbolic of the chosen successor already taking the mantle of Catholic education from his weakened and frail predecessor, who only had a few months to live. But given that Manning's main opposition to the bill stemmed from his belief that only a comprehensive reworking of the education system would suffice, as opposed to this bill's tinkering, this difference of opinion between mentor and successor loses much of its magnitude. Vaughan conceded that greater popular or local control over the schools was acceptable as long as it was based on the rights of parents not ratepayers. As such, Vaughan argued that parents required greater education on the subject so that 'when a political contest comes, all will be forearmed, thoroughly prepared, and trained to fight to the last for the rights and independence of voluntary schools'.[18] It is hard not to notice, once again, the militancy of his rhetoric.

One of the other interesting developments that came from the education debate that year was the plan to create Catholic school boards in the Salford Diocese as a pre-emptive strike against the expected cry for popular control that Vaughan knew would follow the fee grant aid legislation. The proposed Manchester and Salford school board was to consist of fifteen members, seven of them laymen, who would enquire into the management of the Catholic schools with the intention of improving their efficiency, especially with regard to finances and inspections.[19] By October, the plan had evolved into an organization called the Diocesan Board of Education, which reported to Bishop Vaughan and would oversee the Catholic schools of the diocese. Two-man school management committees would be elected by parents whose children attended the schools, and these would be overseen by the Diocesan Board of Education.[20] This creation was exactly what Bishop Hedley had suggested the Catholic community needed while in the midst of the debate over free education. He had written to his clergy in August:

> If our people were intelligently united with us, the pastors, in promoting good education and jealously watching its efficiency, we should be able to forestall the legislation we are threatened with by pointing to a popular control already existing.[21]

Vaughan already had designs on expanding this Diocesan Board of Education idea to other dioceses, much like he did in 1884 with the Voluntary School Association. Thus, in the year prior to his accession to the archbishopric, Vaughan was already showing signs of proactive and innovative educational leadership, qualities that would serve him and the community well in the next decade.

It was within the next few years that Catholics embarked on a campaign to achieve educational reform. No longer satisfied with their educational handout, Catholics now wanted full equality. If their schools were doing what was required by the state and achieving similar results as the board schools, then they wanted commensurate treatment.[22] This campaign came directly from the top of the hierarchy as now Cardinal Vaughan's fingerprints could be found on all facets of the movement.[23] In January 1894, Vaughan circularized the bishops with a plan that he believed would position Catholics for the best possible outcome. It revealed adept political foresight for a denomination which has been portrayed as having no political sense, other than blatant self-righteousness.[24] Vaughan had communicated with several Liberals in Parliament who assured him they would support a Catholic claim to an exceptional and solitary solution to their educational grievances. These lawmakers, however, would not support Catholic claims if they remained aligned with the Church of England. Vaughan realized that the Conservatives could not attack an exclusive Catholic solution too harshly without undermining their own position on voluntary schools. Then, he added, 'if defeated we should fall back upon a claim to share any advantage the Anglicans might obtain from the legislature'.[25] Perhaps this might seem duplicitous, but it was certainly politically tactful. The cardinal was confident this was the proper time to launch such an effort because he knew that no great offence would be taken by the Anglicans if Catholics tried to obtain an exclusive solution, because the Archbishop of Canterbury had recently insulted them by stating: 'the Roman Catholics are not to be trusted as allies'. In a final piece of political acumen, Vaughan confided that no private bill from and intended for the Catholics would ever reach a second reading but that releasing the bill 'will simply be a taking up of position and a declaration of policy'.[26] He would be simultaneously testing the political waters and stirring up public interest in the plight of the Catholic schools at a time when the party usually more receptive to denominational education was out of power as the Conservatives had lost successive elections in 1892 and 1894.

Named 'The Roman Catholic Rate-Aided School Act of 1894', this proposal boldly demanded a share of the education rate for Catholic schools which met certain conditions. First, these Catholic schools must open themselves to local inspection, in addition to the standard governmental inspectors who had been visiting schools since Catholics entered the system in 1848.[27] This offer to receive local inspectors from the district from which the schools would receive rates was an olive branch to those who had wanted some form of popular control in the wake of the Fee Grant Act of 1891. Another important component of this Catholic proposal was the request that, if Catholics took the initiative to build a school on their own in a location of their own choosing which satisfied the requirements of the Education Department, then 'such school shall not be deemed unnecessary ... and shall be entitled to aid by annual grants from the Education Department and from the rates'. And according to the bill, the bishop would still control religious education and the conscience clause would still be in effect for parents who objected to the religious instruction.[28]

Some Catholic educationists remained unsatisfied with the way the proposal had been written. One of the men with whom Vaughan had great experience was Canon George Richardson, who served as missionary rector of St Augustine's Schools, Manchester, as well as chief religious inspector for the Salford diocese. Richardson wrote to the cardinal to warn him that too much of the proposal was left unclear. He cautioned that the proposed local inspector 'may become ... an organizing mischief maker', whose powers must be made more clear and 'must be excluded from having anything to do with the religious work'. He also suggested that a veto should exist for bishops who, acting as the 'Catholic authority', could take care of 'dangerous teachers'. Finally, Richardson told Vaughan that the bill was obviously not ready and should be vetted by many Catholic committees to eliminate any chance of misinterpretation before submission to Parliament.[29]

Meanwhile, Vaughan took this demand for a just educational solution on the road. At a large rally in Birmingham, Vaughan proposed a resolution that demanded from the government that 'the children of the poor should receive a religious education at the public expense'. Revealing that his stance was not wholly intransigent, Vaughan added that the local education authority 'had a right to see ... that the money contributed from the rates was not improperly spent' and that popular control could come from parental representatives of children in denominational schools. But acceding to unrestricted popular control of the ratepayers was out of the question.[30]

John Bilsborrow, Bishop of Salford from 1892 to 1903, attended a Catholic rally at the Temperance Hall in Bolton on 14 February to generate greater support for the Catholic desire for a share of the rates. The flyer which advertised the rally also contained a slightly revised reprinting of Manning's *Fifty Reasons Why the Voluntary Schools of England Ought to Share the School Rates*.[31] Bilsborrow explained in his letter to the *Manchester Courier* that Catholics would only support those politicians who helped them in the battle for educational equality.[32] At their Low Week meeting in April, the bishops unanimously adopted a list of resolutions on elementary education summarizing their belief in parental rights, religious liberty and their desire for a 'full share of public money, whether from the rates or from the taxes, as any other Public Elementary School in the country'.[33] They wanted equal treatment with the board schools. Bishop Bagshawe and other Nottingham Catholics spoke before a well-attended meeting at the Circus Street Hall on 29 May 1894 to publicize the resolutions. The bishop said Catholics should not have to relinquish their religious rights to receive equality in education and warned that Catholics would only give their votes to those politicians committed to such equality. A local Jesuit, Father Edgcome, added to the heightened emotions of the meeting by returning to the military analogy, saying Catholics were on the eve of a great battle and they 'must have their ammunition ready so that they might go in and win'.[34]

By the middle of the year, the hierarchy decided not to press this exceptional and solitary proposal on Parliament on the premise that it had no chance of passing and, perhaps, because of second thoughts about working with a party associated with radicalism. As a consolation, they decided to use the demands contained within the proposal as a test question for Catholic voters at the November school board elections instead. Accompanying this strategy was a full-scale organizational effort by clergy and laymen to ascertain the strength of the Catholic vote, select appropriate candidates and provide that information to the Catholic voters, the number of which they believed had doubled since the last school board election in 1891. By July, they hoped to gain seats in seven London constituencies, where they were poorly represented, as well as in Leeds, Liverpool, Salford and Newcastle-upon-Tyne.[35] The hierarchy continued to press this strategy upon Catholic voters until the November elections. Cardinal Vaughan gave a final speech to Catholics before the elections at St George's Cathedral, Southwark. Speaking before a large crowd, he told them it was their Christian duty to support candidates committed to helping the denominational schools achieve equality with the board schools.[36] Rounding out the Catholic political initiative that year was the effort of the National Union of Catholic Teachers who presented to Parliament a petition signed by 1,351 Catholic teachers complaining of the double burden on Catholics of supporting schools they cannot conscientiously use and their own schools, the costs of which keep rising due to the demands of the Education Department. The Union also formed a parliamentary committee to lobby MPs in future elections to make pledges to give a portion of the rates to voluntary schools.[37] Nothing tangible resulted from this petition despite the large organizational effort. Clearly, 1894 was a year during which many strata within Catholic society became actively involved with the education question. Although they had decided against presenting their proposal for a solitary educational solution to Parliament, Catholic leaders hoped that the next year's parliamentary election might return a government more receptive to their wishes – a Conservative one.

Educational affairs continued to top the Catholic agenda in 1895. Certain bishops, upper clergy and the Catholic laity, including the Duke of Norfolk and five members of the Catholic School Committee, began working on a stripped-down version of their 1894 proposal right before the new year. The result, titled 'An Act for the Furtherance of Free Education in School Board Districts', contained only two clauses: one asked for permission to be able to open an Education Department-approved school wherever at least thirty children required one. As such it would fall under state inspection requirements and would have a board of management consisting of two members elected by the parents and three members determined by the school trustees. The other clause asked for an equal share of the rates.[38] When he sent a copy of this new proposal to *The Times*, Vaughan included a letter of explanation that further expounded on the Catholic grievances in the current system. He again described the financial inequality that existed for supporters of denominational schools and argued that they sought to put all elementary schools on an equal footing for fear of 'the extinction of the denominational schools'. Such a result would be unacceptable, he wrote, because their religious convictions dictated that Catholic children could only attend Catholic schools.[39] After the Low Week meeting in April, the bishops publicized their strategy to support the new proposal. They encouraged the clergy to be vigilant in impressing upon Catholics 'on the platform and through the press' the necessity of the changes this proposal would bring. The bishops asked all Catholic MPs for support of the proposal in the upcoming session of Parliament, and they met with leading statesmen to plan the most opportune and effective time to present it to Parliament.[40] On the Sunday before the election began, bishops such as Edward Ilsley, Bishop of Birmingham from 1888 to 1921, and Thomas Whiteside, Bishop and later Archbishop of Liverpool from 1894 to 1921, used the pulpit to remind Catholic voters to make education the test question for the election and 'to see to it that in their exercise of the franchise the sacred cause of Christian education shall be safeguarded above all other interests'.[41] This meant voting Conservative.

The Conservatives swept back into office with a commanding majority. With a more receptive government in place, the Catholic hierarchy submitted their proposed bill to Parliament. Soon after the election, education again became the dominant political subject, presumably borne into the public discourse by the change in ministries, as well as the bill proposed by the Catholics and a similar one by the Anglicans. In essence, the issue was finally stripped down to whether or not voluntary schools should receive a share of the rates. Catholics and Anglicans, although offering different plans, both demanded some portion of the rates that all taxpayers paid. Even *The Times* reported that the Catholic bill 'is the boldest and the simplest, and possibly the most statesmanlike' of the two, generous words from a traditionally anti-Catholic corner.[42] Nonconformists generally opposed such a scheme. One letter in the *Manchester Guardian* from 'a Taxpayer' warned of the danger to the school boards posed by the denominationalists:

> The time is ripe; the danger is real; the forces of religious tyranny must be met by forces equally earnest on the side of liberty ... We must not allow the priestly hand to snatch new millions of public money.[43]

To this, Patrick Lynch of St Wilfrid's replied the following day arguing that the Catholics did not want to penalize the board schools, only to make the system fair by respecting liberty of conscience and the rights of parents. On the charge of religious tyranny, Lynch agreed that it was a danger, but with a twist: 'Those who wish to cram the School Board system of religious training down the throat of everybody else I regard as the most extreme religious tyrants and bigots of our time'. That was just as obvious proselytism as any other, he concluded.[44]

Sensing an opportunity to strengthen the Catholic agitation in order to coincide with and capitalize on the public debate, Cardinal Vaughan wrote a decidedly provocative letter to *The Times* on 30 September 1895, repeating Manning's call for a comprehensive reform of the educational system rather than piecemeal tinkering. As a common basis for all elementary schools, he suggested that the cost of school maintenance should be the state's responsibility. And he noted the substantial sacrifices that both the Anglican and Catholic Churches had made in order to educate their children according to their religious conscience. Turning up the assault, next Vaughan questioned why they should continue to make such sacrifices when 'education has become a recognized legal public right, to be had at the expense of the State'. The denominationalists were not a minority pleading for crumbs of sympathy but the majority in the country, 'and I submit that [we] ought, without hesitation of apology, to demand a full measure of justice and not to pray and pay for mercy'. In a final statesmanlike and ecumenical gesture, Vaughan acknowledged that nonconformists also had legitimate grievances in small rural districts where the Anglican Church monopolized education and that their objections must also be met before a true national system could be established.[45]

If his intent was to stir up the pot, Vaughan succeeded. The next day a Protestant replied to Vaughan in complete agreement with the archbishop's opinions. W. Farrer Ecroyd wrote that it was fitting that Vaughan lead the vanguard in this debate because of the dire position of the Catholic schools. He added: 'No settlement can be either just or permanent which does not completely remedy this wrong'.[46] *The Times* again reacted positively to the cardinal's suggestions by welcoming his letter 'as the first important sign that action will be taken on a matter which is of grave concern'.[47] On the other side of the question, however, was the letter from Joseph Parker which, while treating the cardinal with great respect, attempted to repudiate Vaughan's arguments at every turn. In answer to Vaughan's question, 'Why should a heavy financial burden be laid upon the denominational schools which is not laid on undenominational Board schools?', Parker answered, 'Because they are denominational'. This nonconformist believed the price of wanting to teach children in a sectarian religious atmosphere should be the double burden of rates and private subscriptions, even though it was the denominational schools that had been in operation since the beginning of state-funded elementary education over half a century before, not the board schools.[48] Further letters attacking Parker's position as untenable appeared in the press. Sydney Smith, a London-based Jesuit priest, criticized Parker's contention that Catholics should pay extra for their desire to teach children in a Catholic atmosphere:

> [His] merry talk would perhaps sound better if Dr. Parker would first pull his hand out of our pockets and leave us the wherewithal to rejoice in duty instead of taking away nearly all we have to support the schools which happen to please him, but which our children cannot attend except at the risk of losing their faith.[49]

Hence, the kernel of the problem was that nonconformists did not want to equalize the system because they believed that, if denominational schools wished to provide a sectarian education, they should have to pay extra for that right. This was such even though the precedent of denominational schools providing education, with government assistance, was established long before the nonconformist-supported board schools came into existence after 1870. However, the paradigm had shifted. While the denominationalists were still a majority and had over a million more children in more efficient schools, the proponents of non-denominational or secular education, as part of the Liberal party, had become ensconced in Parliament and local government where the important decisions were made. The vacillatory nature of the Church of England did not help either, as it turned several hundred schools over to the school boards. Therefore, while they were in the majority, the supporters of voluntary schools were fighting an uphill battle. Perhaps the key factor that had changed was the ever-increasing cost of schools, and it was now believed prudent to say that denominationalists should pay extra than to provide a comprehensive fair solution for all.

Vaughan lost no time that autumn. He wrote to his bishops on 5 November to stress the urgency of presenting another educational statement to the new prime minister, Lord Salisbury, and to ask for input on the attached draft.[50] Taking advantage of the current public debate and political agitation on education, the Catholic bishops released their declaration the following week. This one, however, he and the Duke of Norfolk, current chairman of the Catholic School Committee, presented personally to Salisbury on 13 November 1895. It first asked him and his government to live up to their campaign promises 'to promote ... any measure which shall place all Public Elementary Schools ... upon a footing of perfect equality'. Then, in reference to the inequality of the current system, it declared,

> our schools are often starved, our teachers underpaid, our pupil teachers overworked, and our apparatus inferior ... while the private resources which might have been spent on the improvement of buildings are absorbed in meeting expenses that ought to be borne by the State.[51]

Again, *The Times* reacted favourably.[52] But the denominationalist and Catholic effort was dealt a serious blow when a Church of England deputation also met with Salisbury and subsequently lessened its demands. The Anglican group told the prime minister that the Church of England did not wish to eliminate private subscriptions and would even consent to a plan in which a certain level of subscriptions was necessary for assistance from the rates. This was a concession that a wealthier body like the Church of England could afford but a poverty-stricken Catholic community could not.

Disappointed by this defection in the ranks, Vaughan and the bishops clarified their earlier declaration to Salisbury with an addendum, sent two weeks after the first. In it, the Catholics again broke from the Anglicans. Citing their poverty in opposition to the Church of England's great wealth, the bishops stated: 'Catholics are more than justified in declining, as Nonconformists decline, to raise voluntary contributions in order to relieve the country from the legitimate consequences of a law which declares education to be at once compulsory and free'.[53] They stated that they could not side with the Anglicans but must 'stand upon the common ground of justice and equity, and demand ... that the law shall declare that the same payment shall be made for secular instruction given in the [denominational] Schools as for that given in Board Schools'. The declaration closed by asking all supporters of denominational education across England to meet and create similar resolutions to use in pressuring Parliament for educational legislation favourable to the denominational cause.[54] Richard Lacy, Bishop of Middlesbrough from 1879 to 1929, made sure his diocese was clear on the hierarchy's stance when he wrote in his Advent pastoral letter that since voluntary schools represent two-thirds of the country's schools, they 'demand ... a measure of full justice' and that the 'profession of religion ... must be no bar to the full enjoyment of civil rights'.[55]

Foreshadowing a strategy the archbishop would employ over the next two years, Vaughan again took his demands on the road and presided over a large demonstration in Bradford on 17 December where he criticized the government for not even providing a subsistence level of school maintenance to voluntary schools.[56] Likewise, Bishops Gordon and Lacy hosted political meetings throughout their dioceses into 1896, two of which were attended by Cardinal Vaughan, and all of them, including an exceedingly large one at Middlesbrough, attended by both Catholics and Anglicans.[57]

A New Education Bill

The year 1896 proved to be one of Vaughan's busiest in the political struggle for education and revealed the continuing maturation of Catholic grass-roots political organization and increasing, yet still not potent, influence within the political milieu. It also coincided with the introduction by Sir John Gorst of an education bill that satisfied no one and which did not survive beyond its second reading in Parliament. After a holiday break, the cardinal returned to the circuit in support of the Catholic position in January of that year. With the Duke of Norfolk, Vaughan spoke at St James Hall on 16 January on behalf of voluntary schools, demanding equal payment to any Catholic schools meeting the requirements of the Education Department because Catholics were the poorest community and needed a good education to give them an equal chance of success in life. Tying education together with temporal success seemed a new rhetorical strategy for the cardinal.[58] The following week at a town hall meeting of Birmingham Catholics, Vaughan repeated his soon to be familiar mantra of a 'fair and equal' solution to the education problem through a share of the rates into which all taxpayers paid. He argued that the nonconformist cry for ratepayer control had been overplayed and that managers of voluntary schools were often ratepayers too; they were obviously much more efficient than board school managers because experience had forced them to be.[59] Two days later, Vaughan spoke to an enthusiastic crowd at St Francis Xavier School, Liverpool. After acknowledging England's religious diversity, he opined that the state should solve the education problem in a way acceptable to all groups. He also noted wryly that because the Education Department had spent £43 million on board schools and administration in twenty-four years, voluntary schools could, in all fairness, ask for similar support. But, he claimed, they were not asking for that. They simply wanted a share of the rates along with the recognition of parental rights.[60] The following day, Vaughan's letter to the editor of *The Times* publicly restated his plan for education. Again, building upon the 'newly-created right of each child to receive education at the cost of the State', he outlined his proposal to determine what sum per child was adequate and then to provide that sum to whatever school the parents decided – a late nineteenth-century form of school choice. This plan, he argued, respected the natural law of parental rights and upheld the national interest in educating all children. Vaughan even broached the emerging issue of international competition in his appeal:

> If external dangers are ahead, if heavy calls are to be made upon our national resources, and if we are to be invited to make popular sacrifices, an enlightened patriotism points out that every effort should be made at once ... to place the whole population on an equal footing in respect to the education of their children.[61]

When asked a few days later whether Catholics would respect the wishes of Unitarian or agnostic parents, the archbishop replied in the affirmative. If agnostics or Unitarians built their schools in compliance with the Education Department and produced comparable results, Vaughan concluded, then they should also be treated equally.[62]

Even when meetings occurred at which Vaughan was not present, his centralizing influence was apparent. Bishop Bagshawe organized a meeting of Catholics in the Mechanic's Hall in Nottingham where two resolutions on public education were discussed and approved, including the now familiar notion 'that schools which teach Christian doctrine have a right ... to as much of the public money as is given to Schools which do not teach it'.[63] The Catholic Association met on 28 January and the Earl of Denbigh noted that the upcoming session of Parliament would be heavily involved in the education question. Therefore, as their political duty they should demand fair treatment in the educational system. At the end of the meeting, the association passed a resolution asking for increased grants for Catholic schools and decided to send the resolution to the prime minister and the minister for education.[64] Vaughan also wrote to the bishops in mid-February, asking them to instruct their clergy in missions where educational meetings had not yet been held to schedule meetings and pass resolutions in support of the

Catholic position, all of which should be forwarded to the prime minister.[65] Following his marching orders, Francis Mostyn, vicar apostolic of Wales and future Bishop of Menevia, penned a short note to his clergy in northern Wales, urging them to pass the three resolutions received from the hierarchy on the following topics: 1) parental rights to have children educated in schools of their own religion; 2) equal funding for the maintenance of voluntary schools; 3) equal funding for any school meeting the requirements of the Education Department. These resolutions were to be sent to the prime minister and the Department of Education.[66] Bishop Lacy of Middlesbrough blamed the nonconformists for exacerbating the educational problems in England by refusing to 'make some sacrifice for the principles they uphold' by building their own schools as Catholics and Anglicans had done for years.[67] Clearly, Vaughan's proactive efforts aimed at the upcoming education battle in Parliament were paying dividends, as a great number of Catholics were participating in the struggle for the schools.

John Gorst introduced his education bill in the House of Commons on 31 March 1896. He proposed establishing local educational authorities (LEAs) to act as limited and separate education departments in each county. In addition, Gorst recommended the abolition of rates paid by schools, the abolition of the 17*s.* 6*d.* grant limit per student, the raising of the age of compulsory attendance to twelve years and an increase in the grant to voluntary schools. His agenda, however, was soon evident. Early in his speech he lauded the role of voluntary schools and specifically praised the Catholics who 'boast – and with truth – that they have never surrendered a single one of their schools to a Board'. He admired these poorest of the voluntary schools which survived only by 'begging appeals, by sales of work, by concerts, and by subscriptions of the very poorest people'.[68] His comments elicited great cheers from the Irish members, who were now even more committed to what Colonel Nolan had proclaimed in 1891.

Home Rule MPs, notably John Dillon of Mayo and T. P. O'Connor of Liverpool, vigorously supported this Tory measure in the Commons, despite having to vote against their Liberal allies. Catholics, Dillon said frankly, were simply demanding justice and nothing more and were willing to compromise on the issue of local ratepayer control. He acknowledged the difficulty of voting against his traditional Liberal allies, but, even with a poorly designed bill, he and his fellow Home Rulers had come to realize the importance of education to the Catholics of England. This bill stretched out a 'helping hand to the Catholics' and they must support it.[69] With Home Rule still shelved, Irish political leaders recognized that the Irish in Britain could best be helped through changes in the education system. Collaboration between the Irish MPs and the notoriously anti-Home Rule Vaughan meant that Home Rule was now subordinated to the education question.

In the midst of the parliamentary debate, Vaughan once again took the opportunity to sway public opinion by playing politics in the press. He repeated his theme of equality and fair play in the treatment of elementary education and dauntlessly asked in a letter to *The Times*:

> Are we to persuade the hard-worked and needy ... that the rich have settled that their schools must be maintained by appeals to them for voluntary – I might almost say compulsory – subscriptions, and not out of the rates; and that this policy was settled for them in the summer of 1896 by a Parliament which they returned at great political sacrifices, in order to get rid once and for all of this education difficulty? ... I for one, should not like to deliver to them [this] message.[70]

The bishops released another education declaration in support of Gorst's bill because 'it proposes to recognise by statute Voluntary and Christian schools as an integral part of the national system of elementary education'. They urged Parliament to act quickly to protect the rights and liberties of Christian parents from the secularist threat. Vaughan still recognized two major faults in the bill: one, the problem over 'unnecessary' schools remained open; two, the bill did not address the growing inequality over school maintenance, which was ever increasing due to higher building standards for all grant-aided schools – board and denominational. The bishops acknowledged that they had asked a number of MPs, including the Irish, to help amend the bill to fit Catholic interests.[71] On the day after *The Times* published the cardinal's letter, Dillon again told the Commons that Catholics wanted equal and fair treatment for their schools and for all schools. His great fear rested on the LEAs, and he wanted reassurances from the government that these local councils would allow minority representation. This meant using the cumulative vote in their selection as had been done in the process of designing the selection of school boards in 1870. Otherwise, he believed those councils could and would act prejudicially towards Catholics.[72]

While the bishops quickly tried to gather financial and demographic information about their schools to forward to the Irish MPs to be able to meet the coming attack of the secularists, Catholic activity continued.[73] Reflecting a rising Irish population in southern Wales, Bishop Hedley reported that despite an increased number of children in attendance his schools were now filled to capacity in Cardiff, as several hundred Catholic children were forced to attend non-Catholic schools in the area.[74] Bishop Bilsborrow addressed the annual conference of the National Union of Catholic Teachers in Manchester, expressing the hope that the bill would remove some of the financial difficulties facing Catholics. Mr Murray of Liverpool offered a resolution expressing the Union's appreciation for the leadership of the hierarchy in defending the denominational schools and demanding educational equality. Further resolutions that day and the next articulated the teachers' support for the efforts of the hierarchy to make the bill more amenable to Catholics.[75] Clearly, Catholic opinion on the bill was uniform; they agreed with some of its changes but believed it did not go far enough. Consensus existed from the archbishop down to the teachers.

The bill was later withdrawn because its architects had loaded it with measures to introduce an entirely new system of local control, which, John Dillon argued, had killed any chance of helping the voluntary schools because their supporters could not tolerate such sweeping changes.[76] The Rev. Michael Francis Glancey, diocesan inspector of schools for Birmingham, heaped the blame for the failure of the bill at the feet of the Anglicans, who he claimed did not want to cooperate with Catholics because of bigotry. Perhaps, he argued provocatively, 'they thought it too strange to be true that the Catholic Lamb would lie down peacefully and guilelessly with the Anglican Wolf'.[77] Thus, even ignoring Glancey's exaggerated rhetoric, the two potential partners on the side of denominational education did not unite successfully. The Catholic hierarchy immediately released an educational appeal for public consumption decrying the educational *status quo* and, referring to a comment made by John Gorst in the summer debate, reminded the politicians that voluntary schools required equitable financial support because if they were to close, it would cost the country £25 million to replace and £2,280,000 annually to maintain them. The country could not afford to allow this to happen.[78] Vaughan even sent a copy of this declaration to the retired Gladstone, his and Manning's veteran adversary on education for over two decades, to keep him informed of the Catholic push for educational equality.[79]

In the larger political context, the failure of the education bill reflected a split in the Unionist coalition between the Salisbury Conservatives and the Chamberlain Liberal Unionists. As early as March of that year, Vaughan had recognized and noted this split in a letter to Lady Herbert. Given the ministerial disagreement on the bill, Vaughan worried that Catholics might not receive a satisfying outcome that year.[80] He was right; a solution to please Catholics and other supporters of denominational education did not come that year and 1897 would prove that the failure of Gorst's bill had only been another act of a continuing drama.

Making the Final Turn, 1897–1902

The final six years of the education struggle witnessed a continuation of the political activity that English Catholics had employed since the late 1880s under Cardinal Manning and had increased with much vigilance and tenacity under Cardinal Vaughan. The archbishop persevered in his leadership role, hoping finally to achieve an acceptable educational solution for his patient but increasingly outspoken and assertive Catholic flock.

Their embarrassment from the failed bill of the previous summer still smarting, Salisbury's ministry introduced a scaled-down and less ambitious education bill on 1 February 1897 with the specific intent of assisting voluntary schools. Vaughan had anticipated the legislation as early as October 1896 when he asked his bishops to be prepared for a new bill, especially if it would offer them the carrot of a share of the rates with the stick that an equal share be provided by voluntary subscriptions. 'It will be impossible for us to acquiesce in such a proposal', he concluded.[81] As in the previous year, Vaughan also began politicking in the press prior to the introduction of the bill, perhaps hoping to influence its content.[82] On the day of the bill's presentation in Parliament, Vaughan told a Catholic audience at St Mary's School, Westminster, that he knew the upcoming government bill would not satisfy all of their 'just demands' but would be a 'first instalment towards a great act of justice'. But he questioned why teachers in voluntary schools who work off the same syllabus, provide the same standard of education and whose students take and pass the same examinations as the board schools 'should be compelled to receive a lower salary simply because they augment the secular instruction given in the Board Schools with instruction in an extra science – that of their own religion'.[83]

In the House of Commons, Catholic MPs continued their assault from the year before. On 16 February, T. P. O'Connor argued that Catholics were not afraid of local popular control, as long as safeguards were kept for religious teaching. Revealing that Home Rule, dormant since Parnell's fall and the failure of Gladstone's second Home Rule bill in 1893, was still intertwined with the education question, O'Connor grew indignant at reports that Liberals were telling the Irish they would lose Home Rule permanently by supporting this bill. He asked, 'Were Irishmen to sacrifice their most profound religious convictions to serve the political interests of their country?'[84] Obviously, they would not. It was no accident that O'Connor's speech in the Commons coincided with the release to the press of what had become the hierarchy's annual proclamation on education. Another signed letter from all of the Catholic bishops declared that any attempt to create two judicial systems, one for the rich and one for the poor, would certainly be met with popular resistance; thus, they questioned how the government could justify an educational system that created similar inequalities.[85] John Dillon spoke frequently on behalf of the interests of Catholic schools during the subsequent parliamentary debates on the bill. He expressed his concern about the proposal to form voluntary school associations because he did not want Catholic schools in any formal association with Anglican schools; he pressed for a separate Catholic association, as well as discretion on the part of the Education Department to provide the necessary aid to those voluntary schools that needed it the most, rather than simply being forced to give it to all whether they needed it or not.[86]

In the end, the Voluntary Schools Act passed, but only with the promise to nonconformists that a similar bill would be passed later in the year to help needy board schools.[87] The new Act finally addressed some the Catholics' biggest complaints about the educational system. It repealed the onerous 17*s.* 6*d.* limit on grant aid, exempted schools from paying rates, ended Robert Lowe's system of payment by results and increased the grant to denominational schools. Denominationalist cooperation was evident, at least in the north, as Anglicans, Catholics and Wesleyans supported the bill. A flyer distributed by supporters of the bill in Bolton called the attention of ratepayers to the pure injustice of the system since 1870. Line by line, it compared how much funding the board schools had received historically from rates compared to how much the voluntary schools had received. When board schools were revealed as having received five, six and seven hundred pounds versus absolutely nothing for their denominational counterparts, the point was rather compelling, especially when there were over 2,000 more children on the voluntary rolls.[88]

Although Vaughan approved of the bill, he only saw the measure as a stopgap. His journal entries reflected a man still angered and frustrated by the inequality of the system, despite the recent legislative victory. He wrote:

> We must get down to the bedrock of principle if we hope for an enduring settlement. Short of that ... acknowledgment that equal work deserves an equal wage ... every new concession must be accepted merely as a new vantage-ground for fresh agitation ... A free education has been declared by Parliament to be the birthright of every English child, and yet the managers of our Catholic ... schools are driven with one hand to snatch at the hard earnings of the poor and with the other to hire the antics of some friendly acrobat as an excuse for taking shillings at a bazaar or charity tea.[89]

Despite the provisions contained in this bill, the archbishop continued working with Anglicans to reach the settlement that would please all of them, a share of the rates. By early summer, he was hopeful of continuing progress after having met with several Church of England bishops who assured him that the tide was turning in their favour among the Anglicans. Frequent meetings at Archbishop's House with key political members of the Irish party and prominent English Catholic politicians like Edward Talbot and the Duke of Norfolk were commonplace through the remainder of 1897. In a letter to Lady Herbert, Vaughan humorously mused at how the education question had destroyed what were once considered insurmountable barriers between the staunchest English Catholic aristocrats and the most radical Irish politicians: 'Meetings are taking place two or three times a week at this house – the Duke [Norfolk] sitting beside anti-Parnellites and Parnellites'.[90] Such remarkable harmony would not last indefinitely but was indicative of education's power to transcend some of the deepest crevices in the Catholic community, if only for a few years.

The following year was quiet on the education front compared with 1896 and 1897. Catholics diligently formed additional voluntary school associations to comply with the new education Act and looked ahead to when that down payment would be replaced by payment in full. Events in 1899 once again brought distress to Catholic circles. And it would not be until the passage of the Balfour Act in 1902 that the English Catholic conscience could again be at ease on the matter of education.

What brought matters to a head in 1899 was a critical letter received by the Catholic School Committee from G. W. Kekewich of the Education Department. Kekewich informed the committee that Catholic contributions had decreased significantly in the year since the Voluntary Schools Act became law. The decrease amounted to over £14,000 or approximately 16 per cent. Kekewich pointed out that the Act had been passed to enable schools to maintain or increase their efficiency but not to provide a reason for school supporters to reduce or discontinue their contributions. Then, in a statement that showed how far the original intent of the Education Act of 1870 had been misapplied, even by the government, Kekewich reminded them that Parliament had already provided sufficient free schools (read: board schools) and that if parents wanted their children to attend a 'religious' school, they would have to pay extra for that privilege.[91] In contrast to this nascent view, Vaughan believed that wanting your child to attend a school of your choice was not only consistent with natural law but was a right, not a privilege, guaranteed to every parent by the government's programme of compulsory and free education. This was exactly the absurd situation that he had described in 1896:

> The State condemns Catholics, either to accept a gratuitous education which they disapprove or to pay a penal contribution for an education which they approve. In the first case, the State directly violates liberty of conscience; in the second, it respects liberty of conscience in consideration of a cash payment, but violates its own boast of gratuitous education.[92]

Again, the difference of opinion came down to an understanding of what the Education Act of 1870 was designed to do. Catholics and other denominationalists viewed the situation through a Burkean lens, obligating them to uphold the original intent of Forster that the board schools were only to 'fill up the gaps' of a system in which the voluntary schools remained the standard. Most nonconformists and secularists, however, saw that Act as a break with the past which introduced a new kind of government-aided school as the standard, thereby relegating the voluntary schools to a subordinate position. This was despite the fact that denominationalist schools remained in the majority with nearly one million more students than board schools through the turn of the century.

The Catholic School Committee's reply to Kekewich provides a glimpse of how far the Catholic community had come since 1850 when they were still cowed and intimidated by anti-Catholicism and state authority. First, they challenged the Education Department's figures. They explained how rents that had been charged to the school managers prior to 1897 had always been listed as voluntary subscriptions as a way to reach the 17*s.* 6*d.* limit. Now that the limit was abolished, they had discontinued this practice. Further, they explained how the constant creation of new schools and division of parishes would necessarily show up on the books as a decline in subscriptions for the old schools. And they attributed the very high levels of contributions in the years just prior to 1897 to 'exceptional strain and effort', whereas comparisons to figures from 1893 were more in line with those of 1898.[93] Then the committee boldly used the actual words of government ministers from the debate in 1897 against the Education Department's stance in 1899. Both A. J. Balfour and the Duke of Devonshire had argued in the earlier debate that voluntary school subscribers might deserve some relief from the increased grant aid in the poorer districts. Using those statements as their basis of argument, the committee refused to agree with the Education Department's implied threat that subscription levels had to be maintained in order to receive the extra grant aid.[94] They pointed out that such a stipulation for receiving the extra grant aid had been excluded from the bill after much debate, and, thus: 'It is not easy to see on what grounds the 17s. 6d. limit was abolished if its principle is still to remain in force'. Concluding their reply, the Catholic School Committee repeated their criticism of required governmental 'improvements' that constantly added to the cost of running a school but were difficult to realize with 'limited and inelastic resources', and again they urged Parliament to enquire into a final equitable solution. Or else, the letter admonished, certain 'unusual and extra legal methods of protest' might occur which they themselves disapproved of, but also could not control.[95] Perhaps both sides could play this game of implied threats. This letter, most likely written with the consent of Vaughan, exhibited a wealth of confidence, self-assuredness and even reciprocal militancy with its veiled threat and revealed a community that was not going to back down on an issue that had become their *raison d'être*. Their certainty that an equitable solution had not yet been reached only fuelled their confidence that at the next educational showdown they and their more numerous denominationalist allies might have enough force to prevail.

Just prior to the general election in 1900, the hierarchy re-released a set of resolutions on education originally sent to the Salisbury ministry in November 1899, an action with clear political intent, especially since they also sent a copy to *The Times*.[96] Its revised preface stated: 'Let it not be said, if the Education Question should come up for final settlement, in the course of the next Parliament, that the Catholic Electorate gave no sign to their representatives of their wish upon this subject'. The Catholic hierarchy was informing lawmakers and the next ministry that the Catholic community would settle for no less than a 'broad national system, based on lines of justice and equity for all'.[97] Vaughan instructed the clergy to inform Catholic voters of the details of the resolutions, and to remind those voters to consider the Conservatives' past openness towards denominational education. Meanwhile, with the hierarchy's blessing, the *Tablet* threw its support behind the Conservatives in the election. Notably, in his letter that prefaced the re-release of those resolutions, Vaughan thanked the Irish MPs who had supported the education cause so vigorously in recent years, while, simultaneously, he asked for help to ensure the victory of the Conservatives. He acknowledged obligingly that English Catholics were 'bound up with the children of St Patrick by many ties of blood and sympathy' and that the Irish university question must be pressed upon the parliamentary candidates along with that of the education question in England.[98] He hoped this balanced statement would quell the nationalist vigour of the Home Rulers, who had let Home Rule sit on the shelf for close to seven years. However, with the reunion of the Irish Parliamentary Party under the leadership of John Redmond in 1900 and its rekindled nationalist goals, the Irish were bound to split once more between Home Rule and the education issue.[99] Still, the election returned the Conservatives and a pleased Vaughan planned to continue working towards their goal. More importantly, he had made the praiseworthy effort to assuage Irish opinion, as Manning had done in 1886, to ensure Irish political support in any future education legislation.

The Big Push

The struggle for education reached its climax and, according to Vaughan, a fair resolution in 1902 when Parliament passed A. J. Balfour's Education Bill. This mammoth legislation dominated the parliamentary agenda from March to December, the longest continuous period of debate on one bill in Parliament's history to date. From Archbishop's House in Westminster to Parliament to the dioceses and local parishes, the Catholic community initiated its most unified and well-organized effort on education to that point. Not only did the debate reflect the climax of the century-long educational controversy, it also reflected the culmination of fifty-five years of Catholic struggle with and within the state education system. From arguing over whether or not even to enter the state system, half a century had unified the English Catholics towards their goal of an equal system that did not penalize their right of religious conscience. This more than any other issue enabled their maturation from a reclusive and rather passive community to a conspicuous, self-confident and, when appropriate, tenaciously aggressive community committed to obtaining equal treatment under the law.

As they had done in previous years when educational legislation was expected, the hierarchy publicly issued its revised list of resolutions on education. Released in November 1901, the resolutions primarily touched upon the subject of the rumoured county councils or LEAs that would replace the school boards. First and foremost, the bishops asked that a guarantee be secured to allow at least one representative from each school association to sit on the county councils. This was offered as a way to help prevent the county councils from favouring the board schools. Next, the bishops asked for the right to open schools wherever they deemed them necessary. Foreshadowing one of the more contentious issues to be debated in 1902, the bishops also demanded that school managers retain the right to hire and dismiss teachers. Finally, as they had stated consistently for close to a decade, the bishops declared that they would willingly concede to public oversight of their schools on matters unrelated to religious teaching.[100]

Reminiscent of the Cross Commission's majority report in 1888, Prime Minister Balfour's bill, introduced on 24 March 1902, intended to replace the myriad school boards with county and borough councils that would oversee both denominational and nondenominational schools and would have the choice whether to extend rate-aid to the denominational schools if they desired. In return for rate-aid, Balfour intended for the denominational schools to allow the councils to oversee their secular instruction and appoint two of the six managers.

A confidential itinerary of a general meeting of the Catholic School Committee in April hinted that perhaps that organization was not quite prepared for the fight this bill would bring. Out of several agenda items planned for that meeting, only one mentioned the bill, now headed towards its second reading in May. The committee planned to 'urge on the Government the importance of dealing with the question of further aid for Voluntary Schools in the present Session of Parliament'.[101] Strangely, this revealed no sense of urgency, especially since it was the seventh item on the agenda, and the wording was indistinguishable from any number of resolutions and declarations made over the past decade; in fact, it presented a much weaker argument than some of the petitions that had been sent to Whitehall since Vaughan became archbishop.

The reason for this lack of urgency on the part of the Catholic School Committee is unclear, unless, perhaps, it knew beforehand that the Catholic representatives in Parliament planned to pursue assiduously a settlement acceptable to Catholics. Since Vaughan was the grand architect of the Catholic strategy and he oversaw the operations of the Catholic School Committee, it is feasible to believe that they were informed of the coming Irish Catholic parliamentary push. Also, the lack of urgency could have meant that the committee was waiting to meet with the bishops to develop a cohesive and organized plan in response to the existing bill. That meeting followed on 9 May at Vaughan's residence. Two days later, the day of the second reading, the hierarchy released a list of their comments on and objections to the bill as it stood. No doubt, the publication was spirited down to Whitehall in time for that day's debate. It was clear that the Catholic push was under way, and this was this first united declaration on the controversial bill's proposals.

On several items, this declaration of 11 May represented the Catholic line in the sand. They did not consent to the proposal to allow the LEAs to nominate more than a third of the managers, nor did they approve of the plan to set apart the ongoing costs of 'ordinary repairs' and 'structural improvements' from what had hitherto been called normal maintenance and put that responsibility solely on the school trustees. They demanded that the optional clause, which allowed councils to choose whether or not to provide rate-aid to voluntary schools, be stricken from the bill. They repeated the familiar demand that no school be deemed unnecessary if it complied with governmental requirements. Also, they insisted that any appeal from a dismissed teacher should go to the Education Department and not the LEAs; if a teacher was dismissed for religious reasons, then 'the religious tenets or requirements of the Denomination to which the school belongs be held as sufficient ground for dismissal'. Vaughan, as signatory to the declaration, also divulged the creation of a 'Watching Committee' which remained in constant communication with him and met as often as necessary to monitor the movement of the bill in Parliament. Finally, Vaughan told his bishops and members of the Catholic School Committee that they should be prepared to meet immediately if events necessitated doing so.[102]

While London acted as a focal point for various Catholic meetings, the evidence reveals that the other dioceses were again energized and active. Father Glancey addressed the Birmingham School Board and urged the approval of the main principles of the bill, with a few exceptions such as asking for the withdrawal of the option clauses. In response to nonconformist grumblings that they would refuse to pay the rates if voluntary schools were allowed to receive them, Glancey defiantly stated: 'I would remind them that there is no possible argument by which they justify refusing to pay rates, that would not have justified us Catholics in refusing to pay rates to the board schools' since 1870.[103] Bishop Bilsborrow presided over a large meeting at the Free Trade Hall in Manchester on 7 May, the intended purpose of which was to 'safeguard the interests of Catholic Schools'. Three resolutions that would be sent to Parliament were discussed at the meeting. First, these northern Catholics commended the bill in general as being a positive step. On the motion of Dean Patrick Lynch, now Rector of St Wilfrid's, Manchester, the second resolution asked the government to strike out the 'optional clause', as well as to allow managers to continue to select textbooks. The third resolution insisted that the government amend the wording in the maintenance part of the bill so as not to add the additional burden of repairs and improvements to the voluntary schools.[104] In Wales, Bishop Hedley expressed his approval of the idea that all schools would receive funding from the rates for the high cost of maintenance, but warned his clergy that they must remain vigilant in insisting that they keep control over two-thirds of the management positions and over the hiring of teachers. He also encouraged the clergy to rouse the laity into more action to help the overburdened priests.[105]

Just over two weeks after the second reading of Balfour's bill, the leaders of the many Catholic Voluntary Schools Associations met at the Westminster Palace Hotel on 27 May with the Duke of Norfolk presiding. They passed their own set of three resolutions. Their intent had grassroots implications as they declared that all of the Catholic Voluntary Schools Associations should meet immediately in their respective districts to prepare to contact Parliament on behalf of Catholic educational interests. A full-scale lobbying process had begun. The resolutions also noted that a special committee of the bishops had met on 16 May, five days after the second reading, and urged that Parliament should do its utmost to keep clauses 9 and 10 in the bill.[106]

Autumn of that year saw prominent Lancashire Catholics such as Bilsborrow and Lynch use the regional press to publicize their views on the education bill, much as Vaughan had done for almost a decade in the London press. Lynch wrote several letters to the editor of the *Manchester Guardian* to clarify the local clerical perspective on the bill. He stated that it was the management clause that most frightened them, and in reference to the possibility of local management he stubbornly claimed that Catholics would never consent to school management hostile to their religious conscience. When attacked in the press by a nonconformist who vowed not to pay for 'alien' doctrines like Catholicism, Lynch replied angrily. He explained that denominationalists would be handing over their schools to the LEAs free of charge, for, if they closed them down, then the local council would be extremely burdened with the cost of building several new schools. 'That is the price we pay for the teaching of our distinctive creeds', he added defensively, and that more than paid for their right to have 'our religious teaching in our schools'.[107] Bishop Bilsborrow articulated his views in four lengthy letters to the editor in late October in the same paper. He reiterated the Catholic devotion to the principle of parental rights, questioned why nonconformists had not built schools where they were needed as Catholics had – a problem he argued was to blame for the introduction of the Forster bill in the first place, undercut nonconformist arguments for not supporting 'Rome on the rates' and justified why only Catholic teachers would suffice in Catholic schools.[108]

With the passage of these resolutions for the attention of Parliament and there being so many efforts in the press to inform and persuade, it is necessary to examine how the Catholic MPs reacted to the bill. Both the Irish hierarchy and Cardinal Vaughan pressured the Irish MPs to support the right of denominational schools to receive a share of the rates.[109] On the day of the bill's first reading, T. P. O'Connor presented the Catholic position. He used the plight of his constituents in Liverpool as an illustrative example. The poor dock workers, he said, paid out of their minimal earnings a tax to support their Protestant brethren's schools and a tax to support their own denomination's schools. He expressed his gratitude to Balfour that the bill attempted to ameliorate the 'gross and unfair inequality' of this system, and he told the house that his fellow Irish Catholic MPs would do their utmost to preserve equality for all schools and not harm any other schools in the process.[110] John Dillon brought his oratorical mastery to the subject in the midst of the debate prior to the second reading. He proved to be the most determined Catholic representative during the entire debate. Dillon reiterated the fundamental Catholic beliefs in dogmatic and catechismal teaching, the primacy of religious and moral training and the formation of character over the 'acquisition of learning'. He playfully taunted his nonconformist friends on the subject of religious teaching by stating that 'nothing is dogma in which they believe, but that everything is dogma in which we believe and they do not'. He stated that these determined nonconformists went around believing that 'orthodoxy is our doxy, while heterodoxy is every other person's doxy', while missing the point that both voluntary and board schools taught religious formularies that could be interpreted as dogmatic. In the end, he gave his support to the bill because it recognized the right of parental choice in education and allowed denominational schools to be built where they were desired.[111]

It must be remarked that these Irish MPs held fast to the united Catholic front, even when under extreme political pressure from the likes of David Lloyd George, who tried to drive a wedge between them and the English hierarchy.[112] Dillon strenuously opposed an amendment that would have only abolished school boards in small counties and boroughs but not in large urban areas because he believed it would have penalized the urban voluntary schools, many of which were Catholic. This stance aligned him and the Catholics with the Tory prime minister, now Balfour upon Salisbury's resignation in July. Later, Dillon even challenged Balfour over some of his concessions, which the Irishman believed would be harmful to Catholics, such as the establishment of lay control over religious teaching.[113] Dillon even went so far in pursuit of a solution favourable to Catholics which would also not harm any other denomination that he drew the criticism of the *Tablet* for one of his amendments. He had been angered by a proposal to deny nonconformists in small rural areas a stake in the management and teaching of the schools and he proposed what he considered a fair solution. Yet, he still advocated the hierarchy's position when he demanded that the majority of a voluntary school's managers be from its denomination.[114] Dillon's efforts even attracted the ire of one of his fellow Irish MPs, the renowned anti-clerical Home Ruler, Michael Davitt, who condemned Dillon for helping Vaughan in the education battle that summer.[115]

Other Catholic MPs such as Colonel Nolan of Galway and Jasper Tully of Leitrim entered the debate in October when the controversial Kenyon–Slaney amendment, which made all of the school's managers, not just the priests, responsible for religious education, was under consideration. Angering both high-church Anglicans and Catholics, the amendment passed and was viewed as a sop to the nonconformists in that it was proposed to help restrict the progress of ritualism, the nineteenth-century movement to revive more Catholic liturgical practices in the Church of England.[116] Colonel Nolan protested to little avail that this amendment would harm Catholic schools since it might mean that Protestant managers could influence and ultimately control the religious teaching in their schools. Although the denominational managers of each school (four of six) were to be in the majority for the time being, Nolan asked 'what was to prevent a future Liberal Government from reversing the position?' If that happened, he argued, then Catholics would be forced to forsake the grants altogether.[117] Tully echoed Nolan's fears, adding that this amendment would 'be the thin edge of the wedge by which Roman Catholics sooner or later might have their schools confiscated'.[118]

Vaughan closely monitored the evolution of the bill as it passed through the Commons and into committee stage. When the Kenyon–Slaney amendment was under consideration, Vaughan wrote to his bishops to ensure their unity in protest against the 'one-third having any voice at all in religious matters' but to maintain their support of the bill without that addition.[119] Much like Manning before him, Vaughan visited Commons frequently to check on the bill's progress and lobby sympathetic ears. In order to keep up with the intricacies of the bill, he and a select subcommittee from the Catholic School Committee met each week to examine the different clauses being presented and debated. Vaughan even contacted John Redmond, the leader of the newly reunited Irish Parliamentary Party, in an effort to make sure the Irish remained steadfast in their support of the bill without the Kenyon–Slaney amendment. 'We are convinced that we are not likely ever to get a more satisfactory settlement of the education problem', he wrote to the Irish leader.[120] This gesture from a man whose reputation was against Home Rule and who was often labelled as anti-Irish revealed just how important the passage of this bill was to him and the hierarchy and how he would attempt what was necessary politically to achieve that goal.

Vaughan also resumed the public information strategy he had adopted from 1895 to 1897 by publishing his and the hierarchy's positions in letters to the editor. When amendments were proposed, Vaughan went on the attack in the press. He decried such recommendations as the Kenyon–Slaney amendment and openly suggested that it was 'better [to] remain as we are, poor but free, than put our heads into such a noose'.[121] This fear was echoed by the Arthur Hinsley, headmaster of St Bede's Grammar School near Bradford and future Archbishop of Westminster and cardinal, when he gave a paper at a meeting of the Catholic Truth Society in Newport in September. Referring to the amendment, Hinsley noted that Catholics needed to be careful that opponents of the bill, namely nonconformists, did not capture and make it their own with such damaging amendments, like the nonconformist opponents did to the Education Act of 1870.[122] When a proposal to reduce the weekly classroom time allowed for religion (from five days to two days) was floated in the debates Vaughan thundered against this 'revolutionary and destructive measure'. Catholics would simply reject and ignore it, he argued.[123] That same day he wrote to Lady Herbert that the recent debates on the education bill had been most vexatious to him, but he was confident Catholic politicians would safeguard the school management clauses.[124]

In the House of Lords, Henry Matthews, Viscount Llandaff and former home secretary for Salisbury, attacked the Kenyon–Slaney amendment because it undermined the Catholic view of education by allowing all six managers a stake in the religious education of the children. These managers, Llandaff noted, would also be responsible for repair of the schools and to that point he added with sarcasm, 'Imagine the zeal with which these two foreign managers will go about collecting subscriptions to repair the schools in which doctrines are taught which they abhor'. He also worried about whether any Catholics at all would ever sit on an LEA without some amendment to guarantee a Catholic voice in their important educational work.[125] A week later, no such amendment had yet been proposed, so Llandaff proposed one himself, explaining it as a way 'to save these schools from being wholly unrepresented on a committee which is to deal with a variety of subjects which touch their pockets and affect in the strongest way the whole of the educational prosperity of the school'. The Duke of Devonshire, who was directing the bill through the Lords, told Llandaff flatly that his amendment would not be accepted but, because of Llandaff's persuasive argument, he inserted into the bill wording that would make it easier for Catholics to have their minority voice heard.[126] The Kenyon–Slaney amendment brought the Duke of Norfolk into the debate, as well. He questioned the sanity of saving denominational schools out of concern for respecting the religious conscience of the parents, but at the same time including an amendment that would give a committee of managers, two of whom might not be of that religion, control over that religious education.[127] Despite the strenuous opposition to this feature of the bill from denominationalists, the amendment remained and the Balfour bill finally passed into law in mid-December after an arduous nine-month debate.

In general, Catholics were pleased. Patrick Lynch, writing in the *Dublin Review*, argued that 'the most striking quality of the new Act is its justice'. In addition to support from the rates, the new Education Act gave Catholics an equal opportunity to share maintenance funds, precisely what the bishops had wanted. Even though Catholics accepted certain restrictions, Lynch was pleased to write that: 'Our Catholic schools will continue to be Catholic. They will continue to be Catholic property; and the Catholic religion will be taught in them by Catholic priests and Catholic teachers as it was before'. Despite the measure's shortcomings, one of which would mean that Catholics would still have to raise money for mortgages, for example, Lynch concluded by stating 'the Education Act of 1902 is a great Act'.[128] The archbishop concurred with Lynch's assessment. He believed this was the best compromise Catholics would receive. Even with all building and repair costs, plus debt service, still a burden after the Act, the precedent for fairness had been set by allowing access to the rates for all. This goal had fuelled Vaughan's decade-long campaign. As he reported to the Holy See,

> the general effect of the new law is to make Christian and Catholic education a part of the law and constitution of England. In principle, we have made a large and important advance – which the dissenters and radicals will continue to attack.[129]

Vaughan's final letter to *The Times* on the subject captured not only his opinion on the Act but also perhaps his final resignation to a more compromised conclusion. Whereas for close to a decade, Vaughan had argued for the necessity of one national system of education for all schools, he now realized, after the long, protracted struggle of 1902, that a single system with equal rules for all was not a possibility. The year's education struggle had taken its toll on his health and one can read the overwhelming fatigue in his last sentence: 'Let us agree to live and let live, for we shall never come to agree in one system of education till we all come to agree in one faith'.[130] The battle over and the compromised goal achieved, the archbishop died six months later.

Conclusion

It is clear that Catholic political effort on behalf of their schools did not wane after the death of Cardinal Manning; it actually increased. This is not to say that Manning was an obstacle to Catholic efforts, but that the political conditions were better in the 1890s for a resolution that pleased Catholics. There is no question that Irish MPs were much more helpful and vociferous in the educational debates from 1891 to 1902, no doubt because of the split in the Irish party between the Parnellites and the anti-Parnellites and the second failure of Home Rule in 1893, which shelved Home Rule for the remainder of the decade. They agreed to support the educational position of the bishops in Parliament, not necessarily because they were in full agreement with the English bishops – in fact they often disagreed on other subjects such as Home Rule – but because elementary education in England and Wales was an Irish issue, too. It should be noted that many of these Irish MPs actually lived in England for much of the year and some held jobs there; hence, they were close to the subject of educating the Catholic poor even if they represented persons from Irish constituencies.[131] Additionally, they hoped that when Home Rule gained enough momentum to again surface in Parliament that they could expect better support from the Catholic hierarchy in return. Home Rule compromised the education effort in the 1880s and early 1890s; after Gladstone's second Home Rule bill failed in 1893, however, the path was clear to pursue a Catholic educational agenda until 1902 without the Irish question hindering its progress. That enabled Vaughan to be more successful than he otherwise would have been despite his coolness towards Home Rule.

Another factor that affected the political climate was the conservative ascendancy that began in 1886 and then solidified in 1895. Given that Catholic educationists had drifted towards the Conservatives since the 1870s because of the Tory position on education, having a Conservative ministry was to their advantage. This was so despite the fact that it has been shown that Catholics were taken for granted by the Conservative party, which often spouted anti-Catholic rhetoric in order to hold its Unionist base and did not have to rely upon Catholic votes to survive. Despite their loyalty to the Conservative ministry, Catholics received very few concessions from the party they had drifted towards due to the Conservative wish to hold the Unionist coalition.[132] Yet, Cardinal Vaughan was no doubt an English Tory, and this would have made his reception and opinions easier to accept by the prime minister. He wrote to Salisbury frequently on the question of the voluntary schools, beginning when Vaughan was still Bishop of Salford and continuing through to 1902, when Salisbury resigned due to ill health. Also, Salisbury made a distinction between the Catholics he condemned regularly, the troublesome Irish, and those Catholics who supported his ministry, mainly hereditary English Catholics such as Vaughan and the Duke of Norfolk. Given these factors it can be surmised that their shared political sensibilities enabled the Catholic case for education to receive a better hearing than it would have had under a Liberal administration, which would have spent much political capital appeasing its radical, secularist wing. Finally, the effect of the Boer War on the electorate cannot be discounted either. The election of 1900, held when the war turned decidedly in favour of Great Britain, returned a large Conservative majority with 60 per cent of the seats, largely due to the party's war policy and success. Even Cardinal Vaughan believed that no other government could have passed such an education bill.[133]

Both locally and nationally, the Catholic community overcame its natural class and ethnic divisions to come together in support of education, if only for that issue. The years from 1880 to 1902 saw Catholic political efforts emanating from both the local and national level with varying degrees of success and revealed growing confidence and at times noticeable militancy. In the actions of Manning and Vaughan and other members of the hierarchy, a far-reaching, proactive solution was pursued by clearly establishing the basic principles of the Catholic philosophy of education, making that philosophy known to all concerned Catholics and working to have that philosophy accepted and respected in government policy.

8 CATHOLIC EDUCATION AND IDENTITY AFTER THE BALFOUR ACT: THE BATTLE ENDS BUT THE FIGHT CONTINUES

The Roman Catholic elementary school system in England and Wales after the 1902 Balfour Act was markedly different from that which first accepted state financial assistance over a half a century before. The same can be said about the Catholic community. The pursuit of a fair resolution to the education difficulty grew into an obsession that dominated the Catholic agenda for half a century. Certainly, Catholic leaders recognized other problems that required attention and effort to improve the lives of the faithful in England and Wales. Clerical and lay leaders worked persistently to better housing and working conditions, combat public drunkenness, improve Catholic devotional life and fight leakage from the faith. But the struggle for the schools brought more Catholics together on the same subject and facilitated more action than any other effort. A subject that consistently dominated the Church's policy over so many decades and under the guidance of so many leaders during an era that often witnessed rancorous fights about its implementation and tested sectarian resolve was bound to become part of that community's lifeblood, something by which that community was immediately identified. Victorians knew that Catholics took education seriously; the proof, as this study has shown, existed in the multitude of petitions, speeches, sermons, editorials, meetings and reports generated by a motivated religious community committed to the educational well-being of its children. The proof existed in the archbishops visiting the House of Commons during important votes on educational matters or in state authorities offering to cut side deals with the Catholics, not because they feared the result of angering the Catholic populace but because they respected Catholic dedication and resilience on the subject and what the Church was trying to do with very limited means. The proof was also in what the Church did accomplish with those limited means, a feat that neither Anglicans nor Wesleyans nor even secularists could ignore or match.

When the Committee of Council on Education informed the Catholic Poor School Committee in December 1847 that Catholic schools could begin receiving state grants, the Catholic elementary school system was meagre at best. There existed 236 Catholic schools spread across England and Wales, 143 of those coming from the three Church districts that included London (London District), Birmingham (Central District), and Liverpool and Manchester (Lancashire District). The number of schools reflected as a percentage of the number of Catholic churches/chapels was 44 per cent (236 of 532).[1] Fifty-five years later, the sixteen Catholic dioceses together boasted a total of 1,056 elementary schools, the diocese of Salford supporting 260 alone.[2] This represents a 347 per cent increase in the number of Catholic elementary schools from 1847 to 1902. Incidentally, this figure mirrors almost exactly the percentage increase in the number of Catholic priests during that same period; there were 697 priests in England and Wales in 1847 and 3,073 in 1902, a percentage increase of 341 per cent.[3] The correlation between the two should be no surprise. As the Catholic population increased, the need for priests and elementary schools increased in like manner. However, the number of schools reflected as a percentage of the number of Catholic churches/chapels in 1902 had risen to 67 per cent (1,056 of 1,568), 23 per cent above the percentage in 1847.[4] This figure indicates that the opening of schools outpaced that of churches and reflects the hierarchy's priority of school buildings over churches near the beginning of this study at the 1852 Westminster Synod, as well as the need to keep classroom numbers manageable.

A different measurement of Catholic success in the struggle for the schools is indicated in school attendance figures. The best figures for average attendance in Catholic schools at the beginning of this study are recorded as those who are 'receiving education'; in 1846, 30,207 Catholic children received elementary education.[5] When the Education Act of 1870 passed, according to the figures John T. Smith has provided there were 71,666 students in average attendance at Catholic schools. That number rose dramatically to 269,191 students by 1902.[6] If we compare the figures from 1870 to 1898, then the number of children in average attendance at Catholic schools rose 241 per cent; this compares quite favourably with their fellow voluntary school supporters as the Anglicans increased their number of children in average attendance from 882,432 to 1,880,124, or 113 per cent, while the Wesleyans only saw an increase in average attendance of 6 per cent.[7]

For a more regional analysis, the figures from the Westminster diocese support the national trend. Average Catholic elementary school attendance increased from 8,648 in the academic year 1857–8 to 29,957 during the year 1902–3, a rise of 246 per cent.[8] In the diocese of Salford, educational statistics reveal an increase of 141 per cent in average attendance and 75 per cent increase in number of Catholic children on the rolls of Catholic elementary schools between the yeas of 1873 and 1903.[9] All of these increases dwarf any other religious community and are only superseded by the explosive growth of the board school system, which saw its average attendance rise astronomically from 6,472 in 1870 to 2,072,911 in 1898. It is no wonder that the Catholics saw the future of their schools jeopardized when the non-sectarian and increasingly secularized board school system grew so rapidly. Yet its exponential growth can be viewed as a constant reminder to Catholics that, despite their successes, they could not rest on their laurels; they needed to continue to meet the challenge of the board school system head on, which they did, as their resources would allow. Such expansion did not come cheap. According to a note in the Westminster Diocesan Archives from 1896, the hierarchy calculated that Catholic school expansion had cost the community £1,850,000 since 1870.[10] Vaughan even decided at the beginning of the educational battle of 1902 not to publicize the Church's capital debt on its schools, which stood at £700,000, for fear that it might 'cause anxiety and misunderstanding'. He also indicated that yet another crisis fund would be necessary once the ramifications of the Education Act became apparent.[11]

Thus, a transformation of the Catholic community had occurred in the last half of the nineteenth century, and the struggle for education represented the primary factor in that change. Measuring changes in the identity of a community is a slippery task that must rely upon documented changes in behaviour and rhetoric as evidence. In the case of the Roman Catholics, we have seen how their language on education grew more confident and militant as the half-century progressed, especially after the ramifications of the 1870 Act became manifest. It has also been shown that activities ranging from small meetings with the other bishops to extra-parliamentary, large-scale rallies with hundreds of lay Catholic attendees not only increased when education was the topic *du jour* such as in 1870 and 1891, but also began occurring even when there was no specific legislation being debated at all, as in 1882. Hence, the subtle transformation from reactive to proactive becomes apparent.

A meeting in Salford to celebrate the creation of the Voluntary School Association in 1884 reflects a striking increase in determination on the part of Roman Catholicism to settle the education question. Aggressive and insistent rhetoric, tenacious confidence, political designs, a mixture of clerical and lay voices – all of these are evident in the speeches from this meeting. Bishop Vaughan mocked those proud leaders of Manchester, the 'home of free trade', for not applying the same economic standard to education. It was protectionism of the highest degree, he cried, that taxed denominational schools exorbitantly while providing unlimited funds to the board schools. John Kershaw and Charles O'Neill both moved resolutions intended to stir up Catholic protests as political pressure. Realizing the futility of achieving any helpful changes under the current Liberal administration, O'Neill hoped for better circumstances after the next general election when a party could be increased which could more closely pursue the goals of Catholics with the backing of the Irish Church hierarchy and who, if 'old antipathies and old objections' could be removed, could work to 'remove the injustices of which Catholics were now complaining'. Obviously, O'Neill meant the Home Rule party. Following O'Neill's fiery oratory, Rev. J. Burke read a petition that was to be sent to Parliament, which asked for redress of their grievances, and then expressed his hope that the 'voice of the eloquent sons of Catholic Ireland would ring through the Houses of Parliament' and tell the law-makers that Catholics would 'never be content with any system that violates the principles of religious liberty and interferes injuriously with the religious and Catholic training of children'.[12]

Subsequently, after two correspondents wrote to the editor of the *Manchester Guardian* to complain about Catholic requests, a very public and increasingly belligerent five-week exchange occurred between Father Kershaw and Dr John Watts, a prominent local Protestant. 'We want freedom and fair play, and we refuse without a struggle to be ground down in the State mill into the uniformity of an invertebrate Christianity', Kershaw railed towards his adversary. Later, after Watts wrote that the main reason Catholic educational demands could not be recognized in this matter was because they taught a 'dangerous error', Kershaw exploded:

> Who has got a right to make this assertion? Are we not all – Catholics, Protestants, Jews, and Secularists – equal in the eyes of the law? Do we not bear the burthens of the State? Are we not bound to treat all alike, and do we not all expect equal justice?'[13]

This was the voice of the Catholic educationist in the latter part of the century. It was tenacious in the face of entrenched opposition. It was self-righteously angry, militant and adamant about its virtue. It stressed the legacy of equality and liberty and civil rights. And it showed no signs of the reclusive legacy of English Catholicism from the penal era that had blanketed Britain's eighteenth and early nineteenth centuries. This education battle had transformed the Catholic community.

Catholic unity on this subject was much more elusive. Whereas A. C. F. Beales argued over half a century ago that Catholics stood united on the education front from the beginning of the struggle, this book makes a different claim.[14] As long as Bishop Ullathorne lived, there existed some disagreement even among the bishops, as he accepted but distrusted government assistance after Catholics entered the system, until his death.[15] Yet in the thirty-second year of his episcopacy in Birmingham, this critic and sceptic could still produce a powerful and indignant Advent pastoral attacking the board school system as the second coming of the Reformation because both threats to Catholicism were imposed upon them without their consent and calling for Catholics never to rest until fairness was achieved in what he later called 'the cause of God'.[16]

There was pronounced disagreement on various issues between Inspector Thomas W. Marshall and Secretary Thomas W. Allies, two leading Catholic educationists, which surfaced during the Newcastle Commission hearings.[17] As late as 1891, bishops were pleading for unity among the clergy and Catholic laymen, and Catholic letters to the editor of the *Tablet* were bemoaning the failure of Catholic organizational skills consistently to ensure the election of Catholics onto school boards.[18] Even in 1902, the year that revealed their most unified educational effort hitherto, we find differences of opinion between the head Catholic spokesman in Parliament, John Dillon, and the hierarchy over the issue of giving up the cumulative vote.[19] Obviously, absolute Catholic unity was chimerical, an idealistic mirage that never fully materialized.

Yet, despite this evidence in the midst of the debate over the Balfour Act, it was clear that, although they were disagreeing with one another on educational matters, they were still fighting the same battle. Deciding whether or not to accept government grants for primary schools in the 1850s was a much more serious disagreement than haggling over the finer details of a bill that would finally grant rate-aid to the Catholics in 1902. The crevasses that had existed so painfully in Catholic society at mid-century were at least now traversable. Further, Irish Catholic MPs assisted English Catholic bishops attain an educational solution primarily intended for resident Catholics of Irish descent. And they cooperated with old English Catholic aristocrats and middle-class Catholics to do so. The extensive lay and clerical efforts of the 1880s and 1890s were certainly an improvement over the sporadic, hierarchy-led efforts of ten and twenty years before. By the final two decades of the century, it was clear that the message so eloquently and persistently presented by Wiseman, Manning, Vaughan, Turner, Cornthwaite, Goss, Bagshawe and others had pervaded Catholic society. Hundreds of petitions signed by Catholics from around the country in response to the changing education code of 1881 being presented to Parliament or late-night, emergency meetings with the esteemed Duke of Norfolk in close quarters with Parnellites and anti-Parnellites are testaments to the increasing success of the hierarchy at cultivating general Catholic support for the education battle.

If the nearly complete unity on education in 1902 represents a high water mark in Catholic cooperation, the tide would soon begin to ebb again. As indicated by John Dillon's letter to his Liberal ally in December 1903, the years after the passage of the Balfour Act were anything but settled.[20] Liberal nonconformists, antagonized by having to support denominational schools from their rates, began a campaign of passive resistance in opposition to the new Education Act. Led by Dr John Clifford, a nonconformist minister, energized dissenters began refusing to pay rates in April 1903. Within three years, over 70,000 summonses were issued to resisters, and those who did not pay were subject to distraint of their goods until the debt was paid. The government also faced a blatant refusal by LEAs in Wales, organized and led by future Liberal leader David Lloyd George, to pay any money to denominational schools.[21]

When the Liberals finally regained control of the government in 1905 under Prime Minister Henry Campbell-Bannerman, they prioritized modifying the education system as created by the Balfour Act, especially for those nonconformists living in rural, one-school, usually Anglican, districts. The president of the Board of Education, Augustine Birrell, tried to appease all sides with his education bill in 1906 and, as with most compromises, pleased no one. His changes intended to place all voluntary schools under the full guidance of the LEAs if they wanted to keep their funding, abolish religious tests for teachers and make LEAs responsible for hiring teachers. Under the new bill, denominational religious teaching would be limited to two days each week and held outside school hours. But the clause that sparked much controversy promised denominational teaching each day at schools in urban areas with over 5,000 residents. This had been inserted to appease the English Catholics, a worthy tribute from their adversaries to the Catholic effort in the previous half century on behalf of their schools. While the bill received firm Liberal nonconformist support, it was opposed vigorously by Anglicans and Catholics, despite the special clause for Catholics. When contacted by *The Times* on 11 April about the Catholic hierarchy's opinion of the bill, Monsignor Martin Howlett, administrator of Westminster Cathedral, replied bluntly: 'The Bill will be fatal to Catholic interests'. Howlett also indicated that while the bishops had discouraged public Catholic protests to that point, they could not longer do so as applications from Catholics around the country for public meetings and demonstrations poured in as Catholics planned to 'receive the Bill with the bitter hostility it deserves'.[22] After much debate that summer and given the Liberal majority in Commons, Birrell's bill passed the lower house, but it was subjected to such severe scrutiny and change in the House of Lords that it died there.[23]

In the end, 1902 had not brought the fight for education to a close. As Cardinal Vaughan had reflected in one of his last public statements before he died, it was clear that a system of education to please everyone was not possible until all shared the same faith.[24] The fears of John Dillon and other political pragmatists had come true once a Liberal government held the reins of power. The recent gains of the denominationalists had come under threat again. Alas, the campaign had to continue. Another general, the often irascible Francis Alphonsus Bourne, Archbishop of Westminster from 1903 to 1935 and future cardinal, took Vaughan's place to lead the forces against their educational enemies. With the help of other clerical and lay Catholics at his side, they once again fired up the rhetoric and the extra-parliamentary activities to which Monsignor Howlett referred. The demonstration in support of Catholic schools at Albert Hall on 5 May 1906 was reported to have been 60,000 strong.[25] But despite this rousing support, some of those internal crevasses reappeared in the autumn. A rather public disagreement between the Duke of Norfolk, the archbishop and the Irish MPs concerning the steps taken during the bill's arduous passage through Parliament had rattled the Catholic community and undermined some of the consensus that had been achieved only four years before.[26]

That said, a recent study of the English Catholic Church of the twentieth century suggests that the Church entered the new century with confidence, passion and not a little defensiveness that could easily manifest itself as tenacious defiance.[27] The half-century struggle for the schools is what engendered those traits and altered Catholic identity, leaving it worlds removed from its quiescent past and energized, yet intermittently fractious, for the educational warfare that was to come in the twentieth century.

NOTES

The following abbreviations are used throughout the notes:

BAA	Birmingham Archdiocesan Archives, Birmingham.
LAA	Liverpool Archdiocesan Archives, Liverpool.
LEDA	Leeds Diocesan Archives, Leeds.
LRO	Lancashire Record Office, Preston.
NDA	Nottingham Diocesan Archives, Nottingham.
PRO	Public Record Office.
PTL	Pitts Theology Library, Emory University, Atlanta, Georgia.
SDA	Salford Diocesan Archives, Burnley.
TNA	The National Archives, Kew, Richmond, Surrey.
WAA	Westminster Archdiocesan Archives, Kensington, London.

1 A Church Divided and the Educational Solution

1. N. P. Wiseman, *The Religious and Social Position of Catholics in England: An Address Delivered to the Catholic Congress of Malines, August 21, 1863* (Dublin: James Duffy, 1864), p. 16.
2. For more on this liberal Catholic organ, see J. Altholz, *The Liberal Catholic Movement in England: The Rambler and its Contributors 1848–1864* (London: Burns & Oates, 1962).
3. 'Short Notices', *Rambler*, July 1850, p. 82.
4. For the purposes of this study, the phrase 'English Catholicism' or 'English Catholic' will refer to all of the dioceses restored in 1850, including those in Wales. The education battle was waged for, and the Catholic Poor School Committee acted on behalf of, Catholics in both England and Wales. It is simply a matter of convenience and historiographical convention to refer to both groups using this terminology.
5. Passages from this book were previously published in E. G. Tenbus, '"We Fight for the Cause of God": English Catholics, the Education of the Poor, and the Transformation of Catholic Identity in Victorian Britain', *Journal of British Studies*, 46:4 (October 2007), pp. 861–83; © 2007 by of University of Chicago Press, used with permission.

6. See M. D. R. Leys, *Catholics in England 1559–1829: A Social History* (London: Longmans, Green and Co., Ltd., 1961), pp. 93–125: R. Foster, *Modern Ireland, 1600–1972* (London: Penguin Books, 1989), pp. 205–11.
7. J. Bossy, *The English Catholic Community 1570–1850* (London: Darton, Longman & Todd, 1975), p. 297. For example, see D. Gwynn, *The Second Spring, 1818–1852: A Study of the Catholic Revival in England* (London: Catholic Book Club, 1944).
8. Bossy, *The English Catholic Community*, pp. 327–9.
9. M. Heimann, *Catholic Devotion in Victorian England* (Oxford: Clarendon Press, 1995), pp. 70–99, 137–44.
10. In this text, the term ultramontane (or ultramontanism) is broadly defined as that party within the nineteenth-century Catholic Church that advocated greater papal power and centralized control from Rome and supported the doctrine of papal supremacy.
11. Bossy, *The English Catholic Community*, p. 297. See also p. 364.
12. Ibid., p. 322.
13. E. R. Norman, *The English Catholic Church in the Nineteenth Century* (Oxford: Clarendon Press, 1984), pp. 206, 208.
14. D. Mathew, 'Old Catholics and Converts', in G. A. Beck (ed.), *The English Catholics, 1850–1950* (London: Burns & Oates, 1950), pp. 223–42, on pp. 236–7.
15. Ibid., pp. 232–6.
16. D. Gwynn, 'Growth of the Catholic Community', in Beck (ed.), *The English Catholics*, pp. 410–41, on p. 418.
17. The three volumes edited by Swift and Gilley have done much to enlighten historians on the life of the Irish in Britain: R. Swift and S. Gilley (eds), *The Irish in the Victorian City* (London: Croom Helm, 1985); R. Swift and S. Gilley (eds), *The Irish in Britain 1815–1939* (London: Pinter Publishers, 1989); R. Swift and S. Gilley (eds), *The Irish in Victorian Britain: The Local Dimension* (Dublin: Four Courts Press, 1999).
18. Bossy, *The English Catholic Community*, p. 308. See also G. Connolly, 'Irish and Catholic: Myth or Reality? Another Sort of Irish and the Renewal of the Clerical Profession among Catholics in England, 1791–1918', in Swift and Gilley (eds), *The Irish in the Victorian City*, pp. 225–54, on p. 226.
19. M. A. G. O'Tuathaigh, 'The Irish in Nineteenth-Century Britain: Problems of Integration', in Swift and Gilley (eds), *The Irish in the Victorian City*, pp. 13–36, on pp. 15–16.
20. L. H. Lees, *Exiles of Erin: Irish Migrants in Victorian London* (Ithaca, NY: Cornell University Press, 1979), pp. 190, 244–6, 249, 196–7.
21. O'Tuathaigh, 'The Irish in Nineteenth-Century Britain', pp. 19–20.
22. Bossy, *The English Catholic Community*, pp. 313–15.
23. Lees, *Exiles of Erin*, p. 181.
24. Connolly, 'Irish and Catholic', pp. 228–30.
25. Bossy, *The English Catholic Community*, pp. 315–16. See also E. Larkin, 'The Devotional Revolution in Ireland, 1850–1875', *American Historical Review*, 88:3 (June 1972), pp. 625–52.
26. T. G. McGrath, 'The Tridentine Evolution of Modern Irish Catholicism, 1563–1962: A Re-Examination of the "Devotional Revolution" Thesis', *Recusant History*, 20:4 (1991), pp. 512–23.
27. O'Tuathaigh, 'The Irish in Nineteenth-Century Britain', pp. 25–6. See also Lees, *Exiles of Erin*, pp. 172–97, for her exposition on the ways in which London Irish Catholics practised a weak form of post-Tridentine Catholicism, yet still remained allegiant to the Church.

28. W. B. Ullathorne, *Notes on the Education Question* (London: Richardson & Son, 1857), pp. 9–10. For a recent study of Bishop Ullathorne, see J. Champ, *William Bernard Ullathorne 1806–1889: A Different Kind of Monk* (Leominster: Gracewing, 2006).
29. Altholz, *The Liberal Catholic Movement in England*, pp. 7–24.
30. Norman, *The English Catholic Church*, p. 158.
31. O'Tuathaigh, 'The Irish in Nineteenth-Century Britain', p. 26.
32. Heimann, *Catholic Devotion in Victorian England*, p. 159.
33. See J. D. Holmes, *More Roman than Rome: English Catholicism in the Nineteenth Century* (London: Burns & Oates, 1978); Beck (ed.), *The English Catholics*; V. A. McClelland and M. Hodgetts (eds), *From Without the Flaminian Gate: 150 Years of Roman Catholicism in England and Wales, 1850–2000* (London: Darton, Longman & Todd, 1999); and S. Gilley (ed.), *Victorian Churches and Churchmen: Essays Presented to Vincent Alan McClelland* (Woodbridge, Suffolk: Boydell Press, 2005).
34. V. A. McClelland, *Cardinal Manning: His Public Life and Influence, 1865–1892* (London: Oxford University Press, 1962); E. S. Purcell, *Life of Cardinal Manning: Archbishop of Westminster*, 2 vols (London: MacMillan Company, 1898).
35. D. E. Selby, 'Henry Edward Manning and the Education Bill of 1870', *British Journal of Educational Studies*, 18:2 (June 1970), pp. 197–212; D. E. Selby, *Towards a Common System of National Education: Cardinal Manning and Educational Reform, 1882–1892* (Leeds: University of Leeds, 1977); R. Gray, *Cardinal Manning: A Biography* (London: Weidenfeld & Nicholson, 1985); D. Quinn, 'Manning as Politician', *Recusant History*, 21:2 (1992), pp. 267–85; J. Pereiro, *Cardinal Manning: An Intellectual Biography* (Oxford: Clarendon Press, 1998); J. von Arx, 'Manning's Ultramontanism and the Catholic Church in British Politics', *Recusant History*, 19:3 (1989), pp. 332–47; and J. von Arx, 'Cardinal Manning and His Political Persona: The Education Act of 1870', in Gilley (ed.), *Victorian Churches and Churchmen*, pp. 1–11.
36. Altholz, *The Liberal Catholic Movement in England*; M. G. Holland, *The British Catholic Press and the Educational Controversy, 1847–1865* (New York: Garland Publishing, 1987); D. Quinn, *Patronage and Piety: The Politics of English Roman Catholicism, 1850–1900* (Stanford, CA: Stanford University Press, 1993); and M. J. Hickman, *Religion, Class, and Identity: The State, the Catholic Church, and the Education of the Irish in Britain* (Aldershot: Avebury Press, 1995). Hickman's book probably comes closest to a comprehensive study of the Church and elementary education. She argues that the state and Catholic Church collaborated to use education to make the Irish into British citizens, thus anglicizing potential future troublemakers for both state and Church. Interestingly, I found no evidence of this collaboration or intent in my sources, especially with regards to the assistance of Irish Home Rule MPs in the political battles over education in the 1890s.
37. M. Whitehead, 'A View from the Bridge: The Catholic School', in McClelland and Hodgetts (eds), *From Without the Flaminian Gate*, pp. 217–44. See also M. Whitehead, '"Briefly, and in Confidence": Private Views of Her Majesty's Inspectors on English Catholic Elementary Schools, 1875', *Recusant History*, 20:4 (1991), pp. 554–62.
38. J. T. Smith, *'A Victorian Class Conflict': Schoolteaching and the Parson, Priest and Minister, 1837–1902* (Eastbourne: Sussex Academic Press, 2009). See also J. T. Smith, *Methodism and Education 1849–1902: J. H. Rigg, Romanism, and Wesleyan Schools* (Oxford: Oxford University Press, 1998); J. T. Smith, 'The Priest and the Elementary School in the Second Half of the Nineteenth Century', *Recusant History*, 25:3 (2001), pp. 530–42; and J. T. Smith, 'The Real Milch Cow? The Work of Anglican, Catholic and Wesleyan

Clergymen in Elementary Schools in the Second Half of the Nineteenth Century', *History of Education*, 31:2 (2002), pp. 117–37.

39. K. Aspden, *Fortress Church: The English Roman Catholic Bishops and Politics 1903–63* (Leominster: Gracewing, 2002), pp. 9–11, 302–8.
40. Bossy cites evidence that in the seventeenth century, Monmouthshire and Lancashire held the highest proportion of Catholics at 90 and 94 per 1,000 respectively. A century later in 1767, Lancashire revealed the highest distribution of Catholics, along with country Durham. See *The English Catholic Community*, pp. 404–5, 408–9, 412–13, for evidence of Lancashire's Catholic presence, and see pp. 426–7 for evidence of the explosive growth in the Irish percentage of the Catholic population in Lancashire. By 1851, one year after the restoration of the hierarchy, 75 per cent of practising Catholics in the four major Lancashire towns – Liverpool, Manchester, Preston and Wigan – were of Irish origin. This compares with a 33 per cent Irish presence at the turn of the century. This is based on an approximation of the percentages based on Bossy's figure II.
41. F. Engels, *The Condition of the Working Class in England* (1845), foreword E. Hobsbawm (Chicago, IL: Academy Chicago Publishers, 1994), p. 93.
42. Wiseman, *The Religious and Social Position of Catholics*, pp. 58–9, 60–1.

2 The Status of Catholic Education at Mid-Century

1. See J. Kitching, 'The Catholic Poor Schools, 1800 to 1845: Part I, The Catholic Poor: Relief, Welfare and Schools', *Journal of Educational Administration and History*, 1 (June 1969), pp. 1–8; J. Kitching, 'The Catholic Poor Schools, 1800 to 1845: Part II, The Schools: Development and Distribution', *Journal of Educational Administration and History*, 2 (December 1969), pp. 1–12.
2. See B. Carter, 'Catholic Charitable Endeavor in London, 1810–1840, Part I', *Recusant History*, 25:3 (2001), pp. 487–510; B. Carter, 'Catholic Charitable Endeavor in London, 1810–1840, Part II', *Recusant History*, 25:4 (2001), pp. 648–69.
3. *Proposed Catholic Institute of Great Britain*, 7 March 1838, p. 1, and 12 May 1838, p. 2, New Series, B/A/78, LEDA.
4. Letter from James Smith, Secretary of the Catholic Institute, to Rev. Dr Thomas Youens, Chair, Auxiliary Society of the Catholic Institute, Liverpool, 8 March 1839, as published in the *Catholic Magazine*, April 1839, p. 269.
5. [D. Burke], *The Christian Brothers' History of the Institute, Volume II* (Dublin: Bray Printing Co. Ltd., n.d.), p. 14.
6. See *London and Dublin Weekly Orthodox Journal of Useful Knowledge*, 20 July 1839, pp. 37–64; and *Catholic Magazine*, August 1839, pp. 520–1.
7. *London and Dublin Weekly Orthodox Journal*, 20 July 1839, p. 54.
8. Ibid., p. 38.
9. *Catholic Magazine*, May 1843, p. 318.
10. See *Second Annual Report of the Catholic Poor School Committee* (London: Catholic Poor School Committee, 1849), Appendix D, pp. 71–7.
11. A. C. F. Beales, 'The Struggle for the Schools', in Beck (ed.), *The English Catholics*, pp. 365–409, on p. 367; *Catholic Magazine*, May 1843, p. 317; Kitching, 'The Catholic Poor Schools, 1800 to 1845: Part II', pp. 2–4.
12. *Second Annual Report of the Catholic Poor School Committee*, Appendix C, pp. 50–70; *Catholic Directory* (1847). Rather than twenty-two schools having opened and then

closed in such a short time span, more than likely these numbers are a result of reporting and information-gathering inconsistencies.

13. *Catholic Directory* (1846), p. 153; Beales claims that the number lacking education in 1843 was over 100,000, but that seems much too high given the parish-by-parish statistics from 1845 contained in *Second Annual Report of the Catholic Poor School Committee*, Appendix C, pp. 50–70. 'Report on the State of Elementary Education in Birmingham, Manchester, Liverpool, and several other Towns in Lancashire, 21 October 1840', Appendix to the Minutes of the Committee of Council on Education, p. 78, TNA, PRO, ED 17/4.
14. *Second Annual Report of the Catholic Poor School Committee*, Appendix N, p. 145.
15. Figures taken from ibid., Appendix C, pp. 50–70.
16. Ibid.
17. For more on St Patrick's Charity Schools, see Carter, 'Catholic Charitable Endeavor in London, Part II', pp. 654–6.
18. Since the St Patrick's Boys Schools were operated by the Irish Christian Brothers at mid-century, they refused to allow inspections by the state, and, thus, voluntarily kept themselves outside the government grant system.
19. *Laity's Directory* (1833), pp. 32–3; *Catholic Directory* (1850), pp. 138–9; *Andrew's Weekly Orthodox Journal of Entertaining Christian Knowledge*, 23 May 1835, pp. 286–8; *London and Dublin Weekly Orthodox Journal*, 17 June 1837, pp. 379–80; *London and Dublin Weekly Orthodox Journal*, 13 July 1839, pp. 27–30.
20. *Laity's Directory* (1833), pp. 32–40; *Catholic Directory* (1838), pp. 62–75; B/A/10, New Series, 1 November 1833, LEDA.
21. *Andrew's Weekly Orthodox Journal*, 27 June 1835, pp. 361–2; *London and Dublin Weekly Orthodox Journal*, 24 September 1836, pp. 205–6; *London and Dublin Weekly Orthodox Journal*, 29 July 1837, p. 71; *London and Dublin Weekly Orthodox Journal*, 10 September 1842, pp. 174–5.
22. A. L. O'Toole, *Challenged: The Story of Edmund Rice and the Irish Christian Brothers in Britain since 1825* (Tenbury Wells, Worcestershire: Fowler Wright Books, n.d.), pp. 48–52; J. Coates, 'The Christian Brothers – Part II: Pioneers in Catholic Education in Britain and Ireland Throughout the 19th and 20th Centuries', *Catholic Life* (March 2005), pp. 18–24, on p. 18. The definitive work on the Irish Christian Brothers is W. Gillespie, *The Christian Brothers in England, 1825–1880* (Bristol: Burleigh Press, 1975). See also W. J. Battersby, 'Secondary Education for Boys', in Beck (ed.), *The English Catholics*, pp. 322–36; and E. Cruise, 'Development of the Religious Orders', in Beck (ed.), *The English Catholics*, pp. 442–74.
23. See W. J. Battersby, 'Educational Work of the Religious Orders of Women: 1850–1950', in Beck (ed.), *The English Catholics*, pp. 337–64, on pp. 337–49. For a more complete examination, see B. Walsh, *Roman Catholic Nuns in England and Wales 1880–1937: A Social History* (Dublin: Irish Academic Press, 2002).
24. H. C. Barnard, *A History of English Education from 1760* (London: University of London Press, 1964), pp. 103–4; E. J. Evans, *The Forging of the Modern State: Early Industrial Britain 1783–1870* (London: Longman Group, 1983), p. 233.
25. Letter of Baines to Briggs, 17 March 1843, B1314a, Old Series, LEDA,
26. Letter of Wiseman to Briggs, March 1843, B1315, Old Series, LEDA; letter of Walsh to Briggs, 17 March 1843, B1314, Old Series, LEDA.
27. See Letter of Briggs to Clergy, 22 April 1843, B1322a, Old Series, LEDA, for his letter to his clergy on the need for a 'prompt, strong and universal expression of Catholic feel-

ing' in opposition to the factory bill and directions on how to solicit signatures from the different congregations.

28. Letters of Baines to Briggs, 19 April 1843, 22 April 1843, B1320a, Old Series, LEDA.
29. Letter of Baines to Briggs, 23 April 1843, B1322b, Old Series, LEDA.
30. Letter of Baines to Briggs, 19 April 1843, B1320s, Old Series, LEDA; letter of Baines to Briggs, 26 April 1843, B1324a, Old Series, LEDA; letter of Baines to Briggs, 8 May 1843, B1328a, Old Series, LEDA.
31. Kitching, 'The Catholic Poor Schools, 1800 to 1845: Part II', p. 10.
32. *Rambler*, July 1852, p. 81.
33. Ibid., p. 77.
34. For the purposes of this study, education means primary or elementary education. Certainly secondary and university education were important to the Catholic community, but the needs were greatest for the tens of thousands who would only ever receive a few years of primary education at best.
35. See 'Instruction v. Education', *Rambler*, July 1856.
36. See Norman, *The English Catholic Church*, pp. 160–1, 165–7.
37. R. E. Guy, *The Synods in English: Being the Text of the Four Synods of Westminster* (Stratford-upon-Avon: St Gregory's Press, 1886), p. 268.
38. Pastoral Letter, 21 April 1871, p. 15, Turner ACTA, SDA. For more on Bishop Turner and his educational efforts, see D. Lannon, 'Bishop Turner and Educational Provision within the Salford Diocesan Area, 1840–1870' (MPhil. thesis, University of Hull, 1994); D. Lannon, 'Bishop Turner, the Salford Diocese, and Reformatory Provision, 1854–1872', *Recusant History*, 23:3 (1997), pp. 389–407; and D. Lannon, 'William Turner, First Bishop of Salford, Pastor and Educator', *Recusant History*, 25:2 (2000), pp. 192–217.
39. Pastoral Letter, 9 November 1867, Pastoral Letters of Bishop Turner 1857–70, SDA.
40. Aquinas, *Summa Theologica*, II.II.10.12.
41. Ibid., II.II.154.2.
42. O. Cohausz, *The Pope and Christian Education*, trans. G. D. Smith (New York: Benziger Brothers, 1933), pp. 54–7, 46–9.
43. Pastoral Letter, 13 November 1885, pp. 5–6, Ullathorne Pastorals 1870–88, BAA.
44. Pastoral Letter, 1 December 1871, p. 2, Beverley Diocesan ACTA, LEDA.
45. Henry Edward Manning was ordained and practised as an Anglican priest, rising to the position of Archdeacon of Chicester until his conversion to Catholicism in 1851. He quickly rose through the hierarchical ranks of the newly re-established Catholic hierarchy and, upon Cardinal Wiseman's death in 1865, succeeded to the position of archbishop. He was made cardinal in 1875. While he subscribed to the ultramontane view of papal infallibility and the pre-eminence of the Papal See, he also revealed a keen interest in the social questions of the day, including workers' rights and education. Perhaps more than any other Catholic from this period, Manning left a legacy of strong and active leadership at the head of the Catholic community during these formative years until his death in 1892. The crowd, mostly of London's poor, who lined the streets at his funeral was reportedly the largest since the death of the Duke of Wellington.
46. Manning, Pastoral Letter, as cited in 'Parliament and Catholic Education', *Dublin Review*, 18 (April 1872), p. 414.
47. H. A. Vaughan, *The Dangers of the Education Question and How to Meet Them* (Salford, 1891), pp. 7–8, Vaughan ACTA, SDA.

48. 'Instruction v. Education', *Rambler*, July 1856, pp. 443–4. A later article in the *Rambler* expanded on this definition of education: 'It is to put the whole moral and intellectual creature into order ... to give habits of energy and diligence, to teach self respect and self control ... to inculcate principle, and to draw out into healthy working the pure affections of piety. Education is consequently, in its essence, a religious and sacred work' ('Elementary School-Books', *Rambler*, September 1860, pp. 65–6.
49. Begun in 1836 from a collaboration of London-based Irish lawyer Michael Quin, then Rector of the English College in Rome, future Cardinal and Archbishop of Westminster Nicholas Patrick Wiseman and Irish leader Daniel O'Connell, the *Dublin Review* was published for the educated Catholic into the mid-twentieth century. See Holland, *The British Catholic Press*, pp. 106–8; J. Warren, 'The Dublin Review (1836–75), Its Reviewers and a "Philosophy of Knowledge"', *Recusant History*, 21:1 (1992), pp. 86–98.
50. 'Elementary Education; Our Position, Prospects, and Policy', *Dublin Review*, 13 (October 1883), p. 399.
51. 'Saving Our Schools and Their Catholic Teaching', *Dublin Review*, 110 (January 1892), p. 166.
52. Pastoral Letter, 28 May 1869, p. 96, C/G/69, LEDA.
53. Thomas William Allies served as Secretary for the Catholic Poor School Committee from 1853 until his retirement in 1890, upon which he received his pension of £400 a year and was made a Knight Commander of St Gregory by Pope Leo XIII. See M. H. Allies, *Thomas William Allies* (London: Burns & Oates, 1907), pp. 68–9, 175.
54. House of Commons, 'Answers to the Circular of Questions', *Sessional Papers 1861*, Education General, 25 July 1859, vol. 7, p. 39.
55. Pastoral Letter, 9 November 1867, pp. 2, 3, Turner ACTA, SDA.
56. H. E. Manning, *National Education and Parental Rights* (London: Burns, Oates, & Co., 1872), p. 11. See Letter on Educational Peril, 21 February 1882, p. 11, Vaughan ACTA, SDA, for Bishop Herbert Vaughan of Salford's opinion on the subject. In a letter to his diocese, Vaughan accused the board schools of teaching morality without Christian dogma. He wrote: 'Severed from Christian dogma, morality is like a branch severed from the tree – it is doomed to decay'. The logical result of this lack of morality was 'the spirit of religious indifference' and 'growth of rationalism and unbelief'.
57. H. E. Manning, *A Charge Delivered at the Ordinary Visitation of the Archdeaconry of Chichester in July 1843* (London: John Murray, 1843), pp. 30–1.
58. House of Commons, 'Second Report of the Royal Commission Appointed to Inquire into the Working of the Elementary Education Acts, England and Wales', *Sessional Papers 1887, Education General*, 26 January 1887, vol. 35, pp. 402, 403.
59. D. K. Jones, *The Making of the Education System, 1851–81* (London: Routledge & Kegan Paul, 1977), pp. 14–15; Barnard, *A History of English Education*, pp. 107–8.
60. W. B. Ullathorne, *Remarks on the Proposed Education Bill* (London: Burns & Lambert, 1850), pp. 12, 14.
61. Bishop Goss to Mr. Lloyd, 31 December 1858, RCLV, Goss Letter Books 1855–72, Box 14, 2/427, LRO.
62. Ad Clerum, 28 May 1869, p. 3, Turner ACTA, SDA.
63. H. E. Manning, *Denominational Education: A Pastoral Letter to the Clergy and Laity of the Diocese of Westminster* (London: Burns, Oates, & Co., 1869), p. 7. Virtually the same language was used in another pastoral letter from the entire hierarchy two years later in response to the passage of the Education Act of 1870. See *Pastoral Letter of the Archbishop and Bishops of the Province of Westminster Assembled* (London, 1871), p. 11,

Turner ACTA, SDA; or see H. A. Vaughan, *A Letter on the Educational Peril to Christianity* (Manchester: T. Walker, 1882), p. 7, Vaughan ACTA, SDA, for Bishop Herbert Vaughan's similar views on the subject. What is revealed is consistency of the message across the hierarchy of bishops.

64. J. F. Supple-Green, *The Catholic Revival in Yorkshire, 1850–1900* (Leeds: Leeds Philosophical and Literary Society, 1990), p. 38.
65. Lawrence Toole was born in Liverpool and in his early life was a tailor. After his wife died he entered the priesthood. In 1875, Toole was awarded an honorary Doctor of Divinity by Pope Pius IX for his work in the progress of Catholic education. Interestingly, he served twenty years as a member of the Manchester School Board.
66. 'Religion an Essential Element in the School Education of the Poor: A Paper Read at the Social Science Congress, Manchester, 6 October 1866 by the Very Rev. Canon Toole', Early Bishops Collection Brown–Whiteside, Series 3.II Education, Folio 1: Education up to 1900, LAA.
67. F. Oakeley, *Education to be Real Must be Denominational*, as quoted in 'Parliament and Catholic Education', *Dublin Review*, 18 (April 1872), pp. 418, 419.
68. House of Commons, 'Answers to the Circular of Questions', *Sessional Papers 1861*, Education General, 4 July 1859, vol. 7, p. 292.
69. See P. T. Marsh, *The Victorian Church in Decline: Archbishop Tait and the Church of England, 1868–1882* (Pittsburgh, PA: University of Pittsburgh Press, 1969), pp. 66–81; and Smith, *Methodism and Education*, for Anglican and Methodist views.
70. Pastoral Letter, 14 June 1855, p. 3, MSS 173, Box 2, Folder 2, N. Wiseman Collection, PTL.
71. R. Cornthwaite, *Pastoral Letter for Advent, 1875* (Leeds: John Whitehead and Son, 1875), p. 16.
72. Ad Clerum, 12 February 1871, p. 5, Turner ACTA, SDA.
73. R. Challoner, *The Catholic Christian Instructed in the Sacraments, Sacrifices, Ceremonies and Observances of the Church by Way of Question and Answer* (Baltimore, MD: G. Dobbin & Murphy, 1809), pp. 25–6.
74. B. L. Martaler, *The Catechism Yesterday and Today: The Evolution of a Genre* (Collegeville, MN: Liturgical Press, 1995), pp. 86–9; Heimann, *Catholic Devotion in Victorian England*, pp. 84, 91.
75. R. Challoner, *The Garden of the Soul: or A Manual of Spiritual Exercises and Instructions for Christians, Who (Living in the World), Aspire to Devotion* (Philadelphia, PA: Carey, 1792), pp. 30, 184–5. See Heimann, *Catholic Devotion in Victorian England*, pp. 70–99, for an insightful analysis of devotional practices in the nineteenth century. Her argument maintains that there was little difference devotionally between recusant and later Catholics.
76. Ad Clerum, 12 February 1871, p. 5, Turner ACTA, SDA.
77. H. E. Manning, *A Pastoral Letter to the Clergy and Laity of the Archdiocese of Westminster on Education* (London: Burns & Oates, 1889), p. 8.
78. See H. McLeod, *Piety and Poverty; Working-Class Religion in Berlin, London, and New York, 1870–1914* (New York: Holmes & Meier, 1996), pp. 103–4; and H. McLeod, 'The De-Christianization of the Working Class in Western Europe, c. 1850–1900', *Social Compass*, 27 (1980), pp. 191–214, for his analysis of rising secularism among the working classes of Europe and his three-stage model of that process.
79. Some of this section was previously published under E. G. Tenbus, 'Defending the Faith through Education: The Catholic Case for Parental and Civil Rights in Victorian Brit-

ain', *History of Education Quarterly*, 48:3 (August 2008), pp. 432–51; © 2008 by History of Education Society, used with permission.

80. *Tablet*, 13 January 1844, p. 19.
81. H. E. Manning, *The Grounds of Faith: Four Lectures Delivered to St. George's Church, Southwark* (London: Burns & Lambert, 1852), pp. 97–9, 5.
82. Pastoral Letter, 26 May 1856, p. 2; Synodical Letter, 1859, p. 7, MSS 173, Box 2, Folder 2, N. Wiseman Collection, PTL.
83. See D. M. Lewis, *Lighten their Darkness: The Evangelical Mission to Working-Class London, 1828–1860* (New York: Greenwood Press, 1986), pp. 188–90; and J. Wolffe, *The Protestant Crusade in Great Britain, 1829–1860* (Oxford: Clarendon Press, 1988), pp. 33–43, 180–4, for detailed examinations of these Protestant efforts that affected urban Catholics.
84. Edward G. F. Howard to Charles Langdale, President of the Catholic Poor School Committee, *Catholic School*, March 1855, pp. 110–11. The fourteenth Duke of Norfolk died in 1860.
85. Pastoral Letter, 26 May 1856, p. 1, MSS 173, Box 2, Folder 2, N. Wiseman Collection, PTL.
86. Ad Clerum, 2 June 1858, p. 1, Turner ACTA, SDA. Perhaps out of frustration that Catholic children continued to be lost to the faith in Protestant schools, he repeated the warning, almost verbatim, in similar communications in 1861 and 1863. See Ad Clerum, 30 May 1861, p. 1, and 20 May 1863, p. 1, Turner ACTA, SDA.
87. Falling away from the faith involved two levels of severity. Much Catholic literature at the time used the term 'leakage' to describe a more common phenomenon, which was the cessation of regular practice of the sacraments and attendance at mass. As grave and troublesome as this was for the Church, the more serious, and less frequent, occurrence was open apostasy, which was a more conscious decision to spurn the faith.
88. *Tablet*, 16 November 1844, p. 3. For a similar perspective from the liberal Catholics, see 'Shams and Realities', *Rambler*, March 1854, p. 207.
89. O'Tuathaigh, 'The Irish in Nineteenth-Century Britain', p. 25.
90. See Lees, *Exiles of Erin*, pp. 180–2; Bossy, *The English Catholic Community*, pp. 313–16; Connolly, 'Irish and Catholic', pp. 227–8; O'Tuathaigh, 'The Irish in Nineteenth-Century Britain', pp. 25–6. See also J. Hickey, *Urban Catholics: Urban Catholicism in England and Wales from 1829 to the Present Day* (London: Geoffrey Chapman, 1967), pp. 91–2, where, in his study of Catholics in Cardiff, he employs Easter duties percentages over a twenty-year span to show an even lower percentage – an average of 25.19 per cent – of Irish Catholic practice. Note that these historians do not mean by their figures that poor Irish Catholics had repudiated their faith, but that regular attendance and practice of the sacraments was suffering.
91. *First Annual Report of the Catholic Poor School Committee* (London: Catholic Poor School Committee, 1848), p. 54. See also the *Seventh Annual Report of the Catholic Poor School Committee* (London: Catholic Poor School Committee, 1854), p. 16.
92. *Seventh Annual Report of the Catholic Poor School Committee*, p. 34.
93. Galley Proof of a message to the diocese on the 'Education of the Poor', 19 November 1865, p. 4, MSS 002, Box 11, Folder 8, H. Manning Collection, PTL. The other bishops were not blind to the problem of leakage at the diocesan level either. Bishop George Brown of Liverpool urgently described the desperate situation in Liverpool as one where 'thousands [of children] ... are yearly absorbed into the infidel mass with which they are surrounded'. If education was not fortified with an organized and united effort, he argued, 'Catholic [these children] will soon cease to be'. See Pastoral Letter on the Cath-

olic Poor School Collection, 13 June 1854, pp. 1, 3–4, RCLV Box 40, LRO. For other examples from the bishops, see Ad Clerum, 30 May 1861, p. 1, Turner ACTA, SDA, and Pastoral on the Diocesan Poor and New Mission Fund, 1 December 1893, pp. 5, 6–7, Bilsborrow ACTA, SDA.

3 Educational Obstacles to Overcome

1. Her Majesty's Inspection Report, 1868, St Augustine's Infant School Log Book, SMPr 46/1, LRO. This report reflects the stern efficiency required by the Revised Code as schools were penalized for inadequate examination results or substandard amenities.
2. 'Preface', *Rambler*, 1849, p. iv.
3. 'The Rising Generation: Our Poor Schools', *Rambler*, November 1856, p. 326.
4. 'The Present Catholic Dangers', *Dublin Review*, 41 (December 1856), pp. 462–3, 469–70.
5. Pastoral Letter for Lent, 25 January 1883, pp. 10–15, Pastorals Bagshawe 1874–1901, NDA.
6. George Richardson, 25 April 1849, as cited in the *Second Annual Report of the Catholic Poor School Committee*, p. 143. In August, R. R. W. Lingen, Acting Assistant Secretary of the Committee of Council on Education, wrote to Scott N. Stokes, to reply to Catholic complaints such as Richardson's. Lingen stated that no changes would be forthcoming in the rule that a grant could only match what was raised by the school because Parliament had decided upon this stipulation because of the limited funds available and the state of public opinion which supported this system. Basically, he passed the responsibility onto the legislature. George Richardson (1813–1901) converted to Catholicism in 1833 and became a leading member of the Catholic laity. He served as secretary of the local Poor School Committee, and on the Manchester School Board after the passage of the Education Act of 1870. His eldest son joined the priesthood and also was heavily involved in the educational affairs of the community. See Lannon, 'Bishop Turner and Educational Provision', p. 55, n.
7. 'The Controversy on the Poor-School Grant', *Rambler*, May 1857, p. 339.
8. Wiseman, *The Religious and Social Position of Catholics*, pp. 17–18.
9. *Twenty-Second Annual Report of the Catholic Poor School Committee* (London: Catholic Poor School Committee, 1870), pp. 20–2.
10. 'Catholic Interests and the Late Session of Parliament', *Month*, 13:76 (October 1870), pp. 383–4.
11. *Liverpool Mercury*, 11 December 1865, p. 6.
12. Letter of Goss to Rev. Hugh McCormick, 10 October 1856, 1/341, Goss Letter Books, 1855–72, Box 14, RCLV, LRO.
13. Letter of O'Connell to Cornthwaite, 24 March 1869, C/A/256, Cornthwaite Correspondence, LEDA.
14. Letter of Sherlock to Ullathorne, 19 June 1886, B9207, Documents, BAA.
15. House of Commons, 'Third Report of the Royal Commission Appointed to Inquire into the Working of the Elementary Education Acts, England and Wales', *Sessional Papers 1887*, Education General, 7 June 1887, vol. 36, p. 299.
16. Education Papers, 1864, Ed/4, BAA; Briggs Correspondence, 2 January 1852, B/K/2, New Series, LEDA.
17. 'Elementary Education; Our Position, Prospects, and Policy', *Dublin Review*, 13 (October 1883), pp. 394–5.

18. House of Commons, 'First Report of the Royal Commission Appointed to Inquire into the Working of the Elementary Education Act, England and Wales', *Sessional Papers 1886*, Education General, 9 June 1886, vol. 34, p. 458.
19. *Tablet*, 2 June 1888, p. 903.
20. Pastoral Letter, 1889; Pastoral Letter, 1890, pp. 8–10, Pastoral Letters from English Bishops and Other Papers 1869–93, NDA.
21. Ad Clerum, 20 January 1863, Beverley Diocesan ACTA, LEDA.
22. *Catholic School*, October 1854, p. 97. *Catholic School* was a publication of the Catholic Poor School Committee. See also the *Seventh Annual Report of the Catholic Poor School Committee*, p. 19.
23. *Catholic School*, October 1854, pp. 97–8. St Mary's, Hammersmith, was the male training college established in 1850.
24. *Catholic School*, March 1855, pp. 124, 126.
25. Pastoral Letter, 21 November 1856, B/K/3, New Series, LEDA.
26. 'The Poor-School Question', *Rambler*, August 1855, pp. 83–4, 89–90.
27. Ibid., p. 89.
28. House of Commons, 'First Report of the Royal Commission Appointed to Inquire into the Working of the Elementary Education Acts', vol. 34, p. 329.
29. This decrease was attributed to the poor income that a school master salary would draw compared to another line of work. Additionally, those prospects 'seem to be so poor that there is nothing to induce intelligent boys, or boys of better social position, to enter'. Ibid., vol. 34, p. 456.
30. Pastoral Letter, 30 June 1889, Vol. V, 1888–9, ACTA, LEDA.
31. Manning, *A Pastoral Letter to the Clergy and Laity of the Archdiocese of Westminster*, p. 5.
32. House of Commons, 'Third Report of the Royal Commission Appointed to Inquire into the Working of the Elementary Education Acts', vol. 36, p. 294.
33. *Leeds Mercury*, 19 April 1892, p. 5.
34. Ad Clerum, 16 June 1882, p. 1, Vaughan ACTA, SDA.
35. Diocese of Liverpool, *Report on Religious Inspection* (Liverpool: Rockliff Brothers, 1885), p. 8, Early Bishops Collection Brown–Whiteside, Series 3.I Education, A. Papers on Education and Schools Programme, LAA.
36. House of Commons, 'Third Report of the Royal Commission Appointed to Inquire into the Working of the Elementary Education Acts', vol. 36, p. 295.
37. House of Commons, 'First Report of the Royal Commission Appointed to Inquire into the Working of the Elementary Education Acts', vol. 34, p. 453.
38. Manning, *A Pastoral Letter to the Clergy and Laity of the Archdiocese of Westminster*, pp. 9, 12. Manning repeated a similar desire for a pension fund in a pastoral letter given for the Feast of the Sacred Heart in 1891. See *Tablet*, 13 June 1891, p. 955.
39. St Joseph's School Log Book, Bury, 13 December 1875, 31 July 1876, 11 September 1876, 1 August 1877, SDA.
40. St Mary's School Log Book, Manchester, 3 February 1868, 15 October 1871, 29 April 1872, RCMm 2/1, LRO.
41. Ibid., Her Majesty's Inspection Report, 1870.
42. St Mary's Girls School Log Book, Manchester, 9 January 1865, 8 May 1865, 9 January 1867, 6 January 1868, 14 January 1868, 15 June 1868, RCMm 2/2, LRO.
43. For examples of this problem, see School Inspection Returns 1858, St Patrick's School, Liverpool; St Anne's, Edge Hill, Liverpool; St Anthony's School, Liverpool; St Mary's

School, Liverpool; Holy Cross School, Liverpool; St Wilfrid's School, Preston; St John's Middle School, Wigan, Box 44, RCLV, LRO.

44. Ullathorne, *Notes on the Education Question*, pp. 36–40.
45. *Catholic School*, October 1853, pp. 9, 10–11.
46. 'Nuns as Teachers of Schools', *Rambler*, July 1853, pp. 51–5.
47. House of Commons, 'Reports, Papers and Correspondence Relating to the Commission on Popular Education in England 1861–62', *Sessional Papers, 1861–62*, Education General, vol. 8, pp. 176–7.
48. See Whitehead, '"Briefly, and in Confidence"', for further examination of Her Majesty's Inspectors and Catholic schools.
49. See M. E. W. Fitzgerald, 'Catholic Elementary Schools in the Manchester Area during the Nineteenth Century' (MEd thesis, University of Manchester, 1975), p. 176.
50. 'English Catholic Poor-Schools', *Dublin Review*, 8 (April 1867), pp. 301, 308.
51. *Eleventh Annual Report of the Catholic Poor School Committee*, as cited in *Dublin Review*, 8 (April 1867), pp. 309–10.
52. It is also important to note that under the Revised Code, a child had to be marked present 200 times in order to sit for an examination. The fewer the number of children taking the examinations, the lower the grant amount. Mary Fitzgerald cites a case where no government grant was earned for a boy who had only 199 attendances. See 'Catholic Elementary Schools', p. 190.
53. Ibid., p. 173.
54. St Anne's Infants School Log Book, Liverpool, 7 January 1864, 18 January 1864, 15 February 1864, 7 March 1864, 7 April 1864, LH/1, Sisters of Notre Dame de Namur Archive, Woolton, Liverpool.
55. St Anne's Infants School Log Book, 21 December 1865, LH/1, Sisters of Notre Dame de Namur Archive; St Augustine's Infant School Log Book, Preston, 30 June 1868, SMPR 46/1, LRO.
56. St Augustine's School Log Book, Manchester, 24–8 July 1871, SDA.
57. Ibid., 21–5 July 1871.
58. St Michael's Boys School Log Book, Liverpool, 7 August 1874, 1/123/38, 352 EDU, Liverpool Central Library. References to poor attendance can also be found on the following dates: 15 November 1872, 26 November 1872, 10 January 1873, 28 January 1874, 6 February 1874, 29 January 1875, 5 February 1875. One can see that this was primarily a problem in the winter months, and one that resurfaced year after year.
59. St Mary's Girls School Log Book, 1863–77, Manchester, 27 January 1863–11 January 1864, *passim*, RCMm 2/2, LRO.
60. St Mary's Boys School Log Book, 1863–82, Manchester, 8 March 1864, RCMm 2/1, LRO.
61. St Augustine's Infant School Log Book, 1863–1933, Preston, HMI Report, 1866, SMPr 46/1, LRO.
62. St Joseph's School Log Book, Bury, 18 August, 1875, SDA.
63. St Mary's Infants School Log Book, 1863–94, Burnley, 2 November–24 November 1868, SDA.
64. Adelphi Infant School Log Book, Salford, 24–5 June 1869, 19 July 1869, Faithful Companions of Jesus Archive, Salford, Greater Manchester.
65. Synodal Letter, 1859, p. 5, MSS 173, Box 2, Folder 2, N. Wiseman Collection, PTL.
66. Pastoral Letter, 3 December 1875, p. 879, 1874–5, ACTA, LEDA. Bishop Cornthwaite repeated this warning, in some ways word for word, in a pastoral letter eleven years later,

indicating that the problem had not improved. See Pastoral Letter, 28 November 1886, pp. 15–17, Vol. IV, 1886–7, ACTA, LEDA.

67. Letter of Lacy to Cornthwaite, 3 February 1876, C/A/449, Cornthwaite Correspondence, LEDA.
68. Pastoral Letter, December 1880, p. 14, Pastorals Bagshawe 1874–1901, NDA. Like Bishop Cornthwaite, Bagshawe repeated this theme periodically, the last time coming in a pastoral letter from 1901 in which he beseeched the parents of his diocese to not risk the faith of their children in non-Catholic schools. See Pastoral Letter, 2 February 1901, p. 14, Pastorals Bagshawe 1874–1901, NDA.
69. *Bristol Mercury*, 4 December 1882, p. 3.
70. *Report of the Liverpool Diocesan Mission Fund for the Year 1883* (Liverpool: Rockliff Brothers, 1884), pp. 4–6, Liverpolitana, LAA.
71. Pastoral Letter, 19 October 1882, 3–5, Vol. II, 1881–3, ACTA, LEDA.
72. Letter of G. Lambert to Cornthwaite, 15 August 1880, pp. 1–3, C/A/597, Cornthwaite Correspondence, LEDA.
73. Pastoral Letter, 26 November 1882, p. 12, Pastorals Bagshawe 1874–1901, NDA.
74. Pastoral Letter, 21 February 1881, p. 8, Pastorals Ullathorne 1848–88, BAA.
75. Pastoral Letter, 6 June 1899, pp. 8–9; 9 November 1900, pp. 12–14; Ad Clerum, Feast of St Michael and All Angels 1900, p. 9, Cardiff Province Pastorals 1881–1940, LAA.
76. St Mary's Girls School Log Book, 27 January 1863–30 August 1864; 14 January 1864, RCMm 2/2, LRO.
77. St Augustine's Infant School Log Book, 18 June 1866–22 October 1866; 21 November 1867–25 January 1869, SMPr 46/1, LRO.
78. St Anne's Infants School Log Book, 31 May 1864, 1 June 1864, 5 September 1864, LH/1, Sisters of Notre Dame de Namur Archive.
79. Fitzgerald, 'Catholic Elementary Schools', pp. 189–90.
80. House of Commons, 'Third Report of the Royal Commission Appointed to Inquire into the Working of the Elementary Education Acts', vol. 36, p. 350. Lawrence Conway, Headmaster of Holy Cross School, Liverpool, repeated similar statements during his testimony as well. See ibid., vol. 36, p. 301.
81. See, for example, A History of St. Joseph's Parish, Preston, 1860–1960, p. 27, P126, SDA.
82. Adelphi Infant School Log Book, Salford, 24 and 25 June 1869, 19 July 1869, Faithful Companions of Jesus Archive.
83. St Anne's Mixed School Log Book, Salford, 2 April 1886, 15 November 1886, Faithful Companions of Jesus Archive; St Mary's Infants School Log Book, Burnley, 3 August 1868, 18 August 1868, 28 September 1868, 29 October 1868, SDA.
84. House of Commons, 'Third Report of the Royal Commission Appointed to Inquire into the Working of the Elementary Education Acts', vol. 36, p. 350.
85. Ibid., vol. 36, p. 299.
86. *Tablet*, 31 March 1888, p. 544.
87. *Report of the Liverpool Diocesan Mission Fund for the Year 1883*, pp. 4–6, Liverpolitana, LAA.
88. Letter of Alexander Goss to Rev. Kelly, 23 June 1859, 3/144, Goss Letter Books, 1855–72, Box 14, RCLV, LRO.
89. *Report of the Liverpool Diocesan Mission Fund for the Year 1887* (Liverpool: Rockliff Brothers, 1888), pp. 8–9, Liverpolitana, LAA. See the Diocesan Mission Fund reports

from any large diocese for the year-to-year struggle to provide places of education and worship for a transient and growing Catholic population.

90. *Catholic School*, October 1853, pp. 34–55.
91. St Mary's Boys School Log Book, Manchester, 29 January 1863, 19 January 1864, RCMm 2/1, LRO.
92. St Mary's Girls School Log Book, Manchester, 22 March 1865, RCMm 2/2, LRO.
93. A History of St Joseph's Parish, Preston, 1860–1960, p. 27, P126, SDA.
94. House of Commons, 'Third Report of the Royal Commission Appointed to Inquire into the Working of the Elementary Education Acts', vol. 36, p. 294. His testimony was corroborated by Constance Fox, who told the commission that many of her parents were too poor even to purchase copy books. See ibid., vol. 36, p. 353.
95. Whitehead, 'A View from the Bridge', p. 219.
96. *Seventh Annual Catholic Poor School Committee Report*, as cited in ibid., p. 219.
97. For more on Bishop Brown, see P. Doyle, '"A Tangled Skein of Confusion": The Administration of George Hilary Brown, Bishop of Liverpool, 1850–1856', *Recusant History*, 25:2 (2000), pp. 294–303.
98. Pastoral Letter, 13 June 1854, p. 2, Box 40, RCLV, LRO.
99. Pastoral and Ad Clerum Letters of W. A. Ullathorne, 1848–69, Pastoral Letter, 19 May 1865, p. 2, BAA; *Liverpool Mercury*, 25 September 1871, p. 6.
100. 'The Education Crisis', *Month*, 13:76 (October 1870), p. 389.
101. 'The New Education Act', *Month*, 13:77 (November 1870), p. 611.
102. 'Parliament and Catholic Education', *Dublin Review*, 18 (April 1872), p. 422.
103. See Heimann, *Catholic Devotion in Victorian England*, pp. 125–36, on the development of lay Catholic societies in this period.

4 English Catholics and the Politics of Education, 1847–70

1. Quinn, *Patronage and Piety*, pp. xiv, 63, 184.
2. J. von Arx, 'Catholics and Politics', in McClelland and Hodgetts (eds), *From Without the Flaminian Gate*, pp. 245–71, on pp. 249, 264.
3. J. Altholz, 'The Political Behavior of English Catholics, 1850–1867', *Journal of British Studies*, 4 (November 1964), pp. 89–103, on p. 91.
4. G. Albion, 'The Restoration of the Hierarchy', in Beck (ed.), *The English Catholics*, pp. 86–115, on pp. 100–1; Evans, *The Forging of the Modern State*, pp. 305–6, 421.
5. E. Halevy, *Victorian Years (1841–1895)*, trans. E. I. Watkin (New York: Barnes & Noble, 1961), p. 370.
6. Altholz, 'The Political Behavior of English Catholics', pp. 94–5.
7. Ibid., pp. 95–6.
8. J. J. Dwyer, 'The Catholic Press, 1850–1950', in Beck (ed.), *The English Catholics*, pp. 475–514, on p. 484. What most shocked long-time *Tablet* readers, including Irish MPs, was its strong opposition to the disestablishment of the Irish Church. See *Tablet*, 16 January 1869, p. 366.
9. Altholz, 'The Political Behavior of English Catholics', p. 96; Norman, *The English Catholic Church*, p. 185.
10. *The Times*, 6 June 1851, p. 5.
11. Quinn, *Patronage and Piety*, p. 46.
12. *Manchester Guardian*, 3 April 1862, p. 4.
13. Quinn, *Patronage and Piety*, pp. 66–7.

14. *Reynolds's Magazine*, 16 February 1851, p. 5.
15. E. Larkin, *The Roman Catholic Church and the Home Rule Movement in Ireland, 1870–1874* (Chapel Hill, NC: University of North Carolina Press, 1990), p. 109.
16. See *The Times*, 7 May 1856, p. 6; 9 July 1859, p. 6; 29 July 1859, p. 6; 9 August 1859, p. 6; 12 January 1860, p. 12; 5 May 1860, p. 6; 17 August 1860, p. 7; 25 August 1860, p. 6; 29 June 1861, p. 7; 12 April 1862, p. 6.
17. *The Times*, 28 November 1866, p. 3; 1 December 1866, p. 10; 7 December 1866, p. 10. Henry Manning wrote an open letter to Edward Cardwell, Secretary for the Colonies, in 1864 criticizing the foreign policy of Palmerston and likening it to the role of France in the late eighteenth and early nineteenth centuries as a supporter of seditious causes. This letter came after the administration received Garibaldi as an official guest. See H. E. Manning, 'The Visit of Garibaldi to England', in *Miscellanies*, 3 vols (London: Burns & Oates, 1877–88), vol. 1, p. 146.
18. *The Times*, 11 June 1857, p. 8; 13 June 1857, p. 12.
19. *The Times*, 11 February 1858, p. 6.
20. Maynooth was a Catholic seminary in Ireland to which the British government gave an annual grant. The annual parliamentary grant had begun during the Napoleonic era to quell Irish Catholic unrest. In 1845, Prime Minister Robert Peel proposed tripling the grant amount and making it a permanent item in the government's budget. A great outcry of anti-Catholicism followed, but, with Whig support, Peel's measure passed. See W. L. Arnstein, *Protestant versus Catholic in Mid-Victorian England: Mr. Newdegate and the Nuns* (Columbia, MO: University of Missouri Press, 1982), pp. 6–7, 18–19, 34, 56.
21. *The Times*, 28 February 1852, p. 3.
22. *The Times*, 21 May 1852, p. 4; 26 May 1852, p. 2.
23. *The Times*, 16 June 1852, p. 3.
24. This topic is covered comprehensively in Arnstein's study on anti-Catholicism. See *Protestant versus Catholic*, pp. 62–73, 108–22, 125–35, 178–81, 198–9.
25. Hansard's *Parliamentary Debates*, 3rd series, 116 (1851), cols 979, 983.
26. W. B. Ullathorne, *A Plea for the Rights and Liberties of Religious Women with Reference to the Bill Proposed by Mr. Lacy* (London: Thomas Richardson & Son, 1851), p. 21.
27. Hansard's *Parliamentary Debates*, 3rd series, 127 (1853), cols 99, 102–3.
28. *The Times*, 3 June 1853, p. 8.
29. Hansard's *Parliamentary Debates*, 3rd series, 128 (1853), col. 561.
30. Hansard's *Parliamentary Debates*, 3rd series, 177 (1865), cols 1066–7, 1069, 1637.
31. Hansard's *Parliamentary Debates*, 3rd series, 177 (1865), cols 1642–3.
32. Arnstein, *Protestant versus Catholic*, pp. 67–9.
33. *The Times*, 6 April 1870, p. 5; 9 April 1870, p. 5.
34. *The Times*, 9 April 1870, p. 12.
35. *The Times*, 11 April 1870, p. 11.
36. J. P. Marmion, 'The Beginning of the Catholic Poor Schools in England', *Recusant History*, 17:1 (1984), pp. 67–83.
37. Although this occurred before the official restoration of the Catholic hierarchy in 1850 with the naming of bishops to English sees, the correspondence of the time often referred to the vicars apostolic as bishops (some of them held historic bishoprics outside Great Britain) and the entire group as the Church hierarchy. Technically, however, they were vicars apostolic not English bishops until 1850.
38. B. Ward, *The Sequel to Catholic Emancipation: The Story of the English Catholics Continued Down to the Re-Establishment of their Hierarchy in 1850*, 2 vols (London: Longmans,

Green & Co., 1915), vol. 2, p. 54; J. T. Ward and J. H. Treble, 'Religion and Education in 1843: Reaction to the "Factory Education Bill"', *Journal of Ecclesiastical History*, 20 (April 1969), pp. 79–110, on p. 99.

39. *The Second Annual Report of the Catholic Institute of Great Britain* (London: Richards, 1847), p. 5.
40. Letter of Kay-Shuttleworth to Charles Langdale, 5 February 1847, as cited in ibid., p. 12.
41. Letter of Briggs to Unnamed Colleague, 1847, pp. 1–2, B1664b, Old Series, LEDA.
42. Letter of Briggs to Langdale, 14 April 1847, pp. 1–4, B1666b, Old Series, LEDA.
43. Letter of Griffiths to Langdale, 27 April 1847, 1–3, B1666, Old Series, LEDA.
44. Letter of Kay-Shuttleworth to Charles Langdale, 5 February 1847, as cited in *The Second Annual Report of the Catholic Institute of Great Britain*, pp. 12–13; Norman, *The English Catholic Church*, p. 167.
45. Norman, *The English Catholic Church*, pp. 167–8. Norman contends that the formation of *Tablet* editor Frederick Lucas's Association of St Thomas of Canterbury, a more radical and democratic body urging political action in the realm of education, helped expedite the demise of the Institute and its replacement by the Poor School Committee because of the hierarchy's concern about Lucas's radical tendencies.
46. *Tablet*, 20 March 1869, p. 673; Marmion, 'The Beginnings of the Catholic Poor Schools', p. 71.
47. Letter of Langdale to Vicars Apostolic, 11 November 1847, pp. 1–2, B1690a, Old Series, LEDA.
48. Vicars Apostolic to Catholic Poor School Committee, 1848, as cited in Norman, *The English Catholic Church*, p. 168.
49. Beales, 'The Struggle for the Schools', p. 367. Catholics could not accept building grants right away due to problems over the trust deeds of the planned schools. A model trust deed was finally completed a few years later, thus allowing building grants.
50. *Second Annual Report of the Catholic Poor School Committee*, p. 27.
51. *Catholic Standard*, 13 April 1850, p. 7.
52. Joint Pastoral to our Beloved Brethren and Children in Jesus Christ, the Catholic Clergy and Laity of England, p. 2, Box 35, RCLV, LRO.
53. *Rambler*, August 1852, p. 56.
54. *Rambler*, November 1849, p. 526; *Rambler*, January 1850, p. 104; Letter of Langdale to Vicars Apostolic, April 1849, pp. 1–3, B1547, Documents and Letters, BAA.
55. Pastoral Letter, 28 July 1851, p. 1, Pastoral Letters of Bishop Turner, SDA; Lenten Pastoral, William Hogarth, Bishop of Hexham, 13 February 1852, p. 2, B/K/2, New Series, LEDA; Lenten Pastoral, Thomas Joseph Brown, Bishop of Newport and Menevia, 20 February 1852, p. 7, B/K/2, New Series, LEDA.
56. Pastoral Letter, George Brown, Bishop of Liverpool, June 1852, p. 1, B/K/2, New Series, LEDA; Pastoral Letter, Thomas Grant, Bishop of Southwark, 24 July 1852, pp. 1–2, B/K/2, New Series, LEDA.
57. Guy, *The Synods in English*, pp. 267–8.
58. Minutes of Catholic Poor School Committee meeting, 3 July 1854, p. 3, B1875, Old Series, LEDA.
59. Letter of Langdale to Ullathorne, May 1853, pp. 1–3, B2919a, Documents, BAA.
60. Pastoral Letter, 13 June 1854, p.2, Box 40, RCLV, LRO.
61. Pastoral Letter, 19 June 1854, p. 3, MSS 173, Box 2, Folder 2, N. Wiseman Collection, PTL.

62. *Catholic Standard*, 20 April 1850, p. 6.
63. *Catholic Standard*, 8 June 1850, p. 7.
64. Letter of Scott N. Stokes to the Committee of Council on Education, 19 May 1849, p. 2, ED 11/31/49, TNA, PRO.
65. Letter of Scott N. Stokes to the Committee of Council on Education, 8 August 1849, p.1, ED 11/31/49, TNA, PRO; ibid., 24 August 1849, pp. 1–4.
66. Letter of Scott N. Stokes to the Committee of Council on Education, 4 October 1849, pp. 1–5, ED 11/31/49, TNA, PRO.
67. This letter was in reference to a Committee request for a Catholic boy to serve as a pupil teacher for the 200 Catholic children in Swinton Industrial School. Letter of Scott N. Stokes to the Committee of Council on Education, 12 January 1850, pp. 1–4, ED 11/31/50, TNA, PRO.
68. Letter of Thomas W. Allies to the Committee of Council on Education, 24 October 1856, pp. 1–2, ED 11/31/56, TNA, PRO.
69. Letter of Charles Langdale to the Committee of Council on Education, 17 November 1856, p. 1, ED 11/31/56, TNA, PRO.
70. Letter of Goss to Mr Yates, 14 March 1857, 1/454, and Alexander Goss to Rev. Gillow, 20 May 1857, 2/34, Goss Letter Books 1855–72, Box 14, RCLV, LRO.
71. *First Annual Report of the Catholic Poor School Committee*, p. 17.
72. Ibid.
73. *Twentieth Annual Report of the Catholic Poor School Committee* (London: Catholic Poor School Committee, 1868), p. 14. Those four contributors were the fourteenth Duke of Norfolk, the Earl of Shrewsbury, Colonel Towneley and an unnamed friend of Charles Langdale.
74. *Catholic* School, March 1855, p. 125. Note that by the time this was published for public consumption, the training school had been open for three months. The article, according to an editor's note, had been written the year before.
75. N. Nicholson, 'St. Mary's College Hammersmith: Its Early Development in the Context of Mid-Nineteenth-Century Teacher Training', in M. Eaton, J. Longmore and A. Naylor (eds), *Commitment to Diversity: Catholics and Education in a Changing World* (London: Cassell, 2000), pp. 115–62, on pp. 120–1, 124.
76. *Eighth Annual Report of the Catholic Poor School Committee* (London: Catholic Poor School Committee, 1855), p. 8.
77. Nicholson, 'St. Mary's Training College, Hammersmith', pp. 125–6, 156.
78. House of Commons, 'First Report of the Royal Commission Appointed to Inquire into the Working of the Elementary Education Acts', vol. 34, p. 459.
79. Much important work has been competed recently on the activities of female religious orders in England and Wales. See Walsh, *Roman Catholic Nuns in England and Wales*; S. O'Brien, 'Terra Incognita: The Nun in Nineteenth-Century England', *Past and Present*, 121 (November 1988), pp. 110–40; S. O'Brien, 'French Nuns in Nineteenth-Century England', *Past and Present*, 154 (February 1997), pp. 142–80; S. O'Brien, 'Religious Life for Women', in McClelland and Hodgetts (eds), *From Without the Flaminian Gate*, pp. 108–41; K. Lowden, 'Women Religious and Teacher Education: A Case Study of the Sisters of Notre Dame in the Nineteenth Century', in Eaton et al. (eds), *Commitment to Diversity*, pp. 67–93.
80. Scott N. Stokes, as cited in *The History of the Training College of Notre Dame, Liverpool 1856–1885* (St Mary's Abbey, Bergholt: St Benedict's Press, 1885), pp. 1–2.
81. Battersby, 'Educational Work of the Religious Orders of Women', p. 348.

82. *Twentieth Annual Report of the Catholic Poor School Committee*, p. 15; Battersby, 'Educational Work of the Religious Orders of Women', pp. 348–9; *The History of the Training College of Notre Dame*, p. 13.
83. Notebook Entitled 'Foundations and Compliments', p. 2, MPh/4, Sisters of Notre Dame de Namur Archive.
84. She was the daughter of Lord and Lady Stafford, and married the Hon. Edward Petre, nephew to the twelfth Duke of Norfolk, in 1829. After her husband's death in 1848, she entered as a postulant into the Sisters of Notre Dame de Namur and worked as assistant to the Mother-General in Belgium. She was intricately involved in the deliberations with Mr Allies of the Poor School Committee, and played a leading role in the creation of the Mount Pleasant training college for women. See *Sister Mary of Saint Francis: Assistant to the Mother-General of the Sisters of Notre Dame of Namur, Belgium* (London: Burns & Oates, 1951), pp. 25–45.
85. House of Commons, 'First Report of the Royal Commission Appointed to Inquire into the Working of the Elementary Education Acts', vol. 34, p. 339. The third female training college was the Wandsworth Training College built by the Sacred Heart nuns in 1870.
86. Pastoral Letter, 18 June 1857, pp. 1–2, MSS 173, Box 2, Folder 2, N. Wiseman Collection, PTL.

5 English Catholics and the Politics of Education, 1870

1. *The Times*, 25 June 1885, p. 4.
2. Ibid.
3. Ullathorne, *Notes on the Education Question*, p. 72.
4. Letter of Turner to Briggs, 10 February 1857, pp. 1–2, B/A/312, Briggs Correspondence, New Series, LEDA.
5. Notes on Resolutions Adopted at Bishops Meeting in London, April 1857, B1917, Briggs Correspondence, Old Series, LEDA.
6. Lenten Indult, 28 February 1859, p. 6, Pastorals Etc. 1848–88, BAA. A similar admission came in a pastoral letter in 1865 in which he was grateful for the government aid that had allowed his diocese to increase the number of poor schools to 85, up from 39 in 1843. See Pastoral Letter, 22 November 1865, pp. 8–9, Pastorals Ullathorne 1850–69, BAA.
7. Letters between Charles Langdale and F. Stephen of the Committee of Council on Education between September 1858 and May 1859 do indicate that Langdale and the Poor School Committee asked to have a Catholic representative on the Education Commission, but did so after the other Assistant Commissioners had already been appointed and begun their inquiries.
8. *Rambler*, February 1859, p. 106.
9. Letter of Langdale to Bishops, 18 October 1858, pp. 1–2, B1864b, Old Series, LEDA; Cardinal Wiseman quoted in Lenten Indult, 28 February 1859, p. 6, Pastorals Etc. 1848–88, BAA.
10. Ad Clerum, 9 November 1858, p. 1, Pastoral Letters of Bishop Turner, SDA; Lenten Indult, 28 February 1859, pp. 12–13, Pastorals Etc. 1848–88, BAA.
11. House of Commons, 'Report of the Commissioners on the State of Popular Education in England and with an Index', *Sessional Papers 1861*, Education General, vol. 1, 680–2.
12. Letter of Goss to Edwards, 16 June 1859, p. 1, 3/133, Goss Letter Books 1855–72, Box 14, RCLV, LRO.

13. See *The Times*, 12 February 1862, p. 6; 28 February 1862, p. 7.
14. *The Times*, 1 March 1862, p. 6.
15. See *The Times*, 7 March 1862, p. 6; 12 March 1862, p. 6; 14 March 1862, p. 6; 18 March 1862, p. 5; 21 March 1862, p. 7; 22 March 1862, p. 6; 25 March 1862, p. 7. A partial explanation for the lack of parliamentary activity by the Irish bloc was that they were heavily involved in other legislative matters at the time. Three days prior to Lowe's introduction of the new code on 13 February, John Pope Hennessy introduced a bill to reform the Poor Laws in Ireland. Debate on Hennessy's bill occurred the day after Lowe's introduction, and then again in March, at which time several Irish Catholic MPs spoke on the floor. See Hansard's *Parliamentary Debates*, 3rd series, 165 (1862), cols 101–2, 341–2, 1959–62, 1965–6.
16. Handwritten Notes from Bishops Meeting at Low Week, 29 April 1862, pp. 1–3, B4111, Documents and Letters, BAA.
17. *Liverpool Mercury*, 8 February 1867, p. 3.
18. Letter of Goss to Manning, 17 February 1868, p. 1, 5/188, Goss Letter Books 1855–72, Box 14, RCLV, LRO.
19. Pastoral Letter, 28 May 1869, pp. 93–4, Beverley Diocesan ACTA, LEDA.
20. Letter of Lord Howard to Bishop Cornthwaite, 30 June 1869, p. 4, C/E/38, Cornthwaite Education Files, LEDA.
21. Ibid., pp. 1–4.
22. Letter of T. W. Allies to Bishop Cornthwaite, 14 May 1862, p. 1, C/A/61, Cornthwaite Education Files, LEDA; Ad Clerum, 10 July 1868, pp. 1–2, Beverley Diocesan ACTA, LEDA.
23. Pastoral Letter, 28 May 1869, p. 93, LEDA.
24. Letter of Manning to Lord Howard, 9 April 1869, pp. 1–3, B4724, Documents and Letters, BAA.
25. McClelland, *Cardinal Manning*, p. 61. See also K. T. Hoppen, *The Mid-Victorian Generation 1846–1886* (Oxford: Clarendon Press, 2003), pp. 219–20. With the land reform process in Ireland temporarily shelved, Gladstone believed that the disestablishment of the Anglican Church of Ireland would purchase Irish goodwill and unify his party.
26. *Tablet*, 5 December 1868, p. 148.
27. Letter of Goss to Rev. Wilford Cooper, 30 August 1868, p. 1, 5/198, Goss Letter Books 1855–72, Box 14, RCLV, LRO.
28. 'Popular Education in England', *Dublin Review*, 10 (January 1868), p. 136.
29. *Tablet*, 16 January 1869, p. 366.
30. *Tablet*, 6 February 1869, p. 465.
31. Herbert Alfred Vaughan was born of a recusant family from Herefordshire. After studies in England and Belgium, Vaughan befriended Manning in Rome. He opened St Joseph's Foreign Missionary College in 1869, acquired ownership of the *Tablet* in the same year, and took a mission to America to Christianize freed slaves. In 1872 Vaughan became Bishop of Salford and immersed himself in the Catholic education effort nationally. Vaughan succeeded Manning as Archbishop of Westminster in 1892, became a Cardinal in 1893, and led the successful capital campaign to build the current Westminster Cathedral. He died in 1903, just months after the tiring educational conflict over the Balfour Bill in 1902.
32. *Tablet*, 6 February 1869, p. 465.

33. *Twenty-First Annual Report of the Catholic Poor School Committee* (London: Catholic Poor School Committee, 1869), pp. 10–11; see also 'The Primary Education of the Poor', *Month*, 11:62 (September 1869), p. 233.
34. Manning, *Denominational Education*, p. 9.
35. *The Times*, 21 January 1869, p. 9.
36. *Tablet*, 6 February 1869, p. 465. Note that the parliamentary debate over Forster's education bill was still a year away.
37. W. B. Ullathorne, *Catholic Education: The Address Delivered at the Catholic Meeting in the Town Hall, Birmingham, November 15th, 1869, by the Right Rev. Bishop Ullathorne* (Birmingham: M. Maher & Son, 1869), pp. 4–12, B4778, Documents and Letters, BAA.
38. *Tablet*, 22 January 1870, pp. 101–2.
39. Ibid., pp. 107–8. See McClelland, *Cardinal Manning*, ch. 3, for the standard account of the archbishop's role in the Catholic response to the Education Act of 1870. Note that Howard's letter also ran concurrently in the *Catholic Times*.
40. *Tablet*, 12 February 1870, p. 197. According to McClelland, the entire hierarchy was not in Rome. Manning left Bishop Brown of Newport in charge, but the 72-year-old Bishop, while still intellectually active, remained in Wales much of the year and also did not get on well with the Duke or Lord Howard. See McClelland, *Cardinal Manning*, pp. 77–8.
41. *Tablet*, 19 February 1870, pp. 225–6.
42. T. Burke, *Catholic History of Liverpool* (Liverpool: C. Tinling & Co., 1910), p. 188.
43. *Tablet*, 5 February 1870, p. 169.
44. *Tablet*, 26 February 1870, p. 261.
45. *The Times*, 11 March 1870, p. 5.
46. *The Times*, 17 March 1870, p. 6. See also *The Times*, 16 March 1870, p. 5; 19 March 1870, p. 6; 22 March 1870, p. 5; 24 March 1870, p. 6.
47. *The Times*, 30 March 1870, p. 6. See *The Times*, 13 May 1870, p. 5, for a parliamentary petition from a group of the most influential lay Catholics warning Parliament not to pass a bill that would violate the consciences and liberties of Catholics.
48. Letter of Manning to Gladstone, 24 February 1870, British Library, Add. MS 44,249, ff. 139–40.
49. *The Times*, 28 February 1870, p. 10.
50. *Tablet*, 12 March 1870, p. 330.
51. *Tablet*, 26 March 1870, p. 385.
52. 'The Ministerial Education Bill', *Dublin Review*, 14 (April 1870), pp. 437–8.
53. 'The Education Bill', *Dublin Review*, 15 (July 1870), p. 125.
54. McClelland, *Cardinal Manning*, p. 67; Selby, 'Henry Edward Manning and the Education Bill of 1870', p. 204. See also Beales, 'The Struggle for the Schools', pp. 373–7.
55. Selby, 'Henry Edward Manning and the Education Bill of 1870', p. 200. Manning relates this to Gladstone in a letter dated 7 March 1870, British Library, Add. MS 44,249, ff. 144–5.
56. Letter of Manning to Gladstone, 7 March 1870, British Library, Add. MS 44,249, ff. 144–5.
57. McClelland, *Cardinal Manning*, p. 68.
58. Letter of Manning to Gladstone, 20 March 1870, British Library, Add. MS 44,249, ff. 146–7.
59. Letter of Manning to Gladstone, 6 April 1870, p. 1, MSS 002, Box 13, Folder 6, H. Manning Collection, PTL.

60. Letter of Gladstone to Manning, 26 March, 1870, British Library, Add. MS 44,249, ff. 148–9, 150–1.
61. Statement of Bishops from Poor School Committee, 12 March 1870, p. 1, C/E/5, Cornthwaite Education Files, LEDA; *The Times*, 14 March 1870, p. 4. McClelland states that he was assured by the archivist at the English College in Rome that no such official meeting took place, yet Allies here is reporting a statement from the bishops on 12 March (*Cardinal Manning*, p. 80, n.). *The Times* also reported on 14 March that the *Weekly Register* contained details of a three-hour meeting of the bishops on 28 February where the education bill was discussed with Manning presiding.
62. Selby, 'Henry Edward Manning and the Education Bill of 1870', pp. 210–11.
63. Letter of Manning to O'Sullivan, 26 August 1870, pp. 1–3, B4839, Documents and Letters, BAA.
64. See Selby, 'Henry Edward Manning and the Education Bill of 1870', pp. 211–12.
65. Manning, *National Education and Parental Rights*, p. 43.
66. *The Times*, 13 May 1870, p. 5.
67. Letter of Lord Howard to Bishop Cornthwaite, 18 May 1870, pp. 1–4, C/E/40, Cornthwaite Education Files, LEDA.
68. *The Times*, 14 June 1870, p. 5
69. *The Times*, 5 July 1870, p. 5.
70. Hansard's *Parliamentary Debates*, 3rd series, 203 (1870), cols 851–4, 1183–4.
71. *The Times*, 8 September 1870, p. 6. This figure shows a fivefold increase in the need for Catholic educational provision in Liverpool since 1848, when the number of Catholic children was around 5,000.
72. Pastoral Letter, 1 September 1870, Series I, Box II C/15, LAA.
73. *The Times*, 26 October 1870, p. 6.
74. Letter of Norfolk to Cornthwaite, 13 October 1870, pp. 1–4, C/E/40, Cornthwaite Education Files, LEDA.
75. Pastoral Letter, 21 October 1870, pp. 183–92, p. 1, Beverley Diocesan ACTA, LEDA.
76. Pastoral Letter, 27 October 1870, pp. 3–7, Pastorals Ullathorne 1870–88, BAA.
77. Letter of Norfolk to Cornthwaite, 25 November 1870, p. 1, C/E/8, Cornthwaite Education Files, LEDA.
78. Letter of Allies to Cornthwaite, 20 December 1870, p. 1, C/E/10, Cornthwaite Education Files, LEDA. The amounts provided were: Westminster, £7038 16*s.*; Beverley, £2546 16*s.*; Birmingham, £2000; Clifton, £192; Hexham, £2800; Liverpool, £9498 16*s.*; Menevia, £1500; Northampton, £40; Plymouth, £272; Salford, £2600; Shrewsbury, £1400; Southwark, £2400; West Scotland, £6000; East Scotland, £3000; North Scotland, £100. This reflects the inclusion of three Scottish districts that now were under the purview of the Poor School Committee, especially Glasgow which had a very large Irish Catholic population.
79. See Selby, 'Henry Edward Manning and the Education Bill of 1870', pp. 203–4; McClelland, *Cardinal Manning*, pp. 70–1.
80. For that criticism, see Purcell, *Life of Cardinal Manning*, vol. 2, p. 494.
81. See Selby, 'Henry Edward Manning and the Education Bill of 1870', p. 211.
82. *The Times*, 8 March 1870, p. 7; 9 March 1870, pp. 5–6; 11 March 1870, p. 5; 12 March 1870, p. 7; 28 March 1870, p. 6; 22 July 1870, p. 7.
83. Quinn, *Patronage and Piety*, p. 26.

6 English Catholics and the Politics of Education, 1871–90

1. Letter of Manning to Cullen, 30 May 1873, as cited in S. Leslie, *Henry Edward Manning: His Life and Labours* (London: Burns, Oates & Washbourne, 1921), p. 176.
2. *Tablet*, 1 April 1871, p. 386. The paper certainly reflected the more conservative outlook of Herbert Vaughan, who had purchased the *Tablet* in 1868 and was sole proprietor and editor until his appointment as Bishop of Salford in 1872, when George Elliot Ranken took over as editor. See Dwyer, 'The Catholic Press', p. 485.
3. *Tablet*, 22 April 1871, pp. 483–4. See also the *Twenty-Third Annual Report of the Catholic Poor School Committee* (London: Catholic Poor School Committee, 1871).
4. 'Results of the Education Act', *Month*, 16:91–2 (January–February 1872), pp. 125–7.
5. 'Parliament and Catholic Education', *Dublin Review*, 21 (January 1872), pp. 413, 421–2.
6. The Elementary Education Act of 1873 changed the relationship of voluntary schools to the school boards. Under the Act of 1870, voluntary schools could choose not to have inspection, and thereby not receive Privy Council grants, and their only penalty would be to suffer the competition if a board school was built nearby. With the Act of 1873, parents sending their children to such 'independent' voluntary schools had to prove to a magistrate that their children could pass an examination of their age group or they faced a possible fine. Consequently, Catholics believed this Act went further to harm any of their schools which chose not to participate in the governmental system.
7. 'Secularism in Elementary Education', *Dublin Review*, 25 (July 1875), pp. 64, 68–9, 72–3, 80–1.
8. Quinn, *Patronage and Piety*, pp. 26–31.
9. Catholic Education Crisis Fund Committee Code of Rules, 1871, C/E/11, Cornthwaite Education Files, LEDA.
10. *Birmingham Daily Post*, 29 May 1871, p. 5; see also Pastoral Letter, 21 April 1871, pp. 1–19, Beverley Diocesan ACTA, LEDA.
11. Documents and Letters, B4913, 1871, BAA.
12. Letter of Norfolk to Cornthwaite, 25 March 1871, pp. 1–6, C/E/49; letter of Allies to Cornthwaite, 4 July 1871, pp. 1–4; letter of Cornthwaite to Allies, 6 July 1871, p. 1; letter of Allies to Cornthwaite, 7 July 1871, pp. 1–4; letter of Cornthwaite to Allies, 9 July 1871, pp. 1–3; letter of Allies to Cornthwaite, 14 July 1871, pp. 1–5; letter of Cornthwaite to Allies, 16 July 1871, p. 1; letter of Allies to Cornthwaite, 17 July 1871, pp. 1–2, C/E/50, Cornthwaite Education Files, LEDA.
13. List of Schools in the Diocese of Birmingham to which a Grant has been Paid from the Catholic Education Crisis Fund, 1871, p. 1, B5097, Documents and Letters, BAA.
14. Pastoral Letter, 6 October 1871, pp. 217–29, Beverley Diocesan ACTA, LEDA; *Report of the Catholic Education Crisis Fund at Expiration of the Second Year* (London: W. Davy & Son, 1873), p. 5, C/E/16, Cornthwaite Education Files, LEDA.
15. Pastoral Letter, 25 October 1872, pp. 259–68, Beverley Diocesan ACTA, LEDA.
16. *Report of the Catholic Education Crisis Fund*, pp. 1, 6, C/E/16, Cornthwaite Education Files, LEDA.
17. Letter of Manning to Bishops, 22 February 1871, p. 1, B4905, Documents and Letters, BAA; Ad Clerum, 1 March 1871, p. 143, Beverley Diocesan ACTA, LEDA.
18. *The Times*, 16 March 1871, p. 8.
19. *The Times*, 19 July 1871, p. 11.
20. Ad Clerum, 14 November 1873, pp. 1–2, Liverpolitana, LAA.

21. *The Times*, 6 March 1872, p. 7.
22. *The Times*, 1 March 1873, p. 6; 4 March 1873, p. 5; 5 March 1873, p. 6; 6 March 1873, p. 8; 7 March 1873, p. 7; 8 March 1873, p. 6; 14 March 1873, p. 6; 21 March 1873, p. 5; 28 March 1873, p. 6; 22 April 1873, p. 6.
23. Due to its designation as an Anglican institution, Trinity College, Dublin, was not open to Irish Catholics, and due to their secular education and non-denominational nature, the Queens colleges, located in Belfast, Cork and Galway, were places Catholics would not attend. While the Irish hierarchy wanted to have its own state-endowed university, Gladstone offered in his bill a university for Dublin to which other denominations could then add their own colleges. The proposed college was to have a non-denominational governing body and its curriculum was to be secular. See Quinn, *Patronage and Piety*, pp. 27–8; G. I. T. Machin, *Politics and the Churches in Great Britain 1869 to 1921* (Oxford: Clarendon Press, 1987), p. 53.
24. *The Times*, 5 March 1873, p. 5.
25. Gladstone resigned after the bill failed, but, when Disraeli refused to form a ministry, Gladstone was forced to remain in office as a lame duck until the election in 1874. For the Catholic political role in this episode, see Quinn, *Patronage and Piety*, p. 28; and Machin, *Politics and the Churches*, pp. 54–61.
26. *The Times*, 22 March 1873, p. 11.
27. See Catholic petitions in *The Times*, 10 June 1873, p. 8; 12 June 1873, p. 6; 14 June 1873, p. 7; 17 June 1873, p. 6.
28. Pastoral Letter, 12 August 1873, pp. 8–23, Beverley Diocesan ACTA, LEDA.
29. Machin, *Politics and the Churches*, p. 65.
30. *Tablet*, 7 February 1874, p. 184, as cited in Quinn, *Patronage and Piety*, p. 29.
31. Machin, *Politics and the Churches*, p. 67.
32. This clause allowed the fees of poor children to be paid at denominational schools due to their parents' poverty. This especially angered nonconformists because their property rates could be used to support Anglican schools. In reality, the clause was not invoked very often.
33. Burke, *The Catholic History of Liverpool*, pp. 211–14.
34. Letter of Bright to Gladstone, 26 January 1874, as cited in J. P. Rossi, 'English Catholics, the Liberal Party, and the General Election of 1880', *Catholic Historical Review*, 63 (July 1977), pp. 411–27, on p. 412.
35. Letter of Vaughan to Lady Herbert of Lea, 11 February 1874, in *Letters of Herbert Cardinal Vaughan to Lady Herbert of Lea 1867 to 1903*, ed. S. Leslie (London: Burns & Oates, 1942), p. 245.
36. Quinn, *Patronage and Piety*, pp. 30–1, 71.
37. Purcell, *Life of Cardinal Manning*, vol. 2, p. 519.
38. Rossi, 'English Catholics, the Liberal Party, and the General Election', p. 414.
39. Ibid., p. 415; Machin, *Politics and the Churches*, pp. 104–5; Purcell, *Life of Cardinal Manning*, vol. 2, pp. 524–5. See also Manning's Lenten Pastorals, *The Times*, 4 March 1878, p. 10; 25 February 1879, p. 10.
40. Rossi, 'English Catholics, the Liberal Party, and the General Election', p. 417.
41. H. Owen, *The Education Acts, 1870–1902, and Other Acts Relating to Education* (London: Knight & Co., 1903), p. 310.
42. *The Times*, 21 June 1876, p. 7.
43. *The Times*, 12 July 1876, p. 10.

44. See Hansard's *Parliamentary Debates*, 3rd series, 229 (1876), cols 1941–5; 230 (1876), col. 1296; *The Times*, 14 July 1876, p. 6; 19 July 1876, p. 8; 20 July 1876, pp. 6–7; 21 July 1876, p. 7; 22 July 1876, p. 8; 25 July 1876, p. 8; 28 July 1876, p. 7; 29 July 1876, p. 7; 4 August 1876, p. 8; 5 August 1876, p. 8; 9 August 1876, p. 7.
45. *The Times*, 25 July 1876, p. 8.
46. *The Times*, 4 August 1876, p. 8.
47. Letter of Manning to Ripon, 14 June 1876, British Library, Add. MS 43,545, ff. 4–6.
48. *The Times*, 29 August 1876, p. 3. Pope Pius IX made Manning a Cardinal in 1875.
49. *Birmingham Daily Post*, 29 August 1876, p. 8; *Angelus*, September 1876, p. 216, NDA.
50. See *The Times*, 14 June 1876, p. 9; 15 June 1876, p. 6; 16 June 1876, p. 6; 20 June 1876, p. 6.
51. Pastoral Letter, Lent, 1876, p. 10; Pastoral Letter, Advent 1876, pp. 8–9, Pastorals Bagshawe 1874–1901, NDA.
52. Rossi, 'English Catholics, the Liberal Party and the General Election', p. 418.
53. As cited in Machin, *Politics and the Churches*, p. 114.
54. Rossi, 'English Catholics, the Liberal Party, and the General Election', pp. 419–20; *Machin, Politics and the Churches*, p. 115.
55. Norman, *The English Catholic Church*, pp. 195–6.
56. Rossi, 'English Catholics, the Liberal Party, and the General Election', p. 425.
57. Machin, *Politics and the Churches*, p. 116.
58. *Report of the Committee of Council on Education with Appendix, 1871–72*, ED 17/37, TNA, PRO; *Report of the Committee of Council on Education with Appendix, 1872–73*, ED 17/39, TNA, PRO; *Report of the Committee of Council on Education with Appendix, 1881–82*, ED 17/52/150–1, TNA, PRO.
59. Handwritten document titled School Statistics in the Diocese of Liverpool, March 1877, S3 1 B/1, LAA.
60. Document titled Salford Diocesan Education Board, 10 November 1870, ACTA Turner, SDA. The third page of this document shows deficiency statistics. See also *Educational Statistics of the Diocese of Salford* (Salford: J. Roberts, 1873), pp. 3–10; *Educational Statistics of the Diocese of Salford* (Salford: J. Roberts, 1877–8), pp. 8–9; *Educational Statistics of the Diocese of Salford* (Salford: J. Roberts, 1881), p. 10.
61. *The Times*, 1 July 1878, p. 10. This is evidence that marks Manning's intentions on the path towards the royal commission four years prior to the evidence Selby uses as the beginning of Manning's crusade. He begins with Manning's writings in 1882.
62. Selby, *Towards a Common System of National Education*, p. 2.
63. *The Times*, 22 September 1880, p. 8.
64. *The Times*, 15 June 1881, p. 12.
65. M. Sturt, *The Education of the People: A History of Primary Education in England and Wales in the Nineteenth Century* (London: Routledge & Kegan Paul, 1967), pp. 346–7.
66. Memorandum on Mr Mundella's Proposals, 7 November 1881, Vaughan ACTA, SDA.
67. *Thirty-Second Annual Report of the Catholic Poor School Committee* (London: Catholic Poor School Committee, 1879), pp. 18–20; *Thirty-Fourth Annual Report of the Catholic Poor School Committee* (London: Catholic Poor School Committee, 1881), pp. 25–7; *Thirty-Fifth Annual Report of the Catholic Poor School Committee* (London: Catholic Poor School Committee, 1882), pp. 18–20.
68. Manning, 'Is the Education Act of 1870 a Just Law?', in *National Education* (London: Burns & Oates, 1890), p. 22.
69. Letter of Manning to Cross, 1 November 1882, British Library, Add. MS 51,269, ff. 235–6.

70. Selby, *Towards a Common System of National Education*, p. 4.
71. *A Letter on the Educational Peril to Christianity*, 21 February 1882, pp. 11, 15, Vaughan ACTA, SDA.
72. *The Times*, 18 April 1882, p. 10.
73. Petition to the House of Commons, May 1882, pp. 1–5, Vaughan ACTA, SDA. It is important to note that instructions for petitioning Parliament were included in this notice of the petition. In order that the petition would not be discarded due to its not adhering to the proper rules of parliamentary procedure, the instructions were detailed. For example, petitions must be written on one side only of large sheets with the heading plainly written on the top. At least three signatures were required on the sheet with the wording of the petition. Before being sent to Parliament, petition sheets had to be 'gummed or pasted' together 'so as to form a roll'. Any loose sheets were rejected and if they were signature sheets, did not count. As long as they weighed less than two pounds, they could be sent free of postage, but they had to have the words 'Parliamentary Petition' written on the outside of the envelope. A letter in the same mailing was required to go to the MP, asking him to present the petition and listing the number of signatures. See also Petition against School Rates for Board Schools, 20 July 1883, Vaughan ACTA, SDA; or To the Honourable the Commons of the United Kingdom of Great Britain and Ireland in Parliament Assembled, October 1893, p. 3, Bilsborrow ACTA, SDA. One can attribute such care to their increased concern for making known their political opinions.
74. Ad Clerum, 9 May 1882, #79, Folder E06 Bishops Circulars 1880–90, Box E01–E11, NDA.
75. See *The Times*, 24 May 1882, p. 6, through 11 August 1882, p. 6, for the almost daily introduction of petitions from Catholics in favour of the denominational system and against the education rate.
76. *The Times*, 28 July 1882, p. 7.
77. *Resolutions of the Catholic Bishops in England at their Annual Meeting held at Archbishop's House, Westminster, in Low-Week 1882*, May 1882, p. 1, Leeds Diocesan ACTA, 1881–3, LEDA.
78. Gladstone's reform bill of 1884 broadened the household franchise to the county voter, which increased the total electorate from three million to over five million.
79. J. G. Snead-Cox, *The Life of Cardinal Vaughan*, 2 vols (London: Herbert & Daniel, 1912), vol. 2, p. 91.
80. Ibid., vol. 2, pp. 92–7.
81. Letter of Vaughan to Ullathorne, 4 February 1884, pp. 1–7, R1060; Letter of Ullathorne to Vaughan, 12 February 1884, pp. 1–3, R1061, Documents and Letters, BAA.
82. Letter of Manning to Bishops, 31 May 1884, p. 1, B8452, Documents and Letters, BAA.
83. Ad Clerum, 11 July 1884, p. 1, Vaughan ACTA, SDA.
84. Voluntary School Association: Resolutions of the Bishops Passed at their Annual Meeting Held in Low Week, p. 1, Early Bishops Collection Brown–Whiteside, Series 3.I Education A. Papers on Education and Schools Programme, LAA.
85. Letter of Ripon to Cornthwaite, 31 December 1884, pp. 1–6, C/A/665, Cornthwaite Correspondence, LEDA; J. F. Supple, 'Catholicism in Yorkshire, 1850–1900' (PhD thesis, University of Leeds, 1982), p. 93.
86. J. Kershaw, 'The Catholic Education Question in England and Ireland', *Dublin Review*, 13 (January 1885), pp. 155, 159, 167–8.

87. See R. O'Neil, *Cardinal Herbert Vaughan: Archbishop of Westminster, Bishop of Salford, Founder of the Mill Hill Missionaries* (London: Burns & Oates, 1997), p. 4; and Norman, *The English Catholic Church*, pp. 345–6, for comments on the somewhat direct, abrasive and sometimes aggressive nature of Vaughan's personality.
88. H. A. Vaughan, *Pastoral Letter on the Parental Right and Church Guidance in Education* (Manchester: T. Walker, 1885), p. 8, Vaughan ACTA, SDA.
89. Letter to School Managers, 23 February 1885, p. 1, Vaughan ACTA, SDA. The questionnaire reads: '1. Has your grant been increased or decreased under the new Code, and to what amount? 2. Have you been put to increased expenditure for extra staff and appliances, and to what amount? 3. How many additional hours to the prescribed school-hours per week have children to employ in studies in order to secure satisfying results at the Government examination? 4. Respecting the 17s. 6d. limit, have you forfeited any amount of the grant under the above restrictions during the last twelve months?'
90. Snead-Cox, *The Life of Cardinal Vaughan*, vol. 2, p. 100.
91. Pastoral Letter, 12 February 1885, pp. 7–11, Leeds Diocesan ACTA, 1884–5, LEDA.
92. Ad Clerum, 23 February 1885, pp. 1–3, Liverpolitana, LAA.
93. *Liverpool Mercury*, 2 March 1885, p. 7.
94. *The Times*, 25 June 1885, p. 4.
95. 'How Shall Catholics Vote at the Coming Parliamentary Election?', *Dublin Review*, 14 (October 1885), pp. 406–11.
96. Pastoral Letter, 6 November 1885, p. 7, Liverpolitana, LAA; Ad Clerum, 2 November 1885, 1, B9022, Documents and Letters, BAA.
97. Pastoral Letter, 6 November 1885, p. 7, Liverpolitana, LAA.
98. Pastoral Letter, 18 November 1885, p. 1, #122, Folder E06 Bishops Circulars 1880–90, Box E01–E11, NDA.
99. *The Times*, 2 November 1885, p. 9; *Resolutions of the Catholic Bishops of England on Education*, 31 October 1885, pp. 1–2, Leeds Diocesan ACTA, 1884–5, LEDA; Snead-Cox, *The Life of Cardinal Vaughan*, vol. 2, p. 101.
100. C. H. D. Howard, 'The Parnell Manifesto of 21 November, 1885, and the Schools Question', *English Historical Review*, 62 (January 1947), pp. 42–51, on pp. 44–5.
101. Letter of Joseph Chamberlain to Thomas Wareing, 10 October 1885, pp. 1–3, R1110, Documents and Letters, BAA.
102. *The Times*, 6 November 1885, p. 7.
103. Howard, 'The Parnell Manifesto', p. 45; Machin, *Politics and the Churches*, p. 163.
104. Howard, 'The Parnell Manifesto', pp. 44, 49–51; O'Neil, *Cardinal Herbert Vaughan*, pp. 278–88.
105. Letter of Manning to Cross, 13 November 1885, British Library, Add. MS 51,269, ff. 240–1.
106. Machin, *Politics and the Churches*, p. 165; Selby, *Towards a Common System of National Education*, p. 5.
107. See E. Larkin, *The Roman Catholic Church and the Creation of the Modern Irish State, 1878–1886* (Philadelphia, PA: American Philosophical Society, 1975), pp. 278–82, 366, for Manning's attitudes on this subject. Also, O'Neil, *Cardinal Herbert Vaughan*, p. 286.
108. Letter of Walsh to Manning, 27 December 1885, as cited in Larkin, *The Roman Catholic Church and the Creation of the Modern Irish State*, pp. 356–7.
109. Letter of Walsh to Manning, 23 February 1886, as cited in ibid., p. 365.

110. Letter of Manning to Sir Howard Vincent, 13 May 1886, as cited in ibid., p. 374. Vincent was Manning's godson and the archbishop instructed him not to make his comments publicly known.
111. *The Times*, 5 May 1886, p. 5.
112. Letter of Manning to Vaughan, 11 June 1886, as cited in Leslie, *Henry Edward Manning*, p. 408. See also Larkin, *The Roman Catholic Church and the Creation of the Modern Irish State*, pp. 379–80.
113. Letter of Ullathorne to Manning, 18 June 1886, p. 1, R1611; Letter of Ullathorne to Manning, 22 June 1886, p. 1, R1612, Documents and Letters, BAA; *The Times*, 6 July 1886, p. 5. See also Larkin, *The Roman Catholic Church and the Creation of the Modern Irish State*, pp. 380–1. Larkin has the date that Manning's letter was published listed incorrectly as 5 July.
114. For more on Manning's role on the Cross Commission, see Selby, *Towards a Common System of National Education*.
115. Manning, 'To Amend the Education Act of 1870', in *Miscellanies*, vol. 3, p. 83.
116. Ad Clerum, 22 January 1886, p. 1; Ad Clerum, 27 September 1886, p. 1, Liverpolitana, LAA.
117. Ad Clerum, 30 October 1886, pp. 1–3, Liverpolitana, LAA.
118. Manning, 'Suggestions for a Common System of National Education', in *Miscellanies*, vol. 3, p. 89.
119. The 14th clause forbade the teaching of any 'religious catechism or religious formulary which is distinctive of any particular denomination' in a school supported by local rates. See Owen, *The Education Acts*, p. 210.
120. Manning, 'Suggestions for a Common System of National Education', in *Miscellanies*, vol. 3, p. 87.
121. Selby, *Towards a Common System of National Education*, pp. 24–6, 50.
122. Ibid., pp. 26–7.
123. Ibid., p. 31.
124. Letter of Salisbury to Cranbrook, 12 January 1889, as cited in Machin, *Politics and the Churches*, p. 188. Salisbury was referring to ex-Liberal Joseph Chamberlain who left the Liberal party over Home Rule in 1886 and brought his followers into an alliance with the Conservatives.
125. Letter of Manning to Ullathorne, 20 December 1888, as cited in Leslie, *Henry Edward Manning*, p. 452.
126. E. Larkin, *The Roman Catholic Church in Ireland and the Fall of Parnell, 1888–1891* (Chapel Hill, NC: University of North Carolina Press, 1979), pp. xvii–xxi.
127. Ibid., pp. 110–23.

7 English Catholics and the Politics of Education, 1891–1902

1. *The Times*, 20 August 1895, p. 12; Machin, *Politics and the Churches*, p. 219.
2. See O'Neil, *Cardinal Herbert Vaughan*, pp. 283–91, for an examination of Vaughan's perspective on the Irish and Home Rule.
3. Snead-Cox, *The Life of Cardinal Vaughan*, vol. 2, pp. 103, 106.
4. Letter of Manning to Ilsley, 27 April 1891, pp. 1–2, R1853, Documents and Letters, BAA.

5. Letter of Manning to Sandford, 14 June 1891, as cited in Selby, *Towards a Common System of National Education*, p. 50. McClelland, however, argues that Manning was more amenable to 'this change for the better'. See *Cardinal Manning*, p. 86.
6. *The Times*, 16 June 1891, p. 10.
7. 'Catholic Schools and Popular Control', *Tablet*, 29 August 1891, p. 325.
8. Snead-Cox, *The Life of Cardinal Vaughan*, vol. 2, p. 106.
9. Bishop of Birmingham, William Ullathorne, long-standing sceptic of educational assistance from the government, died in March 1889.
10. For example, see St Alphonsus' School Log Book, Manchester, 17 August 1891, 23 August 1891, SDA.
11. Hansard's *Parliamentary Debates*, 3rd series, 354 (1891), cols 1765, 1766.
12. See *The Times*, 6 June 1891, p. 10; 12 June 1891, pp. 6–7.
13. Hansard's *Parliamentary Debates*, 3rd series, 355 (1891), cols 1387–8.
14. Ad Clerum, 20 August 1891, pp. 1–6, Cardiff Ad Clerums 1881–1940, Cardiff Province, Diocese of Newport and Menevia, LAA.
15. Ad Clerum, 24 August 1891, pp. 3–6, ACTA 1890–1, LEDA. See Ad Clerum, 1 September 1891, pp. 1–3, Pastoral Letters of Bishop Ilsley 1–140, BAA, for the similar message given to clergy in Birmingham.
16. Pastoral Letter, 21 November 1891, pp. 6–16, Pastoral Letters from English Bishops and Other Papers 1869–93, NDA. See also *Bristol Mercury*, 3 December 1891, p. 3.
17. See Pastoral Letter, 21 November 1892, pp. 9–11, Pastoral Letters from English Bishops and Other Papers 1869–93, NDA, for increased numbers in the Diocese of Clifton; or *Report of the Liverpool Diocesan Mission Fund for the Year 1892* (Liverpool: Rockliff Brothers, 1893), pp. 4–5, Liverpolitana, LAA, for the Diocese of Liverpool.
18. H. Vaughan, 'How to Save the Voluntary Schools', *Dublin Review*, 26 (October 1891), pp. 403, 411.
19. Proposed Scheme for Catholic School Boards handwritten draft, 14 February 1891, pp. 1–2, Vaughan ACTA, SDA.
20. Vaughan, 'How to Save the Voluntary Schools', pp. 406–7.
21. 'The Free Education Act', *Tablet*, 22 August 1891, p. 305.
22. Snead-Cox, *The Life of Cardinal Vaughan*, vol. 2, p. 111.
23. Vaughan became Archbishop of Westminster on 8 April 1892 on the death of Manning and was elevated to cardinal 16 January 1893.
24. Quinn, *Patronage and Piety*, pp. 176–84.
25. Handwritten letter to Clergy, 13 January 1894, pp. 1–2, Folder: Education Bills, Box 112, SDA.
26. Ibid., p. 2.
27. *An Act for Assisting Roman Catholic Elementary Schools out of Education Rates* (London: Spottiswoode & Co., 1894), pp. 1–2, Folder: Education Bills, Box 112, SDA.
28. Ibid., p. 3.
29. Letter of George Richardson to Vaughan, 18 January 1894, p. 1, Folder: Education Bills, Box 112, SDA.
30. *The Times*, 2 February 1894, p. 5.
31. Flyer Advertising Catholic Rally on 14 February 1894, Folder: Education Bills, Box 112, SDA. Bilsborrow's flyer omitted numbers 15 and 16 from Manning's original publication, most likely because they listed statistical information that was now out of date. Therefore, this left them with only forty-eight reasons.

32. Letter to *Manchester Courier* of 1 May 1894, as cited in the *Catholic Pulpit and Expositor*, June 1894, p. 7.
33. Resolutions of the Catholic Archbishop and Bishops of England on Public Elementary Education, April 1894, pp. 1–4, Ed/B7, Education Papers 1891–1900, BAA. See also *Liverpool Mercury*, 30 April 1894, p. 6.
34. *Nottingham Daily Express*, 30 May 1894, p. 8.
35. *The Times*, 23 July 1894, p. 11
36. *The Times*, 12 November 1894, p. 7.
37. *The Times*, 23 July 1894, p. 11.
38. *The Times*, 10 January 1895, p. 6; 20 August 1895, p. 12.
39. *The Times*, 10 January 1895, p. 6.
40. *The Times*, 27 April 1895, p. 13; Annual Meeting of the Bishops Agenda, April 1895, p. 1, Ed/B6, Education Papers 1891–1900, BAA.
41. Ad Clerum, 5 July 1895, pp. 1–2, Pastoral Letters of Bishop Ilsley 1–140, BAA; Pastoral Letter, 4 July 1895, p. 1, Liverpolitana, LAA.
42. *The Times*, 20 August 1895, p. 12.
43. *Manchester Guardian*, 27 September 1895, p. 6.
44. *Manchester Guardian*, 28 September 1895, p. 9.
45. *The Times*, 30 September 1895, p. 8.
46. *The Times*, 3 October 1895, p. 10.
47. *The Times*, 30 September 1895, p. 9.
48. *The Times*, 3 October 1895, p. 10.
49. *The Times*, 7 October 1895, p. 7.
50. Letter of Vaughan to Bishops, 5 November 1895, p. 1, #392, Folder V. 1/63–4 Schools 1893–1902, WAA.
51. H. A. Vaughan, *The Rights of Christian Parents in a National System of Elementary Education: Declarations by the Cardinal Archbishop and the Catholic Bishops of England and Wales* (London: Burns & Oates, 1896), pp. 5, 7, Folder: Declarations of the Hierarchy on Education, Box 46, SDA; see also *Education Question: 1: Memorial From Catholics to the Prime Minister 2: Supplementary Declaration* (Liverpool: Rockliff Brothers, 1895), pp. 1–11, Liverpolitana, LAA.
52. *The Times*, 14 November 1895, p. 9.
53. A Further Declaration by the Catholics Bishops on the Education Difficulty, 28 November 1895, p. 2, Folder: Declarations of the Hierarchy on Education, Box 46, SDA. See also *The Times*, 4 December 1895, p. 10.
54. A Further Declaration by the Catholics Bishops, 28 November 1895, pp. 1, 3.
55. Pastoral Letter, 11 November 1895, p. 7, Middlesbrough Pastorals 1895–1922, LAA.
56. *The Times*, 18 December 1895, p. 7.
57. Supple, 'Catholicism in Yorkshire', pp. 94–5.
58. *Reynolds's Magazine*, 19 January 1896, p. 3.
59. *The Times*, 22 January 1896, p. 10.
60. *The Times*, 24 January 1896, p. 8.
61. *The Times*, 25 January 1896, p. 7.
62. *The Times*, 27 January 1896, p. 11; 28 January 1896, p. 6.
63. Notice to Diocese of Nottingham from Bishop Bagshawe, 14 January 1896, p. 1, Folder E06 Bishops' Circulars 1890–1901, Box Bishop Bagshawe E01–E11, NDA.
64. *The Times*, 29 January 1896, p. 11.

65. Letter of Vaughan to Bishops, 13 February 1896, p. 1, #314, Folder V. 1/63–4 Schools 1893–1902, WAA.
66. Ad Clerum, 18 March 1896, p. 1, Cardiff Ad Clerums 1881–1940, Cardiff Province, Diocese of Newport and Menevia, LAA.
67. Pastoral Letter, 10 February 1896, pp. 5–6, Middlesbrough Pastorals 1895–1922, LAA.
68. Hansard's *Parliamentary Debates*, 4th series, 39 (1896), cols 526, 528.
69. Hansard's *Parliamentary Debates*, 4th series, 40 (1896), cols 1212, 1214, 1217–18, 1222, 1224.
70. *The Times*, 10 June 1896, p. 17.
71. *A Declaration by the Cardinal Archbishop and Bishops of the Province of Westminster on the Government Education Bill* (London: Burns & Oates, 1896), pp. 3–8, Folder: Declarations of the Hierarchy on Education, Box 46, SDA.
72. Hansard's *Parliamentary Debates*, 4th series, 41 (1896), cols 870, 1249–50.
73. Ad Clerum, 30 April 1896, Pastoral Letters of Bishop Ilsley 1–140, BAA.
74. Ad Clerum, 9 June 1896, pp. 1–5, Cardiff Ad Clerums 1881–1940, Cardiff Province, Diocese of Newport, LAA. The Diocese of Newport and Menevia was renamed the Diocese of Newport in 1895.
75. *Manchester Guardian*, 7 April 1896, p. 6; 8 April 1896, p. 6.
76. Hansard's *Parliamentary Debates*, 4th series, 41 (1896), cols 1592, 1595.
77. M. F. Glancey, *The Present Position of the Education Question* (Walsall: J. & W. Griffin Publishers, 1896), pp. 5–6, B11698, Documents and Letters, BAA.
78. The Appeal on the Education Question, 10 November 1896, p. 5, Ed/B7, Education Papers 1891–1900, BAA.
79. The Appeal on the Education Question, 1/B/3, St Deiniol's Library, Hawarden.
80. Letter of Vaughan to Lady Herbert of Lea, 19 March 1896, in *Letters of Herbert Cardinal Vaughan*, p. 426.
81. Letter of Vaughan to Bishops, 29 October 1896, #159, Folder V. 1/63–4 Schools 1893–1902, WAA.
82. See his letter to *The Times*, 9 January 1897, p. 12, in which he pleaded, 'is it too much to hope that both political parties might agree to amend the law of 1870 by giving to ratepayers in School Board areas the choice and discretion originally intended?'
83. *The Times*, 1 February 1897, p. 11.
84. Hansard's *Parliamentary Debates*, 4th series, 46 (1897), cols 555, 556.
85. *The Times*, 25 February 1897, p. 4.
86. Hansard's *Parliamentary Debates*, 4th series, 47 (1897), cols 415–16, 1407; 46 (1897), col. 1669.
87. Machin, *Politics and the Churches*, p. 228.
88. Flyer on the Education Question from Bolton, Folder: Education Pamphlets, Box 112, SDA.
89. Snead-Cox, *The Life of Cardinal Vaughan*, vol. 2, p. 122.
90. Letter of Vaughan to Lady Herbert of Lea, 22 May 1897, in *Letters of Herbert Cardinal Vaughan*, p. 429.
91. Letter of G. W. Kekewich to Catholic School Committee, 10 June 1899, p. 1, Folder: Grant Aid, Box 112, SDA. This statement appears to be a far cry from W. E. Forster's intentions to 'fill up the gaps'.
92. *A Declaration by the Cardinal Archbishop and Bishops*, pp. 4–5, Folder: Declarations of the Hierarchy on Education, Box 46, SDA.

93. Letter of Catholic School Committee to Education Department, 29 July 1899, p. 1, Folder: Grant Aid, Box 112, SDA.
94. One Education Department circular received by Vaughan was more to the point: 'In the case of those schools where, after due warning, voluntary contributions are not forthcoming, or are less than might be reasonably expected, it will be the duty of the governing body to reduce the amount of grant. Or even to withhold it altogether.' See Snead-Cox, *The Life of Cardinal Vaughan*, vol. 2, p. 125.
95. Letter of Catholic School Committee to Education Department, 29 July 1899, pp. 1–4, Folder: Grant Aid, Box 112, SDA.
96. *The Times*, 28 September 1900, p. 2.
97. Resolutions on a National System of Elementary Education by the Catholic Hierarchy, p. 1, Bilsborrow ACTA, SDA; Resolutions on a National System of Elementary Education by the Catholic Hierarchy, 27 September 1900, p. 1, Ed/B7, Education Papers, BAA.
98. *The Times*, 28 September 1900, p. 2. Catholics in Ireland were still demanding a Catholic university.
99. Snead-Cox, *The Life of Cardinal Vaughan*, vol. 2, p. 126; Machin, *Politics and the Churches*, p. 249; D. G. Boyce, *Ireland 1828–1923: From Ascendancy to Democracy* (Oxford: Blackwell Publishers, 1992), p. 73.
100. 'The Bishops' Resolutions on Education', *Dublin Review*, 130 (January 1902), pp. 6–9.
101. Circular to Members of the Catholic School Committee, p. 1, Folder: Catholic School Committee, Box 46, SDA.
102. The Education Bill: Meeting of the Bishops and Catholic School Committee, 11 May 1902, p. 1, Folder: Salford Diocesan School Association 1901–2, Box 46, SDA.
103. The Education Bill Address by Father Glancey, 25 April 1902, p. 16, Ed/D1, Education Papers 1902–6, BAA.
104. Announcement of meeting and three resolutions, 7 May 1902, p. 1, Folder: Salford Diocesan School Association 1901–2, Box 46, SDA.
105. Ad Clerum, 5 June 1902, pp. 4–7, Cardiff Ad Clerums 1881–1940, Cardiff Province, Diocese of Newport, LAA.
106. Resolutions generated at a meeting of the Presidents, Vice-Presidents and Secretaries of the Catholics Voluntary Schools Association, 27 May 1902, Folder: Salford Diocesan School Association 1901–2, p. 1, Box 46, SDA. Clause nine referred to the necessity of schools and clause ten dealt with the amount of the aid grant.
107. *Manchester Guardian*, 16 October 1902, p. 7; 21 October 1902, p. 8.
108. *Manchester Guardian*, 7 October 1902, p. 6; 20 October 1902, p. 9; 24 October 1902, pp. 8–9; 28 October 1902, p. 7.
109. F. S. L. Lyons, *John Dillon: A Biography* (Chicago, IL: University of Chicago Press, 1968), p. 219.
110. Hansard's *Parliamentary Debates*, 4th series, 105 (1902), cols 952–3.
111. Hansard's *Parliamentary Debates*, 4th series, 107 (1902), cols 1006–7, 1004–5, 1008.
112. Lloyd George made the following inflammatory remark in the debate on the second reading, 'Cardinal Vaughan, a priest of their own Church, passes them [the Irish] by when they are fallen on the roadside. I am not sure that he did not join in helping their assailants.' When it was pointed out that Vaughan had never made known publicly his opinion on Home Rule, Lloyd George backed down somewhat and instead meekly criticized Vaughan's political support of the Tories: 'Cardinal Vaughan did his very best to help return the hon. Members opposite'. See ibid., col. 1111.

113. Hansard's *Parliamentary Debates*, 4th series, 108 (1902), cols 1207–8; 111 (1902), cols 954–5. See also Machin, *Politics and the Churches*, p. 263.
114. Hansard's *Parliamentary Debates*, 4th series, 112 (1902), cols 1047–8, 1050.
115. Lyons, *John Dillon*, p. 221. Dillon wrote in December 1903 to a Liberal ally of his who had opposed him during the 1902 debate. He explained the difficulty he had found working with the Catholic hierarchy, but that he did so because it was the best action for Irish Catholic education in England. But in the span of a year in which the Liberal nonconformist anger grew to great heights over the passage of the bill, Dillon criticized Vaughan after the fact for adhering to a policy that the Irishman knew would cause an overreaction on the part of the Liberals and possibly lead to the destruction of Catholic schools in England in the future. See letter of Dillon to James Bryce, 24 December 1903, as cited in ibid., p. 221. Yet this argument does not make sense because Dillon could not have known ahead of time how much of a stir the bill would cause, and it appears this was written with the obvious benefit of hindsight and with the political purpose of healing any lingering wounds with the Liberals.
116. Machin, *Politics and the Churches*, p. 264.
117. Hansard's *Parliamentary Debates*, 4th series, 113 (1902), cols 1336–7. See also Hansard's *Parliamentary Debates*, 4th series, 115 (1902), cols 587–8.
118. Hansard's *Parliamentary Debates*, 4th series, 113 (1902), col. 1345.
119. A Suggested Policy re: The Education Bill, 8 October 1902, pp. 1–4, G/A/138, William Gordon Files, LEDA.
120. Snead-Cox, *The Life of Cardinal Vaughan*, vol. 2, pp. 134, 136. See also *The Times*, 26 November 1902, p. 13, for Vaughan's explanation of why he wrote to Redmond. He called it 'an appeal for support to a principle of the natural law'. He also related how he had been misquoted in that letter so that it appeared that the archbishop wanted to insult the nonconformists. Politically speaking it was important for him to clarify this misquotation or else leave nonconformists believing that he wanted the Education Bill to harm their interests. In keeping with his consistent reasoning, Vaughan reiterated that he desired them to 'have things their own way in the education of their own children, even at the cost of a considerable addition to the public burdens'. That was the only way to keep things fair and just.
121. *The Times*, 15 July 1902, p. 8.
122. *Manchester Guardian*, 24 September 1902, p. 10.
123. *The Times*, 19 July 1902, p. 6.
124. Letter of Vaughan to Lady Herbert of Lea, 19 July 1902, in *Letters of Herbert Cardinal Vaughan*, p. 447.
125. Hansard's *Parliamentary Debates*, 4th series, 115 (1902), cols 1231–4.
126. Hansard's *Parliamentary Debates*, 4th series, 116 (1902), cols 870, 873.
127. Ibid., cols 582–3.
128. P. Lynch, 'The New Education Act, 1902', *Dublin Review*, 132 (January 1903), pp. 240–1, 247–8.
129. Letter of Vaughan to the Holy See, January 1903, #230, Folder V. 1/63–4 Schools 1893–1902, WAA.
130. *The Times*, 26 November 1902, p. 13.
131. See, for example, A. O'Day, *The English Face of Irish Nationalism* (London: Gill & MacMillan, 1977).

132. Quinn, *Patronage and Piety*, p. 174; E. D. Steele, 'Salisbury and the Church', in Lord Blake and H. Cecil (eds), *Salisbury: The Man and His Politics* (London: Macmillan Press, 1987), pp. 185–218, on pp. 207, 209.
133. Vaughan to the Holy See, January 1903, #230, WAA.

8 Catholic Education and Identity after the Balfour Act

1. *Catholic Directory* (1847). At the time, the London District included London, Berkshire, Essex, Hampshire, Hertfordshire, Kent, Surrey and Sussex. The Central District included Derbyshire, Leicestershire, Nottinghamshire, Oxfordshire, Shropshire, Staffordshire, Warwickshire and Worcestershire. The Lancashire District included Lancashire, Cheshire and the Isle of Man.
2. W. D. Strappini, *Educational Facts and Figures* (London: Catholic Truth Society, 1903), p. 14, #13, Folder V. 1/63–4, Schools 1893–1902, WAA; *Educational Statistics of the Diocese of Salford* (Salford: J. Roberts & Sons, 1903), p. 27.
3. *Catholic Directory* (1847); *Catholic Directory* (1903).
4. *Catholic Directory* (1903).
5. *Catholic Directory* (1846), p. 153. This is a raw number of Catholic children receiving elementary education. The first average attendance figures reported by government inspectors after Catholics entered the state grant system reveal much lower numbers of Catholics in average attendance (e.g., 1,349 Catholic children in average attendance in 1855) than the figure listed for 1846 (30,207) because inspectors only counted children in schools under inspection. Many Catholic schools, especially those under Irish Christian Brothers direction, refused inspection; thus, their students were not included in the government's statistics. By the late 1850s, a much larger percentage of Catholic schools were under inspection and the numbers reported by inspectors provide a more accurate count of students in average attendance in Catholic schools.
6. Smith, *Methodism and Education*, Appendix B, Statistics of the Committee of Council on Education of Elementary Schools Inspected for Annual Grants, 1854–1898; Strappini, *Educational Facts and Figures*, p. 14.
7. Smith, *Methodism and Education*, Appendix B. The figures for the Wesleyans are from 1878 to 1898 as their students were included with the British schools (nonconformist schools receiving grants through the British and Foreign Society) from 1863 to 1877.
8. *Catholic Directory* (1857–1903).
9. *Educational Statistics of the Diocese of Salford* (Salford: J. Roberts & Sons, 1873), p. 10; *Educational Statistics of the Diocese of Salford* (Salford: J. Roberts & Sons, 1903), p. 4. Although the later reports did not list average attendance, the statistics for the year 1900 maintained that average attendance approximated about 80 per cent of the number on the rolls. Thus, for the 1903 report, the number on the rolls was 53,749, of which 43,000 is 80 per cent.
10. 'Note', #371, Folder V. 1/63–4, Schools 1893–1902, WAA.
11. Letter to Bishops, 7 February 1902, p. 1, #7, Folder V. 1/63–4, Schools 1893–1902, WAA.
12. *Manchester Guardian*, 12 September 1884, p. 8.
13. *Manchester Guardian*, 23 September 1884, p. 6; 31 October 1884, p. 7.
14. Beales, 'The Struggle for the Schools', p. 369.
15. However, it should be noted that despite his earlier opposition to entrance into the state system, Bishop Ullathorne's name was usually included with the other bishops on

educational manifestos released to the press and sent to the government in the 1870s and 1880s. By then, even Ullathorne was on board. See, for example, Pastoral Letter of the Archbishop and Bishops of the Province of Westminster Assembled, 21 April 1871, ACTA Turner 1852–72, SDA.

16. *Birmingham Daily Post*, 27 November 1882, p. 12; Pastoral Letter, 22 June 1886, p. 5, Ullathorne Pastorals 1870–88, BAA.
17. House of Commons, 'Reports, Papers and Correspondence Relating to the Commission of Popular Education in England', vol. 8, pp. 169, 181.
18. *Tablet*, 22 August 1891, p. 305; 12 December 1891, p. 941; 19 December 1891, p. 981.
19. Hansard's *Parliamentary Debates*, 4th series, 108 (1902), cols 1207–8.
20. See note 115 to Chapter 7, above, for the context of this letter.
21. Machin, *Politics and the Churches*, pp. 265–7; Barnard, *A History of English Education*, pp. 214–15; Beales, 'The Struggle for the Schools', pp. 385–6.
22. *The Times*, 12 April 1906, p. 7.
23. Machin, *Politics and the Churches*, pp. 284–9.
24. *The Times*, 26 November 1902, p. 13.
25. *The Times*, 7 May 1906, p. 11; Machin, *Politics and the Churches*, p. 286; G. Wheeler, 'The Archdiocese of Westminster', in Beck (ed.), *The English Catholics*, pp. 151–86, on p. 172.
26. See the letters from January and February 1907 between the aggrieved parties, Bourne Papers Bo/178, WAA.
27. Aspden, *Fortress Church*, pp. 1–14, 307–8.

WORKS CITED

Primary Sources

Archives and Manuscript Collections

Birmingham Archdiocesan Archives (BAA), Birmingham.

British Library, London

Richard Cross Papers.

William Ewart Gladstone Papers.

First Marquis of Ripon Papers.

Faithful Companions of Jesus Archive, Salford, Greater Manchester.

Lancashire Record Office (LRO), Preston.

Leeds Diocesan Archives (LEDA), Leeds.

Liverpool Archdiocesan Archives (LAA), Liverpool.

Liverpool Central Library.

The National Archives (TNA), Kew, Richmond, Surrey.

Nottingham Diocesan Archives (NDA), Nottingham.

Pitts Theology Library, Emory University, Atlanta, Georgia

H. Manning Collection.

N. Wiseman Collection.

St Deiniol's Library, Hawarden.

Salford Diocesan Archives (SDA), Burnley.

Sisters of Notre Dame de Namur Archive, Woolton, Liverpool.

Westminster Archdiocesan Archives (WAA), Kensington, London.

Newspapers and Periodicals

Andrew's Weekly Orthodox Journal of Entertaining Christian Knowledge.

Birmingham Daily Post.

Bristol Mercury.

Catholic Magazine (*Edinburgh Catholic Magazine* before 1837).

Catholic Pulpit and Expositor.

Catholic School.

Catholic Standard.

Dublin Review.

Leeds Mercury.

Liverpool Mercury.

London and Dublin Weekly Orthodox Journal of Useful Knowledge.

Manchester Guardian.

Month.

Nottingham Daily Express.

Rambler (*Home and Foreign Review* after 1862).

Reynolds's Magazine.

Tablet.

The Times.

Public Documents

Catholic Directory (*Laity's Directory of Church Service*, 1833–47) (1833–1902).

Hansard's *Parliamentary Debates*, 3rd series, 110–356 (1850–91); 4th series, 39–116 (1896–1902).

United Kingdom. House of Commons, 'Report of the Commissioners on the State of Popular Education in England and with an Index', *Sessional Papers, 1861*, Education General, vol. 1.

—, 'Answers to the Circular of Questions', *Sessional Papers, 1861*, Education General, vol. 7.

—, 'Reports, Papers and Correspondence Relating to the Commission on Popular Education in England, 1861–62', *Sessional Papers, 1861–62*, Education General, vol. 8.

—, 'First Report of the Royal Commission Appointed to Inquire into the Working of the Elementary Education Acts, England and Wales', *Sessional Papers, 1886*, Education General, vol. 34.

—, 'Second Report of the Royal Commission Appointed to Inquire into the Working of the Elementary Education Acts, England and Wales', *Sessional Papers, 1887*, Education General, vol. 35.

—, 'Third Report of the Royal Commission Appointed to Inquire into the Working of the Elementary Education Acts, England and Wales', *Sessional Papers, 1887*, Education General, vol. 36.

Printed Primary Sources

An Act for Assisting Roman Catholic Elementary Schools out of Education Rates (London: Spottiswoode & Co., 1894).

Anon., *The Education Crisis* (London: Burns, Oates, & Co., 1871).

—, *Pastoral Letter of the Archbishop and Bishops of the Province of Westminster Assembled* (London, 1871).

—, *Report of the Catholic Education Crisis Fund at the Expiration of the Second Year* (London: W. Davy & Son, 1873).

—, *Education Question: 1: Memorial From Catholics to the Prime Minister 2: Supplementary Declaration* (Liverpool: Rockliff Brothers, 1895).

—, *The Education Act of 1902: The Difficulty and Its Solution* (London: Catholic Truth Society, 1904).

—, *The Catholic Attitude on the Education Question* (London: Catholic Truth Society, 1905).

[Burke, D.], *The Christian Brothers' History of the Institute, Volume II* (Dublin: Bray Printing Co. Ltd., n.d.).

Cardinal Archbishop and Bishops, *A Declaration by the Cardinal Archbishop and Bishops of the Province of Westminster on the Government Education Bill* (London: Burns & Oates, 1896).

Catholic Institute of Great Britain, *The Second Annual Report of the Catholic Institute of Great Britain* (London: Richards, 1847).

Catholic Poor School Committee, *Annual Report of the Catholic Poor School Committee* (London: Catholic Poor School Committee, 1848–83).

Challoner, R., *The Garden of the Soul: or A Manual of Spiritual Exercises and Instruction for Christians, Who (Living in the World), Aspire to Devotion* (Philadelphia, PA: Carey, 1792).

—, *The Catholic Christian Instructed in the Sacraments, Sacrifices, Ceremonies and Observances of the Church by Way of Question and Answer* (Baltimore, MD: G. Dobbin & Murphy, 1809).

Cornthwaite, R., *Pastoral Letter for Advent, 1875* (Leeds: John Whitehead and Son, 1875).

Diocese of Liverpool, *Report on Religious Inspection* (Liverpool: Rockliff Brothers, 1885).

Diocese of Salford, *Educational Statistics of the Diocese of Salford* (Salford: J. Roberts, 1873–1903).

Engels, F., *The Condition of the Working Class in England* (1845), foreword E. Hobsbawm (Chicago, IL: Academy Chicago Publishers, 1994).

Glancey, M. F., *The Present Position of the Education Question* (Walsall: J. & W. Griffin Publishers, 1896).

Guy, R. E., *The Synods in English: Being the Text of the Four Synods of Westminster* (Stratford-upon-Avon: St Gregory's Press, 1886).

Liverpool Diocesan Mission Fund, *Report of the Liverpool Diocesan Mission Fund for the Year 1883* (Liverpool: Rockliff Brothers, 1884).

—, *Report of the Liverpool Diocesan Mission Fund for the Year 1887* (Liverpool: Rockliff Brothers, 1888).

—, *Report of the Liverpool Diocesan Mission Fund for the Year 1892* (Liverpool: Rockliff Brothers, 1893).

Manning, H. E., *A Charge Delivered at the Ordinary Visitation of the Archdeaconry of Chichester in July, 1843* (London: J. Murray, 1843).

—, *The Grounds of Faith: Four Lectures Delivered to St. George's Church, Southwark* (London: Burns & Lambert, 1852).

—, *Education and Christendom* (London: Longmans, Green, & Co., 1867).

—, *Denominational Education: A Pastoral Letter to the Clergy and Laity of the Diocese of Westminster* (London: Burns, Oates, & Co., 1869).

—, *National Education and Parental Rights* (London: Burns, Oates & Co., 1872).

—, *The Vatican Decrees in their Bearing on Civil Allegiance* (New York: Catholic Publication Society, 1875).

—, *Free Education* (Newcastle-upon-Tyne: J. B. Barnes, 1885).

—, *How Shall Catholics Vote at the Coming Parliamentary Election?* (London: J. Donovan, 1885).

—, *To Amend the Education Act of 1870* (London, 1885).

—, *Miscellanies*, 3 vols (London: Burns & Oates, 1877–88).

—, *A Pastoral Letter to the Clergy and Laity of the Archdiocese of Westminster on Education* (London: Burns & Oates, 1889).

—, *National Education* (London: Burns & Oates, 1890).

—, *The Dignity and Rights of Labour and Other Social Writings* (London: Burns, Oates, & Washbourne, 1934).

Murphy, T., *The Position of the Catholic Church in England and Wales During the Last Two Centuries* (London: Burns & Oates, 1892).

Ullathorne, W. B., *Remarks on the Proposed Education Bill* (London: Burns & Lambert, 1850).

—, *A Plea for the Rights and Liberties of Religious Women with Reference to the Bill Proposed by Mr. Lacy* (London: Thomas Richardson & Son, 1851).

—, *Notes on the Education Question* (London: Richardson & Son, 1857).

—, *Catholic Education: The Address Delivered at the Catholic Meeting in the Town Hall, Birmingham, November 15th, 1869, by the Right Rev. Bishop Ullathorne* (Birmingham: M. Maher & Son, 1869).

—, *Letters of Bishop Ullathorne* (London: Burns & Oates, 1892).

Vaughan, H. A., *Popular Education in England: The Conscience Clause, the Rating Clause, and the Secular Current* (London: Longmans, Green & Co., 1868).

—, *A Letter on the Educational Peril to Christianity* (Manchester: T. Walker, 1882).

—, *Pastoral Letter on the Parental Right and Church Guidance in Education* (Manchester: T. Walker, 1885).

—, *Acts of Preparation and Consecration to the Sacred Heart of Jesus in Connection with the Recent Outrage in Rome and Our Education Question* (London: Burns & Oates, 1889).

—, *The Dangers of the Education Question and How to Meet Them* (Salford: J. Roberts & Sons, 1891).

—, *The Rights of Christian Parents in a National System of Education: Declarations by the Cardinal Archbishop and the Catholic Bishops of England and Wales* (London: Burns & Oates, 1896).

—, *Letters of Herbert Cardinal Vaughan to Lady Herbert of Lea 1867 to* 1903, ed. S. Leslie (London: Burns & Oates, 1942).

Wiseman, N. P., *Pastoral Letter of H. E. Cardinal Wiseman Enjoining the Collection for the Building of Churches and Schools in the Archdiocese* (London: Burns & Lambert, 1864).

—, *The Religious and Social Position of Catholics in England: An Address Delivered to the Catholic Congress of Malines, August 21, 1863* (Dublin: J. Duffy, 1864).

—, 'Out of the Flaminian Gate', in D. C. Douglas (gen. ed.), *English Historical Documents*, 12 vols in 13 (New York: Oxford University Press, 1953–77), vol. 12.1: 1833–1874, ed. G. M. Young and W. D. Handcock.

Secondary Sources

Albion, G., 'The Restoration of the Hierarchy', in Beck (ed.), *The English Catholics*, pp. 86–115.

Allies, M. H., *Thomas William Allies* (London: Burns & Oates, 1907).

Altholz, J., *The Liberal Catholic Movement in England: The Rambler and its Contributors 1848–1864* (London: Burns & Oates, 1962).

—, 'The Political Behavior of English Catholics, 1850–1867', *Journal of British Studies*, 4 (November 1964), pp. 89–103.

Anon., *The History of the Training College of Notre Dame, Liverpool 1856–1885* (St Mary's Abbey, Bergholt: St Benedict's Press, 1885).

—, *Sister Mary of Saint Francis: Assistant to the Mother-General of the Sisters of Notre Dame of Namur, Belgium* (London: Burns & Oates, 1951).

Arnstein, W. L., *Protestant versus Catholic in Mid-Victorian England: Mr. Newdegate and the Nuns* (Columbia, MO: University of Missouri Press, 1982).

Aspden, K., *Fortress Church: The English Roman Catholic Bishops and Politics 1903–63* (Leominster: Gracewing, 2002).

Barnard, H. C., *A History of English Education from 1760* (London: University of London Press, 1964).

Battersby, W. J., 'Secondary Education for Boys', in Beck (ed.), *The English Catholics*, pp. 322–36.

—, 'Educational Work of the Religious Orders of Women: 1850–1950', in Beck (ed.), *The English Catholics*, pp. 337–64.

Beales, A. C. F., 'The Struggle for the Schools', in Beck (ed.), *The English Catholics*, pp. 365–409.

Beck, G. A. (ed.), *The English Catholics, 1850–1950* (London: Burns & Oates, 1950).

Bossy, J., *The English Catholic Community 1570–1850* (London: Darton, Longman & Todd, 1975).

Boyce, D. G., *Ireland 1828–1923: From Ascendancy to Democracy* (Oxford: Blackwell Publishers, 1992).

Burke, T., *The Catholic History of Liverpool* (Liverpool: C. Tinling & Co., 1910).

Carter, B., 'Catholic Charitable Endeavor in London, 1810–1840, Part I', *Recusant History*, 25:3 (2001), pp. 487–510.

—, 'Catholic Charitable Endeavor in London, 1810–1840, Part II', *Recusant History*, 25:4 (2001), pp. 648–69.

Champ, J., *William Bernard Ullathorne 1806–1889: A Different Kind of Monk* (Leominster: Gracewing, 2006).

Clark, J. C. D., *English Society 1688–1832: Ideology, Social Structure and Political Practice during the Ancien Regime* (Cambridge: Cambridge University Press, 1985).

Coates, J., 'The Christian Brothers – Part II: Pioneers in Catholic Education in Britain and Ireland Throughout the 19th and 20th Centuries', *Catholic Life* (March 2005), pp. 18–24.

Cohausz, O., *The Pope and Christian Education*, trans. G. D. Smith (New York: Benziger Brothers, 1933).

Connolly, G., 'The Transubstantiation of Myth: Towards a New Popular History of Nineteenth-Century Catholicism in England', *Journal of Ecclesiastical History*, 35 (January 1984), pp. 78–104.

—, 'Irish and Catholic: Myth or Reality? Another Sort of Irish and the Renewal of the Clerical Profession among Catholics in England, 1791–1918', in Swift and Gilley (eds), *The Irish in the Victorian City*, pp. 225–54.

Cruise, E., 'Development of the Religious Orders', in Beck (ed.), *The English Catholics*, pp. 442–74.

Donovan, R. K., 'The Denominational Character of English Catholic Charitable Effort, 1800–1865', *Catholic Historical Review*, 62 (April 1976), pp. 201–6.

Doyle, P., '"A Tangled Skein of Confusion": The Administration of George Hilary Brown, Bishop of Liverpool, 1850–1856', *Recusant History*, 25:2 (2000), pp. 294–303.

Dwyer, J. J., 'The Catholic Press, 1850–1950', in Beck (ed.), *The English Catholics*, pp. 475–514.

Eaton, M., J. Longmore and A. Naylor (eds), *Commitment to Diversity: Catholics and Education in a Changing World* (London: Cassell, 2000).

Evans, E., *The Forging of the Modern State: Early Industrial Britain, 1783–1870* (London: Longman Group, 1983).

Finnigan, R., and J. Hagerty (eds), *The Bishops of Leeds 1878–1985: Essays in Honour of Bishop David Konstant* (Keighley: PBK Publishing, 2005).

Fitzgerald, M. E. W., 'Catholic Elementary Schools in the Manchester Area during the Nineteenth Century' (MEd thesis, University of Manchester, 1975).

Foster, G. P., 'Middle England Diocese, Middle England Catholicism: The Development of the Roman Catholic Diocese of Nottingham, 1850–1915' (PhD dissertation, University of Hertfordshire, 2004).

Foster, R., *Modern Ireland, 1600–1972* (London: Penguin Books, 1989).

Gillespie, W., *The Christian Brothers in England, 1825–1880* (Bristol: Burleigh Press, 1975).

Gilley, S., 'Catholic Faith of the Irish Slums: London, 1840–70', in H. J. Dyos and M. Wolff (eds), *The Victorian City: Images and Realities*, 2 vols (London: Routledge and Kegan Paul, 1973), vol. 2, pp. 837–53.

—, 'The Years of Equipoise, 1892–1943', in McClelland and Hodgetts (eds), *From Without the Flaminian Gate*, pp. 21–61.

— (ed.), *Victorian Churches and Churchmen: Essays Presented to Vincent Alan McClelland* (Woodbridge, Suffolk: Boydell Press, 2005).

Gray, R., *Cardinal Manning: A Biography* (London: Weidenfeld & Nicholson, 1985).

Gwynn, D., *The Second Spring 1818–1852: A Study of the Catholic Revival in England* (London: Catholic Book Club, 1944).

—, 'Growth of the Catholic Community', in Beck (ed.), *The English Catholics*, pp. 410–41.

Halevy, E., *Victorian Years (1841–1895)*, trans. E. I. Watkin (New York: Barnes & Noble, 1961).

Hamer, E., 'A Phase in the Struggle for Catholic Education: Manchester and Salford in the Mid-Nineteenth Century', *Recusant History*, 23 (May 1996), pp. 107–26.

Heimann, M., *Catholic Devotion in Victorian England* (Oxford: Clarendon Press, 1995).

Hickey, J., *Urban Catholics: Urban Catholicism in England and Wales from 1829 to the Present Day* (London: Geoffrey Chapman, 1967).

Hickman, M. J., *Religion, Class, and Identity: The State, the Catholic Church, and the Education of the Irish in Britain* (Aldershot: Avebury, 1995).

—, 'Catholicism and the Nation-State in Nineteenth-Century Britain', in Eaton et al. (eds), *Commitment to Diversity*, pp. 48–66.

Hilton, J. A., *Catholic Lancashire: From Reformation to Renewal, 1559–1991* (London: Phillimore, 1991).

Holland, M. G., *The British Catholic Press and the Educational Controversy, 1847–1865* (New York: Garland Publishing, 1987).

Holmes, J. D., *More Roman than Rome: English Catholicism in the Nineteenth Century* (London: Burns & Oates, 1978).

Hoppen, K. T., *The Mid-Victorian Generation 1846–1886* (Oxford: Clarendon Press, 2003).

Howard, C. H. D., 'The Parnell Manifesto of 21 November, 1885, and the Schools Question', *English Historical Review*, 62 (January 1947), pp. 42–51.

Jones, D. K., *The Making of the Education System, 1851–81* (London: Routledge & Kegan Paul, 1977).

Kitching, J., 'The Catholic Poor Schools, 1800 to 1845: Part I, The Catholic Poor: Relief, Welfare and Schools', *Journal of Educational Administration and History*, 1 (June 1969), pp. 1–8.

—, 'The Catholic Poor Schools, 1800 to 1845: Part II, The Schools: Development and Distribution', *Journal of Educational Administration and History* 2 (December 1969), pp. 1–12.

Lannon, D., 'Bishop Turner and Educational Provision within the Salford Diocesan Area, 1840–1870' (MPhil. thesis, University of Hull, 1994).

—, 'Bishop Turner, the Salford Diocese, and Reformatory Provision, 1854–1872', *Recusant History*, 23:3 (1997), pp. 389–407.

—, 'William Turner, First Bishop of Salford, Pastor and Educator', *Recusant History*, 25:2 (2000), pp. 192–217.

—, 'Catholic Education in the Salford Diocese, 1870–1944' (PhD dissertation, University of Hull, 2003).

Larkin, E., 'The Devotional Revolution in Ireland, 1850–1875', *American Historical Review*, 88:3 (June 1972), pp. 625–52.

—, *The Roman Catholic Church and the Creation of the Modern Irish State, 1878–1886* (Philadelphia, PA: American Philosophical Society, 1975).

—, *The Roman Catholic Church in Ireland and the Fall of Parnell, 1888–1891* (Chapel Hill, NC: University of North Carolina Press, 1979).

—, *The Roman Catholic Church and the Home Rule Movement in Ireland, 1870–1874* (Chapel Hill, NC: University of North Carolina Press, 1990).

Lees, L. H., *Exiles of Erin: Irish Migrants in Victorian London* (Ithaca, NY: Cornell University Press, 1979).

Leslie, S., *Henry Edward Manning: His Life and Labours* (London: Burns, Oates & Washbourne, 1921).

Lewis, D. M., *Lighten their Darkness: The Evangelical Mission to Working-Class London, 1828–1860* (New York: Greenwood Press, 1986).

Leys, M. D. R., *Catholics in England 1559–1829: A Social History* (London: Longmans, Green and Co., Ltd., 1961).

Lowden, K., 'Women Religious and Teacher Education: A Case Study of the Sisters of Notre Dame in the Nineteenth Century', in Eaton et al. (eds), *Commitment to Diversity*, pp. 67–93.

Lyons, F. S. L., *John Dillon: A Biography* (Chicago, IL: University of Chicago Press, 1968).

Machin, G. I. T., *Politics and the Churches in Great Britain 1869 to 1921* (Oxford: Clarendon Press, 1987).

Marmion, J., 'The Beginnings of the Catholic Poor Schools in England', *Recusant History*, 17:1 (1984), pp. 67–83.

Marsh, P. T., *The Victorian Church in Decline: Archbishop Tait and the Church of England, 1868–1882* (Pittsburgh, PA: University of Pittsburgh Press, 1969).

Martaler, B. L., *The Catechism Yesterday and Today: The Evolution of a Genre* (Collegeville, MN: Liturgical Press, 1995).

Mathew, D., 'Old Catholics and Converts', in Beck (ed.), *The English Catholics*, pp. 223–42.

McClelland, M., 'Catholic Education in Victorian Hull', in Swift and Gilley (eds), *The Irish in Victorian Britain*, pp. 101–21.

McClelland, V. A., *Cardinal Manning: His Public Life and Influence, 1865–1892* (London: Oxford University Press, 1962).

—, 'The Protestant Alliance and Roman Catholic Schools, 1872–74', *Victorian Studies*, 8 (December 1964), pp. 173–82.

—, 'The Formative Years, 1850–92', in McClelland and Hodgetts (eds), *From Without the Flaminian Gate*, pp. 1–20.

McClelland, V. A., and M. Hodgetts (eds), *From Without the Flaminian Gate: 150 Years of Roman Catholicism in England and Wales, 1850–2000* (London: Darton, Longman & Todd, 1999).

McGrath, T. G., 'The Tridentine Evolution of Modern Irish Catholicism, 1563–1962: A Re-Examination of the "Devotional Revolution" Thesis', *Recusant History*, 20:4 (1991), pp. 512–23.

McLeod, H., 'The De-Christianization of the Working Class in Western Europe, c. 1850–1900', *Social Compass*, 27 (1980), pp. 191–214.

—, *Piety and Poverty: Working-Class Religion in Berlin, London, and New York, 1870–1914* (New York: Holmes & Meier, 1996).

Newsome, D., 'Cardinal Manning and His Influence on the Church and Nation', *Recusant History*, 21:2 (1992), pp. 136–51.

Nicholson, N., 'St. Mary's College Hammersmith: Its Early Development in the Context of Mid-Nineteenth-Century Teacher Training', in Eaton et al. (eds), *Commitment to Diversity*, pp. 115–62.

Norman, E. R., *The English Catholic Church in the Nineteenth Century* (Oxford: Clarendon Press, 1984).

O'Brien, S., 'French Nuns in Nineteenth-Century England', *Past and Present*, 154 (February 1997), pp. 142–80.

—, 'Religious Life for Women', in McClelland and Hodgetts (eds), *From Without the Flaminian Gate*, pp. 108–41.

—, 'Terra Incognita: The Nun in Nineteenth-Century England', *Past and Present*, 121 (November 1988), pp. 110–40.

O'Day, A., *The English Face of Irish Nationalism* (London: Gill & MacMillan, 1977).

O'Neil, R., *Cardinal Herbert Vaughan: Archbishop of Westminster, Bishop of Salford, Founder of the Mill Hill Missionaries* (London: Burns & Oates, 1997).

O'Toole, A. L., *Challenged: The Story of Edmund Rice and the Irish Christian Brothers in Britain since 1825* (Tenbury Wells, Worcestershire: Fowler Wright Books, n.d).

O'Tuathaigh, M. A. G., 'The Irish in Nineteenth-Century Britain: Problems of Integration', in Swift and Gilley (eds), *The Irish in the Victorian City*, pp. 13–36.

Owen, H., *The Education Acts, 1870–1902, and Other Acts Relating to Education* (London: Knight & Co., 1903).

Pereiro, J., 'Truth before Peace: Manning and Infallibility', *Recusant History*, 21:2 (1992), pp. 218–53.

—, *Cardinal Manning: An Intellectual Biography* (Oxford: Clarendon Press, 1998).

Pritchard, P., 'Churchmen, Catholics, and Elementary Education: A Comparison of Attitudes and Policies in Liverpool during the School Board Era', *History of Education*, 20 (1983), pp. 103–19.

Purcell, E. S., *Life of Cardinal Manning: Archbishop of Westminster*, 2 vols (London: MacMillan Company, 1898).

Quinn, D., 'Manning as Politician', *Recusant History*, 21:2 (October 1992), pp. 267–85.

—, *Patronage and Piety: The Politics of English Roman Catholicism, 1850–1900* (Stanford, CA: Stanford University Press, 1993).

Richards, N. J., 'Religious Controversy and the School Boards 1870–1902', *British Journal of Educational Studies*, 18 (June 1970), pp. 180–96.

Roberts, G., 'English Catholics and Politics in the Late Nineteenth Century', *Studies* (Winter 1985), pp. 455–63.

Rossi, J. P., 'English Catholics, the Liberal Party, and the General Election of 1880', *Catholic Historical Review*, 63 (July 1977), pp. 411–27.

Sacks, B., *The Religious Issue in the State Schools of England and Wales, 1902–1914: A Nation's Quest for Human Dignity* (Albuquerque, NM: University of New Mexico Press, 1961).

Selby, D. E., 'Henry Edward Manning and the Catholic Middle Class: A Curricular Study', *Paedagogica Historica*, 10 (1970), pp. 149–70.

—, 'Henry Edward Manning and the Education Bill of 1870', *British Journal of Educational Studies*, 18:2 (June 1970), pp. 197–212.

—, *Towards a Common System of National Education: Cardinal Manning and Educational Reform, 1882–1892* (Leeds: University of Leeds, 1977).

Smith, J. T., 'The Wesleyans, the "Romanists" and the Education Act of 1870', *Recusant History*, 23 (May 1996), pp. 127–42.

—, *Methodism and Education 1849–1902: J. H. Rigg, Romanism, and Wesleyan Schools* (Oxford: Oxford University Press, 1998).

—, 'The Priest and the Elementary School in the Second Half of the Nineteenth Century', *Recusant History* 25:3 (2001), pp. 530–42.

—, 'The Real Milch Cow? The Work of Anglican, Catholic and Wesleyan Clergymen in Elementary Schools in the Second Half of the Nineteenth Century', *History of Education*, 31:2 (2002), pp. 117–37.

—, *'A Victorian Class Conflict': Schoolteaching and the Parson, Priest and Minister, 1837–1902* (Eastbourne: Sussex Academic Press, 2009).

Snead-Cox, J. G., *The Life of Cardinal Vaughan*, 2 vols (London: Herbert & Daniel, 1912).

Sneyd-Kynnersley, E. M., *HMI: Some Passages in the Life of One of H.M. Inspectors of Schools* (London: MacMillan & Company, 1908).

Steele, E. D., 'Salisbury and the Church', in Lord Blake and H. Cecil (eds), *Salisbury: The Man and His Politics* (London: Macmillan Press, 1987), pp. 185–218.

Sturt, M., *The Education of the People: A History of Primary Education in England and Wales in the Nineteenth Century* (London: Routledge & Kegan Paul, 1967).

Supple, J. F., 'Catholicism in Yorkshire, 1850–1900' (PhD thesis, University of Leeds, 1982).

Supple-Green, J. F., *The Catholic Revival in Yorkshire, 1850–1900* (Leeds: Leeds Philosophical and Literary Society, 1990).

Swift, R., and S. Gilley (eds), *The Irish in the Victorian City* (London: Croom Helm, 1985).

—, *The Irish in Britain 1815–1939* (London: Pinter Publishers, 1989).

—, *The Irish in Victorian Britain: The Local Dimension* (Dublin: Four Courts Press, 1999).

Tenbus, E. G., '"We Fight for the Cause of God": English Catholics, the Education of the Poor, and the Transformation of Catholic Identity in Victorian Britain', *Journal of British Studies*, 46:4 (October 2007), pp. 861–83.

—, 'Defending the Faith through Education: The Catholic Case for Parental and Civil Rights in Victorian Britain', *History of Education Quarterly*, 48:3 (August 2008), pp. 432–51.

von Arx, J., 'Manning's Ultramontanism and the Catholic Church in British Politics', *Recusant History*, 19:3 (May 1989), pp. 332–47.

—, 'Catholics and Politics', in McClelland and Hodgetts (eds), *From Without the Flaminian Gate*, pp. 245–71.

—, 'Interpreting the Council: Archbishop Manning and the Vatican Decrees Controversy', *Recusant History*, 26:1 (2002), pp. 229–42.

—, 'Cardinal Manning and His Political Persona: The Education Act of 1870', in Gilley (ed.), *Victorian Churches and Churchmen*, pp. 1–11.

Walsh, B., *Roman Catholic Nuns in England and Wales 1800–1937: A Social History* (Dublin: Irish Academic Press, 2002).

Ward, B., *The Sequel to Catholic Emancipation: The Story of the English Catholics Continued Down to the Re-Establishment of their Hierarchy in 1850*, 2 vols (London: Longmans, Green, & Co., 1915).

Ward, J. T., and J. H. Treble, 'Religion and Education in 1843: Reaction to the "Factory Education Bill"', *Journal of Ecclesiastical History*, 20 (April 1969), pp. 79–110.

Warren, J., 'The Dublin Review (1836–75), Its Reviewers, and a "Philosophy of Knowledge"', *Recusant History*, 21:1 (1992), pp. 86–98.

Wheeler, G., 'The Archdiocese of Westminster', in Beck (ed.), *The English Catholics*, pp. 151–86.

Whitehead, M., '"Briefly, and in Confidence": Private Views of Her Majesty's Inspectors on English Catholic Elementary Schools, 1875', *Recusant History*, 20:4 (1991), pp. 554–62.

—, 'Educational Turmoil and Ecclesiastical Strife: The Episcopal Career of Joseph William Hendren, 1848–1853', *Recusant History*, 25:2 (2000), pp. 263–80.

—, 'A View from the Bridge: The Catholic School', in McClelland and Hodgetts (eds), *From Without the Flaminian Gate*, pp. 217–44.

Wolffe, J., *The Protestant Crusade in Great Britain, 1829–1860* (Oxford: Clarendon Press, 1988).

INDEX

For Product Safety Concerns and Information please contact our EU representative GPSR@taylorandfrancis.com
Taylor & Francis Verlag GmbH, Kaufingerstraße 24, 80331 München, Germany

www.ingramcontent.com/pod-product-compliance
Ingram Content Group UK Ltd.
Pitfield, Milton Keynes, MK11 3LW, UK
UKHW011010180926
475701UK00004B/653

* 9 7 8 1 1 3 8 6 6 1 2 9 5 *